CO-CREATION IN THEORY AND PRACTICE

Exploring Creativity in the Global North and South

Edited by
Christina Horvath and Juliet Carpenter

P

First published in Great Britain in 2020 by

Policy Press, an imprint of Bristol University Press
University of Bristol
1-9 Old Park Hill
Bristol
BS2 8BB
UK
t: +44 (0)117 954 5940
e: bup-info@bristol.ac.uk

Details of international sales and distribution partners are available at
policy.bristoluniversitypress.co.uk

British Library Cataloguing in Publication Data
A catalogue record for this book is available from the British Library

ISBN 978-1-4473-5396-6 paperback
ISBN 978-1-4473-5395-9 hardcover
ISBN 978-1-4473-5399-7 ePub
ISBN 978-1-4473-5398-0 ePdf

Cover design by Clifford Hayes
Front cover image: Leandro 'Tick' Rodrigues

Contents

List of figures and tables

Figures

Tables

Notes on contributors

Inés Álvarez-Gortari is based in Nairobi where she works as a behaviour change researcher at ThinkPlace Kenya. She conducts ethnographic research and engages directly with local communities, involving them in co-creation processes to find solutions to their challenges. Inés is a graduate of the London School of Economics, UK, where she studied Geography as an undergraduate and Urbanisation and Development at postgraduate level. She also holds a postgraduate degree in Social Innovation Management from Amani Institute. Inés worked for four years at Casa Fluminense, a civil society organisation in Rio de Janeiro, Brazil, which advocates for inclusive urban policies for the city's metropolitan region.

Sue Brownill is Professor in Urban Governance and Policy in the School of the Built Environment at Oxford Brookes University, UK. Her research focuses on the spaces of participation created through the interaction of the state with urban social movements. She combines this with longstanding experience of community-led planning and regeneration, both as a practitioner and a researcher. As well as involvement with the Co-Creation project, her recent projects include research into neighbourhood planning and localism in the UK and into participatory approaches to encouraging healthy urban mobility in Brazil.

Juliet Carpenter is Senior Research Fellow at the School of the Built Environment, Oxford Brookes University, UK, working at the interface of debates within a range of disciplines, including geography, urban planning, political science and sociology. From 2017 to 2020, Juliet held a three-year Marie Curie Global Fellowship, in collaboration with the University of British Colombia, Canada, working on an international comparison of urban regeneration and governance in the context of social sustainability. She has a particular interest in exploring arts-based methods as a means of giving voice to marginalised communities in an urban planning context.

Pamela Ileana Castro Suarez is an urban planner, holding an MSc in Property Development from the National Autonomous University of Mexico (UNAM) and a PhD in Urban Design from Oxford Brookes University, UK. Since 2012 she has been a part-time professor at undergraduate and postgraduate levels in urban morphology and urban design, social and self-sustainable economic projects, and urban and regional planning, having been a module teacher since 1993 and a casual lecturer at Oxford Brookes in 2006. Since 2013, she has been head of the undergraduate programme in urbanism. Her main research fields are urban design and morphology, property development, crime prevention through urban design, urban instruments, healthy cities, vulnerable neighbourhoods, public space and children, education and co-creation.

Bryan C. Clift is Senior Lecturer (Associate Professor) in Humanities and Social Sciences at the University of Bath, UK, and Director of the Qualitative Research Centre. His research is oriented around three foci: sport and physical activity in relation to issues of contemporary urbanism, popular cultural practices and representations, and qualitative inquiry. These are inspired by the notable ways in which sport, physical activity, and popular cultural practices contribute to examining the structure and experience of contemporary social formations and issues. His work has recently been published in *Body & Society, Sociology of Sport Journal, Qualitative Inquiry,* and *Cultural Studies <=> Critical Methodologies.*

Maria Sarah da Silva Telles is Professor and Researcher at the Post-Graduation Programme in Social Sciences, PUC-Rio, Brazil. Her teaching and research expertise lie in sociology, particularly urban sociology focused on themes of poverty, social inequality, social mobility, migration, favelas, working-class families, education and indigenous people in the city. Her current projects are about women and the life trajectories of young black people. Her publications include an edited volume with S. Luçan, *Os Sociólogos; Viver na Pobreza: Experiência e representações de moradores de uma favela carioca;* and *Il Genocidio Nero Continua? La Lotta Continua* (Clemente, Silva Telles, Sousa e Silva, and Brandão).

Joanne Davies is a PhD candidate in the Department of Education at the University of Bath, UK. She holds a BA Honours in French and Music from the University of Birmingham, UK, and a CELTA qualification from the University of Cambridge, UK, in teaching English to speakers of other languages. Her PhD explores geographical inequalities in access to elite universities and follows on from her previous work for the education charity, IntoUniversity, and King's College London, UK, in the field of widening participation in higher education.

Annaleise Depper is an engagement practitioner at the University of Oxford, UK, where she supports researchers to collaborate with public and community groups beyond academia. Annaleise previously completed a PhD at the University of Bath, UK, in the Physical Culture, Sport and Health research group. Her research explored young people's experiences of embodied mobility and inequality in low-income communities. Annaleise is particularly interested in using Co-Creative approaches to bring together researchers, practitioners and communities to Co-Create solutions in response to everyday challenges and inequalities.

Simone Fullagar is an interdisciplinary sociologist who leads the Women in Sport research group as Professor at Griffith University, Australia. Simone's research uses feminist post-structuralist and new materialist theory-methods to explore the gendering of health and emotional well-being, as well as sport and leisure practices. Her latest book was published by Palgrave in 2019 – *Feminism and a Vital Politics of Depression and Recovery*. Simone was previously Chair of the Physical Culture, Sport and Health research group at the University of Bath, UK.

José Luis Gázquez Iglesias holds a PhD in International Relations and African Studies from the Autonomous University of Madrid, Spain. He completed his graduate studies at Sciences-Po in Paris, France, and a postdoctoral internship at the Autonomous Metropolitan University Cuajimalpa, Mexico. He has also conducted extensive fieldwork in several cities of Senegal and Europe and a research internship at Cheikh Anta Diop University, Dakar. He currently works as an Associate Professor and Researcher in International Relations and African Studies at the National Autonomous University of Mexico (UNAM). His main research topics are Sufi Islam, transnational migrations and networks, state formation and construction processes in Sub-Saharan Africa and Senegal.

Christina Horvath is Reader in French Literature and Politics at the University of Bath, UK. She holds a PhD in contemporary French literature from University Paris 3 - Sorbonne Nouvelle, France. Her research addresses urban representations in literature and film, with emphasis on artistic expressions of advanced marginality such as contemporary French '*banlieue* narratives' and favela literature in Brazil. She has published widely on contemporary French and Francophone literature, *banlieues* and postcolonial legacies in France. Since 2013, she has been working on the conceptualisation and testing of 'Co-Creation' defined as an arts-based method to promote social justice in disadvantaged urban areas.

Martha King is Arts Producer at Knowle West Media Centre (KWMC), UK, and has developed and delivered a wide range of socially engaged, digital and contemporary arts projects, applying methods of co-creation to explore topics such as data ethics, community-led housing and participatory sensing. She co-authored 'Artists, data, and agency in smart cities' in *Big Data in the Arts and Humanities* (2018) with Roz Stewart-Hall, and co-authored a CHI published paper 'A city in common: a framework to foster technology innovation from the bottom up'. She is KWMC's representative for the 'Co-creating Change' network and is supporting a 'Creative Civic Change' project in Knowle West, 2019–21.

Melissa Mean is Head of Arts at KWMC. For over 15 years she has worked across the arts, urbanism and public participation, and has led projects ranging from setting up a pop-up factory to train local people to design and make furniture, to creating a living archive of tattoo culture. She now leads We Can Make, a citizen-led housing programme. Melissa is also part of Redcliffe Neighbourhood Forum, a community group working on a £100m project to reclaim a dual carriageway in Bristol and create affordable housing and public space in its place.

Vitor Mihessen is Information Coordinator and co-founder of Casa Fluminense, Rio de Janeiro, Brazil. He researches socioeconomic indicators in the Rio Metropolitan Region and also designs and organises capacity building activities, including Casa Fluminense's Public Policies course. Vitor holds a Masters in Economic Science with a specialisation in Public Policies and Governmental Management from universities in Rio. Vitor also studied comparative economic development at the Universidad de Salamanca, Spain. His research interests revolve around urban mobility and its social and economic interfaces. Vitor previously worked at several research and policy organisations in Rio and was chief adviser to the Secretary of Economic Development in the State of Rio.

Niccolò Milanese is a director of European Alternatives, a transnational civil society organisation which promotes democracy, equality and culture beyond the nation-state, with offices in London, Berlin, Rome and Paris where he lives. He is a Europe's Futures Fellow at the Institut für Wissenschaften vom Menschen, Austria. His most recent books are *Citizens of Nowhere: How Europe Can be Saved from itself* (Zed Books 2018) and *Wir Heimatlosen Weltbürger* (Suhrkamp 2019).

Oscar Natividad Puig is a PhD candidate in Planning at Oxford Brookes University, UK, researching the role of social network structures in participatory approaches. An architect and urban planner by training, he has participated in development initiatives for vulnerable communities in South Africa, Haiti, Chile, Nepal, and Panama. Before starting at Oxford Brookes, Oscar managed an asset-based community development project for CoLab MIT. His former education includes a degree in Architecture at Universidad Politécnica de Valencia, Spain, and a Masters at the Harvard Graduate School of Design, USA. His research consistently returns to the role and social responsibility of the designer to incorporate the voice of vulnerable communities.

Eliana Osorio Saez is a PhD candidate in the Department of Education, University of Bath, UK. She holds a BA in Teaching Spanish and English from Universidad Popular del Cesar and an MA in Education: English Didactics from Universidad Externado de Colombia, both in Colombia. She also holds an MA in Education, Leadership and Management from Bath Spa University, UK. Her PhD topic is the use of technology to support parental engagement in schools.

Dianell Pacheco Gordillo graduated from UNAM with a BA in Political Science, with a major in International Cooperation and a Masters in Public Affairs and Government. She has held various positions, including member of the local electoral representation in the Council of the National Electoral Institute, analyst at the Council for the Evaluation of Social Development in Mexico City (EVALUA DF) and Research Assistant at the Faculty of Social and Political Sciences in UNAM. She is currently the Technical Secretary of the H2020 Project 'The Cohesive City: Addressing Stigmatisation in Disadvantaged Neighbourhoods' at UNAM.

María José Pantoja Peschard is Lecturer in the Department of Media and Communications, in the School of Social and Political Sciences at UNAM. She graduated in Philosophy at UNAM. She holds an MLitt in Philosophy from the University of St Andrews, UK, and an MA in Film Studies from the University of East Anglia, UK. She obtained her PhD in Cultural Studies from Goldsmiths, University of London, UK. Her research interests are the relationships between political philosophy, aesthetics and visual cultures.

Ségolène Pruvot is Cultural Director of European Alternatives. She was trained as a political scientist and urban planner at Sciences-Po, France, London School of Economics, UK, and University of Leipzig, Germany. Ségolène has published several articles related to urban planning and to gender equality in print and online. Her latest publication is 'Feminists know how to build bridges' in the volume *'The Right to Truth'* (Kiev: Visual Culture Research Centre, 2019) on Feminist Arts and Social Change. In the past 10 years, Ségolène has investigated the transformative power of the arts in several research and activist projects, such as TRANSEUROPA Festival. She has also collaborated with the URBACT European Programme.

Leandro Rodrigues de Souza, known as 'Tick', is a graffiti artist, activist and cultural promoter working in the favela of Tabajaras & Cabritos, in Rio de Janeiro, Brazil. Originally from North-Eastern Brazil, he grew up in Rio de Janeiro where he has been working as a graffiti artist since 2001. Since 2015 he has been active in the project 'Viva Bairro', which aims to develop community-based tourism around graffiti in Tabajaras. Tick has contributed to three international Co-Creation workshops (Santa Marta, 2018, and Tabajaras and Bath, 2019), several international graffiti events and hosted two large-scale graffiti encounters, each bringing together over 35 artists.

Hector Quiroz Rothe is an urban planner and historian at UNAM. He holds a PhD in Geography from the Université de Paris 3 – Sorbonne-Nouvelle. Since 2004 he has been a full-time professor in the School of Urbanism and a member of the National Research System since 2006. His main research fields are contemporary history of Mexican cities, representations of the city in cinema, and co-creation.

Andrés Sandoval-Hernández is Reader in Educational Research at the University of Bath, UK. His research interests include comparative analyses of educational systems using large-scale assessment data with a focus on educational inequalities and civic education. He is part of different international networks on these topics and is co-editor of *'Teaching Tolerance in a Globalised World'* (Springer, 2018), which investigates the attitudes of secondary school students towards minorities across 38 countries.

Jim Segers co-founded City Mine(d). His current interest lies with tough issues and with the tension between individual capabilities and the need for collective action. He is currently active with City Mine(d) in London on the role of personal competences in local development (in 'Elephant Path' in London's Somers Town area) and in Brussels with the triple challenge facing the electricity sector of fairer pricing, rethinking ageing infrastructure and reducing climate impact (in 'La Pile' in Brussels' Quartier Midi). He holds a BA Hons in Politics, a BSc Hons in Econometrics and is trained as a theatre director.

Itamar Silva is a journalist, researcher, and former director of the Brazilian Institute of Social and Economic Analysis (IBASE) until April 2019. Currently, he is the president of the School Without Walls Association, or Eco. Previously, he was a militant of the Rio de Janeiro Slum Movement, director of FAFERJ, president of the Morro Santa Marta Residents Association. He is a member of the Rio 2004 Social Agenda, Terra do Futuro Network, and ActionAid Brasil. His work focuses on favelas, housing, drug trafficking, and public safety.

Ben Spencer is Research Fellow at Oxford Brookes University, UK. He has a PhD in urban design and a background in community development and lifelong learning. His research in the School of the Built Environment is focused on gerontology, mobility and developing healthy urban environments through community engagement. Recent projects have included the award-winning cycle BOOM research project on understanding older people's cycling (www.cycleboom.org) and the Healthy Urban Mobility research project (www.hum-mus. org) in partnership with colleagues from three universities in Brazil.

Roz Stewart-Hall is Head of Research and evaluation at KWMC. Her role involves supporting KWMC's team and people who participate in projects to reflect on and evaluate their work, as well as reporting to funders. Roz has developed a set of tools and mechanisms for generating evidence and data about the work and impact of KWMC. She has extensive experience of research and evaluation and has worked in the field of socially engaged arts practice since 1991. Roz uses action research approaches to evaluation and aims to embed ongoing reflection into organisational practice and systems.

Karla Valverde Viesca is Professor at the Political Studies Center in the Political and Social Sciences Faculty, UNAM. She is member of the National System of Researchers in Mexico and author of the book, *Construcción Institucional del Desarrollo Social en México* (2015). Karla is coordinator at UNAM of the Co-Creation Project 'The Cohesive City: Addressing Stigmatisation in Disadvantaged Urban Neighbourhoods' and the Project 'Vulnerabilidad Socioterritorial y Proceso Metropolitano en la Región Centro de México' (Socioterritorial Vulnerability and Metropolitan Processes in the Central Mexico Region). She is a member of the Global Participatory Budget Research Board for the Participatory Budgeting Project.

Acknowledgements

We would like to thank all the authors who have contributed to this volume, together with the partners in the Co-Creation project, and the participants of the workshops and creative activities that have fed into our exploration of Co-Creation over the last four years. We hope that this book will be the starting point for further experiments with Co-Creation in the future.

Thanks are also due to the editorial team at Policy Press for their support in producing this book, and to Rose Norman for her assistance in proofreading.

This volume has received funding from the University of Bath and from the European Union's RISE Horizon 2020 research and innovation programme under the Marie Skłodowska-Curie grant agreement No 734770.

Chapters 3, 4 and 8 have received funding and support from the research project based at UNAM, PAPIIT CG300118 'Vulnerabilidad Socioterritorial y Proceso Metropolitan en la Region Centro de México' (Socioterritorial Vulnerability and Metropolitan Processes in the Central Mexico Region).

1

Introduction: conceptualising Co-Creation as a methodology

Christina Horvath and Juliet Carpenter

Introduction

Since the neoliberal turn of the 1980s and the globalisation of trade and information flows a decade later, cities around the world have been faced with the increasingly complex societal challenges of 'spatial segregation, separation and exclusion' (Bauman, 1998: 3). The protection of private property rights and the reduction of state expenditure have resulted in a radical polarisation of the distribution of wealth and power. At the same time, the expansion of the urban lifestyle has turned cities into commodities for those with money, encouraging the formation of market niches in consumer habits and cultural forms (Harvey, 2012: 14). As a result, we are living in increasingly fragmented, conflict-prone cities with privatised public spaces, increasing surveillance and growing divides between gated communities and vulnerable neighbourhoods. While new hierarchies founded on global mobility have sharpened the divide between the extraterritorial elites and the localised groups ever more affected by urban marginalisation, close-knit communities and ideals of urban identity, belonging and citizenship have become increasingly harder to sustain.

Despite the growing number of studies exploring urban disadvantage and territorial stigmatisation, knowledge generation about processes of marginalisation remains largely the remit of academic research, considered as the key source of understanding and insight to enhance societal awareness. Yet it has been increasingly recognised that alternative approaches to producing knowledge can lead to much greater societal benefits. According to Lupton and Dyson (2015), quoted in Campbell and Vanderhoven (2010: 10), 'knowledge of the social world must be deeper and stronger if it is co-produced with actors in that world; research is more likely to effect change if it is owned by people who have a capacity to effect change'. To respond to a growing need for co-produced knowledge, this book proposes to challenge territorial marginalisation by inviting to the dialogue partners who rarely participate in collaborative knowledge practices (Banks et al, 2018), namely non-academic collaborators from the civil society sector and communities carrying knowledges that have previously been passed over, and those outside the Global North, increasingly validated as examples of the 'epistemologies of the South' (Santos, 2018).

This is important for a number of reasons. First, civil society groups matter today because they are situated at the forefront of the creation of a new public sphere. The turn to civil society since the 1980s (Yúdice, 2003; 2009) was a consequence of neoliberal trade liberalisation, privatisation and the reduction of state-subsidised services including health care and education. Since institutionalised political parties were unable to counter austerity and structural adjustment policies, the most innovative actors in setting agendas for social justice moved to grassroots movements, local associations, and national and international non-governmental organisations (NGOs). These civil society actors have opened up new forms of 'progressive struggle in which culture is a crucial arena' (Yúdice, 2003: 88), turning to areas of social life abandoned by the neoliberal state and setting a new agenda for organising civil society. These actors are therefore important collaborators for knowledge production involving subaltern communities (that is, non-elite communities which can become agents of political and social change).

Second, knowledge practices focusing on marginality must necessarily involve communities whose knowledge is emerging from struggles against oppression. As opposed to the 'epistemologies of the North' linked with the objectivity, rationality, neutrality of Eurocentric approaches in knowledge generation, these epistemologies emerge from resistance to colonialism, capitalism and patriarchy. They seek to challenge dominant, Eurocentric ways of scientific knowledge production by identifying and discussing:

> ... the validity of knowledges and ways of knowing not recognized as such by the dominant epistemologies ... either because they are not produced according to accepted or even intelligible methodologies or because they are produced by absent subjects deemed incapable of producing valid knowledge. (Santos, 2018: 2)

According to Santos, what distinguishes the epistemologies of the South from those of the North is that they are embodied, rather than intellectual, and value sensations, emotions, experience and memory. Empathic to suffering, they do not distinguish between knowledge, ethics and politics since 'the politics of sharing or solidarity with the struggle are not possible without an ethic of care' (Santos, 2018: 91). Furthermore, they reject the abstract idea of progress and seek social transformation through solidarity with and listening to the life experiences of social groups that are victims of exclusion and unjust suffering under capitalism, colonialism and patriarchy. Learning from their approaches and methods is therefore vital to elaborate alternative strategies involving disadvantaged communities in knowledge production and achieving cognitive justice.

Collaborations with such politically engaged actors have important consequences for academic partners. They redefine the role of academics, transforming researchers into collaborators in the projects of communities (Bonfil, 1991). This impactful transformation of vertical relationships between researchers and researched into horizontal ones between equal knowledge producers is anchored in a range of ideals which, despite their potential contradictions, all concur in promoting greater social justice in cities. The first one is the 'right to the city' (Lefebvre, 1968), interpreted as a collective rather than individual right to 'reinvent the city more after our hearts' desire' (Harvey, 2012: 4). The second one is the model of the 'socially cohesive city' (Cassiers and Kesterloot, 2012) with its roots in social justice, unity and equality of opportunity for all (Harvey, 1973). The third one is linked to the role of creative practice in these processes, and the hope, shared by Chantal Mouffe (2007), that artistic activism can play a critical role in a society 'by subverting the dominant hegemony and by contributing to the construction of new subjectivities' (Mouffe, 2007: 5). Finally, the last ideal is based on the belief that an 'epistemological shift is necessary' (de Sousa Santos, 2018: viii) in order to change the world by collectively reinterpreting it through a dialogue between the producers of different types of knowledge.

In line with these ideals, the core aim of this volume is to reflect on how collaborations between scholars, activists, stakeholders, artists and communities can be used as a springboard to strengthen resilience to socioeconomic marginalisation in vulnerable urban areas in countries belonging to the different regions of the world. Without claims to global relevance, the contributors of this volume have chosen to focus primarily on two large geographical areas: Western Europe and North America on the one hand and Latin America on the other hand. These regions were chosen for their different sociopolitical evolution and complementary perspectives on arts-based approaches. While the approaches of countries located in the so-called 'Global North' have been marked by the legacies of colonial expansion, nationalism, civil rights movements, individualism and the ideal of the welfare state, Latin American countries in the so-called 'Global South' experienced colonialism followed by independence, modernisation, revolution or military dictatorship, redemocratisation and struggles for emancipation led by indigenous and Afro-descendent populations. Emerging from a Latin American context, emancipatory approaches to art such as the conceptualisation of public art available to the citizenry in post-revolutionary Mexico (Coffey, 2012) or Boal's (1979; 2000) theorisation of the 'theater of the oppressed' in Brazil, drawing on Freire's work (1993), have long been leading the way in exploring new ways of democratising knowledge through arts practice.

While the terms 'Global North' and 'South' might seem practical to refer to regional groupings of case-study countries having similar political and socioeconomic histories, the authors recognise that these categories have originated in the traditionally Eurocentric dichotomy of metropolitan and colonial societies. As such, the authors believe that the binary distinction between these two labels is not only arbitrary but also increasingly porous, as each collection of countries encompasses diverse values and ideologies that defy being grouped together as a common entity. The authors would also like to highlight the fact that the entities designated as 'Global North' and 'South' do not necessarily overlap with what is meant by 'epistemologies of the North and the South'. Scholars from the Global North can be promoters of the epistemologies of the South while academics from the Global South, whether educated internationally or not, may rely on categories and research methods established by the epistemologies of the North, some of which come with embedded biases and hidden agendas resulting from centuries of knowledge regulation in which any knowledge not susceptible to serve the objectives of the colonial rule was invalidated and suppressed.

In the light of this context, this volume aims to use a multidisciplinary framework to propose an original approach to methodology, reconceptualising it as 'Co-Creation', to explore this process as a broadly applicable tool, and to examine its suitability and relevance to challenging marginalisation in various contexts. A key innovation of our approach is to define Co-Creation as a knowledge process that employs creativity through arts-based methods as an alternative way to listen to the voices of marginalised communities and involve them in generating shared understandings of their neighbourhoods and (in)justices in the city. This volume is the first to conceptualise this understanding of Co-Creation and to critically explore it in a range of geographic and organisational settings in both the Global North and South. The comparative approach adopted by this volume has provided the contributors with opportunities to test Co-Creation in various contexts, seeking to address different forms of marginalisation including ethnic, racial, social, postcolonial or generational inequalities, and to discuss these experiences in the light of international debates on cohesive cities and active citizenship.

By involving local residents and practitioners in collaboration with researchers, artists and other non-academic communities, the Co-Creation method aims to promote new interactions between partners based on dialogue, to create new links (for instance between researchers, residents and artists) and to provide a safe environment for shared knowledge production. It encourages participants to share insights and awareness using creative or arts-based practice as catalysts to develop skills, networks and resilience. Co-Creation therefore primarily represents an artist-researcher-stakeholder collaboration which results in producing advances in shared knowledge as well as tangible outputs.

While the authors of this volume recommend using creativity as a catalyst to facilitate trust building, cooperation and interaction between the different actors involved in knowledge production, they are also aware of the risk of cooptation that this advocacy represents for the arts. Yúdice (2003) described top-down strategies of 'channelling the arts to manage the social' (Yúdice, 2003: 12) as the 'expediency of culture', arguing that in the post-Fordist, post-civil rights era the reduction of direct state subvention of social services led to a reorientation of arts and culture to a means with no value other than to solve social problems, a cost-effective instrument to reduce crime, enhance education, create jobs, facilitate urban renovation and consolidate citizenship founded on active participation. This vision of art as a panacea for 'a more vigorous economy, more democratic and effective government, and fewer social problems' (Yúdice, 2003: 14) was encapsulated among others in the New Labour notion of the 'creative economy' which sought to turn the arts into a resource for economy and politics. This vision has resulted in top-down arts projects in a range of countries around the world.

There is, however, another, more political, vision of creative engagement articulated by Chantal Mouffe (2007; 2013) according to which socially engaged artistic and cultural practices can provide communities with opportunities for self-understanding and resistance to the dominant social imaginary. The authors therefore apprehend Co-Creation workshops as agonistic interventions which have the potential to open 'cracks in the system' and to 'allow us, through imagination and the emotions they evoke, to participate in new experiences and to establish forms of relationships that are different from the ones we are used to' (Mouffe, 2013: 97). Through understanding differing viewpoints and 'ways of knowing', from both academic and non-academic perspectives using artistic practice, a shared, agonistic understanding can be developed and translated into recommendations that lead to practical and potentially transformative change (Mitchell et al, 2017).

What is Co-Creation?

This volume defines Co-Creation as a collective creative process that aims to feed into shared understandings of socially just neighbourhoods and cities (Carpenter and Horvath, 2018; Carpenter et al, 2021 forthcoming). Co-Creation simultaneously results in tangible material outputs – for instance, artworks, artefacts or other objects – and knowledge generated by multiple partners. The former are produced using arts or other creative methods. While their aesthetic quality is important, the collaborative process leading to their elaboration is equally, if not more, vital, because it offers multiple opportunities for participants to share perceptions, views and understanding about how to build more socially just places for the future.

The term 'co-creation' itself was initially applied in the business sector in the 1990s, referring to customer contribution to product and service development (Vargo and Lusch, 2004; Ind and Coates, 2013). It has since been applied more broadly in areas such as public participation, collaborative governance and community engagement (Voorberg et al, 2015: 1335). It is in this sphere that this book seeks to redefine the concept in relation to a methodology that engages with communities and helps them produce knowledge and understanding about their neighbourhoods, to deepen their awareness of the social world in close collaboration with artists and academic communities.

Although in recent times 'co-creation' has gained traction in a variety of contexts, it has been used with shifting meaning and often interchangeably with other 'co-' terms. One of these is 'co-production', a term associated with citizens' involvement in the provision of public services. Originating in the work of Ostrom (1990), the concept of 'co-production' was further developed by Jasanoff (2004) in the field of public management research. More recently, critics have highlighted how co-production has also been associated with the reduction of state funding for services in the public sector, where end-users are increasingly called upon to fill the gaps in provision left by austerity cuts (Fotaki, 2015). The term has recently been also adopted in the academic literature (Campbell and Vanderhoven, 2016; Banks et al, 2018), where it is used to describe the 'participatory turn' through which researchers generate knowledge in collaboration with stakeholders and other non-academic partners previously excluded from formal research processes (Ersoy, 2017; Banks et al, 2018). In this context, the process can also be labelled 'co-creation' (Leading Cities, 2015).

The knowledge generating process this book refers to as 'Co-Creation' (used in this volume with capital letters to distinguish it from the previously explained meanings of 'co-creation') draws on many of the principles of 'participatory action research' as a well-established approach to social enquiry (Whyte, 1991; Reason, 1994; Greenwood and Levin, 1998), while it also reflects the core foundations of 'co-operative inquiry' (Heron, 1996). These approaches emphasise the importance of research 'with', rather than 'on', people and have a long-established tradition in social science enquiry, blurring the boundaries between 'researcher' and 'researched' to break down hierarchical barriers in order to encourage mutual learning (Beebeejaun et al, 2014). Our approach to Co-Creation adopts these guiding principles, but takes them one step further, by advocating for systematic collaborations between academic researchers and a range of non-academic partners. These involve three groups in particular: first, groups of local residents who have a stake in the research topic at hand; second, stakeholders who are invested in local structures to affect societal change; and third, artists whose socially engaged practices contribute to voicing diverse experiences and processes at the local level and to generating understanding around spatial justice and social inclusion. The boundaries between these groups are fluid and partners in Co-Creation may sit within one or several groups simultaneously.

A key innovation of our understanding of Co-Creation is the involvement of all participants in a creative, arts-based practice of knowledge production, including academic researchers and members of the non-academic community who together engage in creative methods. By challenging rigid binaries such as 'researchers' and 'researched', 'academic' and 'non-academic', or 'artists' and 'non-artists', this approach seeks to balance the inherent power dynamics that are present in social relationships. Whereas the overarching aim of Co-Creation is underpinned by notions of equality and inclusivity, Co-Creation as a practice inevitably unfolds within an arena of diverse and at times conflicting interests. Researchers, local residents, artists and policy makers may have different ideas about the overall narrative to be developed using Co-Creation, who is best positioned to develop and disseminate the emerging stories, and how these should be presented and applied.

Recognising such deep-rooted power relations embedded within society, Alexandra (2015: 43) offers the conceptual tool of 'political listening' as a way forward, suggesting that 'within this nexus of interdependent yet unequal relationships, a methodological attention to the *politics of listening* offers conceptual inroads into addressing the power asymmetries inherent in participatory knowledge projection' [italics added]. The concept of 'political listening', first identified by Bickford (1996), highlights the presence of conflict and difference and makes communicative interaction necessary. As Bickford notes, 'communicative interaction – speaking and listening together – does not necessarily resolve or do away with the conflicts that arise from uncertainty, inequality or identity. Rather it enables political actors to decide democratically how to act in the face of conflict, and to clarify the nature of the conflict at hand' (Bickford, 1996: 2). Co-Creation involves political listening and complex negotiations to address hierarchies, tensions and disagreements during the Co-Creative process. A further issue for Co-Creation is the need for reflexivity, on the part of all participants in the process, paying attention to positionality, as well as to 'reflexivity, the production of knowledge and the power relations that are inherent in research processes' (Sultana, 2007: 382). If successfully executed, this approach to Co-Creation acknowledges the tensions and power relations that are likely to exist between participants and creates an environment of mutual trust in which participants can both listen to each other and negotiate outcomes through the more subtle, embodied ways of collective creative practice.

Co-Creation in theory and practice

Translating the central aims of Co-Creation into practice is faced with complex challenges due to the infinite variety of contexts, configurations of actors and power relations. To be able to satisfy different needs and address issues that are relevant in certain contexts rather than in others, Co-Creation as a method has to be adaptable. Yet this flexibility should not jeopardise the democratic, inclusive ethos at its core. This makes it difficult to provide a universally valid blueprint applicable in every context. Thus, without pretence to offering precise guidelines, this volume proposes a set of overarching 'principles' (understood here both as a rule and as a foundation for belief and behaviour) which have been shaped through discussions

Figure 1.1: Co-Creation principles.

ETHOS			METHODOLOGICAL APPROACH
	1 EQUAL Co-Creation provides a safe environment for knowledge exchange, in which inequalities are recognised and mitigated against using strategies for power drawn up early on in the process.	**6 EMBEDDED** Participants taking part in Co-Creation workshops are embedded in the urban area where the intervention happens.	
	2 RESPECTFUL All participants commit to respecting each other and the Co-Creation principles.	**7 AWARE** Co-Creation workshops are preceded by a series of stakeholder consultations to ensure that local needs, contextual specificities and existing knowledge are taken into account and that evaluation criteria are co-created with stakeholders at the beginning of the process.	
	3 ETHICAL Ethical issues are handled with care following university procedures, and whenever possible, local labour is remunerated.	**8 PLURIVOCAL** All participants have a voice setting the goal(s) of Co-Creation workshops and the design of the activities is based on a consensus about what will be co-created.	
	4 SHARED The outcomes are the shared property of all participants and cannot be exploited without their previous consent.	**9 ACTIVE** All participants involved in Co-Creation workshops play active roles in preparing, running, documenting and analysing the creative process, be they researchers, artists or communities.	
	5 TRUST-BASED Co-Creation aims to produce trust-based relationships. To facilitate this, participants are encouraged to spend time together, sharing meals and social space.	**10 CREATIVE** Co-Creation workshops use art/ creativity to produce outcomes, both tangible such as works of art or creative products, and intangible, such as networks and shared understanding. These outcomes are captured and evaluated.	

with researchers, artists and practitioners and tested through a range of case studies in both the Global North and South (see Figure 1.1).

These ten principles establish a framework underpinned by a set of ideals and a range of methodological considerations. The first five principles outline an ethos in which all partners are considered equals and treated with respect, existing power relations are acknowledged and strategies are devised to mitigate them. The dialogue between participants is enabled by trust built through lengthy processes facilitated by sharing social space and common meals and working together towards shared creative objectives. Some of the ethical issues addressed here revolve around partners' status as professional or volunteer Co-Creators, with salience for whose time and labour should be remunerated. With regard to ownership and dissemination, the authors believe that collectively produced outcomes should be considered as the shared property of all participants.

The remaining five principles are concerned with methodological issues rather than ethical ones. They argue for initial stakeholder meetings to be held as a way to identify participants' needs and acknowledge pre-existing local knowledge. They also recommend that at least some, if not all, actors should be embedded in the context where Co-Creation is taking place, thereby facilitating the understanding of specific local challenges. They advocate for the active participation of all the partners in the project design as well as in knowledge production and creative activities. However, there may be circumstances in which some of these principles can be disregarded.

Our definition of Co-Creation sees arts practice as embedded in the process of knowledge production. This implies that the production of the understandings and the creation of tangible artefacts are not two isolated processes, but two strongly interconnected facets of the same process. This inevitably raises questions about how knowledge created through creative methods is articulated and interpreted and how it contributes to a deeper understanding of different perspectives about issues related to the neighbourhood, the city and social justice in general.

Another set of questions concerns Co-Creation's relationship with other arts-based methods. What does Co-Creation do differently from other creative methods? Is it impactful in general or only in certain contexts? What are Co-Creation's social benefits and how can they be evidenced? While some critics have cautioned against proclaiming the all-encompassing benefits of arts-based methods in bringing about social change (Low et al, 2012), there is a growing body of literature on arts-based methods in research as a valid approach to troubling social issues (Leavy, 2015). Blodgett et al (2013: 313) suggest that arts-based methods can be used not only by professional artists but also by 'researchers and professionals to assist people in expressing feelings and thoughts that ... are difficult to articulate in words'. Arts-based approaches are increasingly seen as being particularly powerful in enabling agency, and in creating spaces for empowerment, engagement and ownership (Mitchell et al, 2017), while 'investigating topics associated with high levels of emotion' (Prendergast, 2009). Involving artists in research projects can be beneficial because often their 'approaches will be different from established norms, creating an unexpected experience for all collaborators' (Pahl et al, 2017: 131) and their 'interventions can change the way people do things … and might create a new configuration of how space is used and appreciated by those who live there' (Pahl et al, 2017: 132).

However, many arts-based research projects only use art as a trigger to elicit emotions or responses. In these projects, arts-based researchers remain purposely outside the creative process (which differs from the Co-Creation approach), in order to be able to understand participants' views without adopting and reproducing them as their own (Bryant and Charmaz, 2007). Other approaches, however, may ally arts-based and participatory research methods to use the productive tension during the collaborative process of knowledge production to help multiple and conflicting perspectives emerge. This is advocated by Gallagher (2008) who uses arts-based methods to position the researchers as doers instead of observers and to build a shared place in which 'polivocality' helps resist 'closed interpretations' (Gallagher, 2008: 71).

Similarly, in Co-Creation, the authors propose that all participants, including researchers, engage in the creative process as a way of collaboratively Co-Creating knowledge and deepening understanding from different perspectives. In addition, Co-Creation seeks to learn from artists' capacity to challenge and dismantle multiple stigmas attached to disadvantaged neighbourhoods using 'complicated gestures of rewriting, strategies of decontextualising' (Rosello, 1998: 18) and encourage residents of vulnerable neighbourhoods to embrace aspirations, contributing to improve their lives and well-being, and to achieve positive outcomes in terms of health, education, and employment to reposition themselves within society (Kearns, 2003).

Other issues arising concern the finality and the feasibility of the knowledge process. What motivates different actors' participation? Who is meant to apply the results and to what end? How will the collectively produced understanding lead to social change? To what extent do residents actually benefit from working with artists and researchers and what do researchers gain from engaging in creative activities together with communities and artists? How can this impact be evidenced? How can Co-Creation handle hierarchies and conflicting interests that may exist within the communities, and between them and the external partners? For instance, should policy makers or other power holders be admitted to participate in Co-Creation or would this make the creation of a safe space for other participants too challenging? Can state-initiated, top-down attempts at Co-Creation be trusted to come without a hidden agenda? Who is the most credible initiator of

Co-Creation, researchers or artists seeking to reach into communities, or communities reaching out to them? And finally, can Co-Creation be practised in large groups or at a wider community level rather than in the intimacy of a small group framework? Can it be done in a short timeframe or does it require a lengthy phase of relation-building?

These are only some of the questions this volume sets out to explore. Being critically mindful of the links between socially engaged collaborative practice, artistic presence, urban change and displacement, and aware of potential tensions between artistic and academic ways of producing knowledge, the authors of this volume propose to analyse the potential of Co-Creation to offer an alternative lens and a crossover between the epistemologies of the North and the embodied, sensorial and passionate approaches developed by the epistemologies of the South.

Co-Creation in the Global North and the Global South

This book originates in a partnership between two European and two Latin American academic institutions and three European non-profit organisations, brought together in a research project funded under the EU's Horizon 2020 RISE scheme (2017–20) to explore Co-Creation in Western Europe and Latin America. Some chapters draw on research undertaken as part of the project, such as case studies in Rio de Janeiro, Greater Paris or Mexico City. Other contributors reflect on similar practices and their own experience in cities including Bristol, Brussels, Madrid, Swindon and Vancouver. However, rather than the planned outcome of a project, the book is the result of an organic collaboration between artists, researchers, NGOs and community activists who have engaged in an interdisciplinary and cross-national dialogue about knowledge production with communities in different contexts of urban marginality.

Some authors are academics based at the University of Bath, Oxford Brookes University, the National Autonomous University of Mexico (UNAM) and the Pontifical Catholic University of Rio de Janeiro (PUC-Rio). Others are activists from the NGOs European Alternatives (Paris), City Mine(d) (Brussels) and Tesserae (Berlin). Despite their diverse experience as academics, practitioners, activists and in some cases artists, most contributors associated with the Horizon 2020 project have studied in Global North universities and are as, if not more, familiar with the epistemologies of the North than with those of the South. Reversely, corporeal knowledge associated with the epistemologies of the South can also exist in communities based in European or North American geographical settings. For a better representation of community voices and Southern perspectives, however, the pool of authors has been widened to include chapters written or co-written by artists and activists who were not part of the project originally, but who are now associated with it. As a consequence of this, the book is truly Co-Created across disciplines, sectors and continents.

Drawing on a range of Global North and Global South perspectives, this volume seeks to investigate Co-Creation through theoretical reflections supported by analysis of Co-Creation practice using a case-study approach. It is divided into two main parts. Part I seeks to engage with broader theoretical debates about Co-Creation and arts-based knowledge production in the Global North and South, while Part II focuses on Co-Creation in practice and seeks to bridge the gap between academic, artistic and community perspectives.

After this introduction sets the scene for a reconceptualisation of Co-Creation as collaborative arts and knowledge practice, the chapters in Part I critically explore the opportunities Co-Creation opens up for emancipation, civil imagination, artistic citizenship, destigmatisation and new narratives. However, these chapters also point to potential risks such as cooptation by the state or the recycling in new forms of old hierarchies that Co-Creation seeks to disrupt. Brownill and Natividad Puig (Chapter 2) discuss whether existing definitions and conceptualisations of Co-Creation originating from the Global North can adequately describe experiences from the Global South. They focus on the relationship between Co-Creation and the state as a way of illustrating these debates in more depth. In Chapter 3, Pantoja Peschard investigates the role of Co-Creation in challenging official narratives and histories which tend to exclude deprived communities from participating, as well as its relationship to Ariella Azoulay's (2012) concept of 'civil imagination', which is also then linked to the concept of 'artistic citizenship'.

Gázquez Iglesias (Chapter 4) develops this further, exploring the theoretical limitations of the 'Global North–Global South' model and investigates the risks of a hegemonic representational practice that reproduces asymmetry and domination. Here, Co-Creation is suggested as an innovative approach for constructing alternative representational structures, discussed in the context of the Co-Creation workshop that was held in Santa Marta, Rio de Janeiro, in August 2018. Milanese (Chapter 5) then explores the questions of where and when the Co-Creation methodology can be a useful strategy. He reflects upon Co-Creation's ability to open up temporary spaces of collaboration in which the shifting shape and time of the urban can be discerned and made accessible. Depper and Fullagar (Chapter 6) link Co-Creation as inventive practice with contemporary debates within new materialism. They examine the implications of affect and of human and non-human relations in creative collaborations and Co-Creation's material-discursive process. In Chapter 7, Castro Suarez and Quiroz Rothe broaden the field, by exploring the material conditions of Co-Creation in metropolises such as Mexico City and focusing on the role of the built environment in processes associated with Co-Creation. The authors examine a range of art practices taking place in different venues across the city and use the example of the recent FAROS project involving the creation of dedicated art facilities in deprived areas. Finally, Valverde Viesca and Pacheco Gordillo (Chapter 8) investigate the link between community social capital generated in public programmes, advocacy actions and Co-Creation. They draw on the experience of the recent Neighbourhood Improvement Programme in Mexico City to identify the potential role of Co-Creation in participatory processes with a direct impact on policy making.

Part II addresses Co-Creation through a range of practices observed by contributors across the Global North and South. Chapters in this section primarily focus on practices initiated by artist-cultural promoters, artist-researchers, or the state. Some of these were originally designed as Co-Creation while others were established on similar premises and therefore constitute useful examples as comparators for the analysis here. Whereas some chapters explore Co-Creation practice from a predominantly academic perspective, others are authored or co-authored by artists and civil society organisations and examine from their angle how the methodology of Co-Creation might support their activities.

In Chapter 9, Pruvot examines the methodology of Co-Creation in the context of a local authority arts collaboration project in Plaine Commune, in the Greater Paris area, setting the case in the context of debates around the Creative City. The chapter explores whether the Co-Creation methodology could be used by local authorities in rethinking processes of consultation and participation and in creating new modes of governance around urban development projects. Horvath (Chapter 10) then explores Co-Creation from a Global North/Global South comparative perspective, by taking examples of two literary festivals: the Brazilian Literary Festival of Peripheries (FLUP) and the French '*La Dictée des Cités*' (The Dictation of the Suburbs). While the chapter explores the creative potential of these two events to disrupt some of the clichés attached to the French *banlieues* and Brazilian favelas, it also reflects upon the possibilities of Co-Creating on a larger scale than the neighbourhood level.

Carpenter (Chapter 11) then takes the example of a Co-Creative practice in the form of a community-based percussion band in Vancouver, Canada. She demonstrates that while the methodology of Co-Creation holds critical potential as a tool to challenge stereotypes and marginalisation, it nevertheless operates within the structural constraints of deeply embedded power hierarchies and hegemonic discourses that dominate received narratives.

In Chapter 12, Segers draws on insights derived from projects run by the NGO City Mine(d) in Spain and Belgium to reflect on social transformation through the lens of 'tough issues', drawing on the work of de Certeau (1980) to explore the shift within community organisations from '*résistance*' to '*bricolage*'. The chapter argues for the role of a third actor in a social transformation process who, through a creative process such as 'prototyping', becomes tactically linked to key stakeholders. In Chapter 13, King, Mean and Stewart-Hall explore the work of the Knowle West Media Centre, in Bristol (UK), which engages with communities using creative methods to address local issues such as inadequate and unaffordable housing. The chapter shows how creative processes can contribute to nurturing exchanges and developing relationships of trust through Co-Creation. Continuing on the community theme, Álvarez-Gortari, Mihessen and Spencer (Chapter 14) discuss some of the innovative ways and collaborative approaches developed by Casa Fluminense, a non-profit organisation in Rio de Janeiro, Brazil, to influence urban policy and address issues of marginalisation. Although Casa Fluminense's approach shares some of the principles and strengths of Co-Creation, they moved away from using the term Co-Creation itself, as they recognise that on a regional level a truly Co-Creative process is difficult to achieve. In Chapter 15, Clift, Telles, and Silva focus on the history of cultural activism in the favela of Santa Marta organised by the Eco Group and its leader Itamar Silva, a black journalist, organic intellectual, activist, and community organiser in Santa Marta. The chapter explores the history of cultural activism in Santa Marta, Itamar's leadership in building this activism in the neighbourhood, and the role of community stakeholders and researchers in Co-Creation.

Staying in Rio de Janeiro, Rodrigues and Horvath (Chapter 16) explore favela tourism through the lens of Co-Creation, taking the example of the favela Tabajaras and Cabritos in Rio de Janeiro, where graffiti artist Tick (Rodrigues) has been working to design a favela tour focusing on street art. Building on a collaboration between researchers, local residents and the artist, the project investigates Co-Creation's potential to challenge dominant narratives related to favela populations and disrupt established models of favela tourism. Further community perspectives are examined in Mexico City (Chapter 17) where Davies, Osorio Saez, Sandoval-Hernandez and Horvath explore the efficiency of mixed-method research and a quasi-experimental approach in measuring the impact of Co-Creation in an educational setting in Iztapalapa, a marginalised area of the city. The authors claim that, while some aspects of the behavioural change enabled by Co-Creation can be successfully evidenced at a neighbourhood level, others are deeply embedded in the resulting artwork and the affects generated by their creation and sharing, which call for new types of evaluation tools to be developed in dialogue with the epistemologies of the South.

The Conclusion (Chapter 18) seeks to summarise what we can learn from Co-Creation experiences and similar creative initiatives in the Global North and South. Horvath and Carpenter identify key challenges (such as ethical issues resulting from previous hierarchies, practical obstacles in the way of collaborative processes and relational issues) both between Co-Creation partners and between Co-Creation teams and other audiences, such as broader communities, policy makers and the state. Drawing on the contributions in the previous chapters, the authors highlight key underlying themes, in particular drawing out the salient comparative aspects. The book ends with a set of recommendations which can provide guidance for activists, researchers, artists or policy makers and other practitioners setting up Co-Creation workshops and offer directions for further research.

References

Alexandra, D. (2015) 'Are we listening yet? Participatory knowledge production through media practice: encounters of political listening', in A. Gubrium, K. Harper and M. Otañez (eds) *Participatory Visual and Digital Research in Action*, Walnut Creek: Left Coast Press, pp 41–55.

Azoulay, A. (2012) *Civil Imagination: A Political Ontology of Photography*, translated by Louise Bethlehem, London and New York: Verso.

Banks, S., Hart, A., Pahl, E. and Ward, P. (eds) (2018) *Co-producing Research: A Community Development Approach*, Bristol: Policy Press.

Bauman, Z. (1998) *Globalization: The Human Consequences*, Cambridge: Polity Press.

Beebeejaun, Y., Durose, C., Rees, J., Richardson, J. and Richardson, L. (2014) ' "Beyond text": exploring ethos and method in co-producing research with communities', *Community Development Journal*, 49(1): 37–53.

Bickford, S. (1996) *The Dissonance of Democracy: Listening, Conflict, and Citizenship*, Ithaca, NY: Cornell University Press.

Blodgett, A.T., Coholic, D.A., Schinke, R.J., McGannon, K.R., Peltier, D. and Pheasant, C. (2013) 'Moving beyond words: exploring the use of arts-based method in Aboriginal community sport research', *Qualitative Research in Sport, Exercise and Health*, 5(3): 312–31.

Boal, A. (1979; 2000) *Theatre of the Oppressed*, London: Pluto Press.

Bonfil Batalla, G. (1991) *Desafíos a la Antropología en la Sociedad Contemporánea*, Iztapalapa 11(24): 77–90.

Bryant, A. and Charmaz, K. (2007) *The SAGE Handbook of Grounded Theory*, London: SAGE.

Campbell, H. and Vanderhoven, D. (2016) *Knowledge That Matters: Realising the Potential of Co-Production*, Manchester: N8 Research Partnership.

Carpenter, J. and Horvath, C. (2018) *Co-Creation: Addressing Urban Stigmatization, Building Inclusive Cities*, Urban Affairs Association Conference, Toronto, 4–7 April 2018.

Carpenter, J., Horvath, C. and Spencer, B. (2021 forthcoming) 'Co-Creation as an agonistic practice in the favela of Santa Marta, Rio de Janeiro', *Urban Studies*.

Cassiers, T. and Kesterloot, C. (2012) 'Socio-spatial inequalities and social cohesion in European cities', *Urban Studies*, 49(9): 1909–24.

Coffey, M. (2012) *How a Revolutionary Art Became Official Culture: Murals, Museums, and the Mexican State*, Durham: Duke University Press.

de Certeau, M. (1980) *L'Invention du Quotidien*, Paris: Union Générale d'Editions.

de Sousa Santos, B. (2018) *The End of the Cognitive Empire: The Coming of Age of Epistemologies of the South*, Durham: Duke University Press.

Ersoy, A. (ed) (2017) *The Impact of Co-production: From Community Engagement to Social Justice*, Bristol: Policy Press.

Fotaki, M. (2015) 'Co-production under the Financial Crisis and Austerity: a means of democratizing Public Services or a race to the bottom?', *Journal of Management Inquiry*, 24(4): 433–8.

Freire, P. (1993) *Pedagogy of the Oppressed*, London: Penguin.

Gallagher, K. (ed) (2008) *The Methodological Dilemma: Creative, Critical and Collaborative Approaches to Qualitative Research*, London: Routledge.

Greenwood, D. and Levin, M. (1998) *Introduction to Action Research: Social Research for Social Change*, Thousand Oaks, CA: SAGE.

Harvey, D. (1973) *Social Justice and the City*, London: Edward Arnold.

Harvey, D. (2012) *Rebel Cities*, London: Verso.

Heron, J. (1996) *Co-operative Inquiry: Research into the Human Condition*, London: SAGE.

Ind, N. and Coates, N. (2013) 'The meanings of co-creation', *European Business Review*, 25(1): 86–95.

Jasanoff, S. (ed) (2004) *States of Knowledge: The Co-Production of Science and Social Order*, London: Routledge.

Kearns A. (2003) 'Social capital regeneration and urban policy', in R. Imrie and M. Raco (eds) *Urban Renaissance? New Labour, Community and Urban Policy*, Bristol: Policy Press, pp 36–60.

Leading Cities (2015) 'Co-creation Connectivity: addressing the citizen engagement challenge', available from https://leadingcities. org/research/co-creation-connectivity-2/ [accessed 16 March 2018].

Leavy, P. (2015) *Method Meets Art: Arts-based Research Practice*, New York: Guilford Press.

Lefebvre, H. (1968) *Le Droit à la Ville*, Paris: Anthropos.

Low, B., Brushwood Rose, C., Salvio, P. and Palacios, L. (2012) '(Re)framing the scholarship on participatory video production and distribution: from celebration to critical engagement', in E-J. Milne, C. Mitchell and N. de Lange (eds) *Handbook of Participatory Video*, London: AltaMira Press, pp 49–64.

Lupton, R. and Dyson, A. (2015) [slides for an informal research programme presentation], 23 September 2015.

Mitchell, C., de Lange, N. and Moletsane, R. (2017) *Participatory Visual Methodologies: Social Change, Community and Policy*, London: SAGE.

Mouffe, C. (2007) 'Artistic Activism and Agonistic Spaces', *Art and Research*, 1(2), available from http://www.artandresearch.org.uk/ v1n2/mouffe.html.

Mouffe, C. (2013) *Agonistics: Thinking the World Politically*, London: Verso.

Ostrom, E. (1990) *Governing the Commons: The Evolution of Institutions for Collective Action*, Cambridge: Cambridge University Press.

Pahl, K., Escott, H., Graham, H., Marwood, K., Pool, S. and Ravetz, A. (2017) 'What is the role of the artists in interdisciplinary collaborative projects with universities and communities?' in K. Facer and K. Pahl (eds) *Valuing Interdisciplinary Collaborative Research*, Bristol: Policy Press, pp 131–152.

Prendergast, M. (2009) 'Introduction' in M. Prendergast, C.D. Leggo and P. Sameshima (eds) *Poetic Inquiry: Vibrant Voices in the Social Sciences*, Rotterdam: Sense Publishers.

Reason, P. (ed) (1994) *Participation in Human Inquiry*, London: SAGE.

Rosello, M. (1998) *Declining the Stereotype: Ethnicity and Representation in French Cultures*, Hanover, NH: University Press of New England.

Sultana, F. (2007) 'Reflexivity, positionality and participatory ethics: negotiating fieldwork dilemmas in international research', *ACME: An International E-journal for Critical Geographies,* 6(3): 374–85.

Vargo, S.L. and Lusch, R.F. (2004) 'Evolving to a New Dominant Logic for Marketing', *Journal of Marketing*, 68(1): 1–17.

Yúdice, G. (2003) *The Expediency of Culture: Uses of Culture in the Global Era*, Durham: Duke University Press.

Yúdice, G. (2009) 'Cultural diversity and cultural rights', *HIOL: Hispanic Issues On Line*, 5: 110–37.

Voorberg, W.H., Bekkers, V.J.J.M. and Tummers, L. (2015) 'A systematic review of co-creation and co-production: embarking on the social innovation journey', *Public Management Review*, 17(9): 1333–57.

Whyte, W. (ed) (1991) *Participatory Action Research*, London: SAGE.

PART I

Co-Creation in theory

2

Co-creation and the state in a global context

Sue Brownill and Oscar Natividad Puig

Introduction

Co-creation[1] narratives are gaining global currency, with initiatives and governments around the world increasingly using the term to label their activities across very different contexts, in an example of what McCann and Ward (2011) refer to as 'policy mobility'. This chapter critically explores the implications of this in two ways. First, by drawing on debates about the need for theory to 'see from the South' (Watson, 2009), it discusses whether existing definitions and conceptualisations of co-creation, which tend to come from the Global North, can adequately characterise and understand the experience of the Global South. Such debates overlap with decolonial approaches seeking to challenge the geopolitics of knowledge production, which are of particular relevance to considerations of co-creation (see for example Mignolo, 2000; Quijano, 2007). This chapter therefore asks the question: is co-creation a colonising concept or can it be explored in ways which break down dichotomies and change relations between the Global North and South as well as addressing other examples of marginalisation and exclusion?

Second, the chapter focuses on the relationship between co-creation and the state as a way of illustrating these debates in more depth. In liberal democracies, the ideal of co-creation sees communities and the state working together in addressing inequalities, allowing voices to be heard, providing emancipatory potential and thus changing the relationship between the state and its publics. But as Pritchard's (2017) critique among others points out, in both the Global North and South, such initiatives can be coopted by the state and other agencies as a way of devolving responsibilities, implementing growth-oriented urban agendas and organising voluntary effort leading to the potential cooption of groups and initiatives into a restrictive narrative of co-creation. In other more extreme cases, an oppressive and militarised state can close down spaces of co-creation. How do projects and communities navigate these differing contexts, and what forms of co-creation emerge within them?

These questions are significant ones for a project that brings together partners from the Global North and South, but the origins of which could arguably be seen as adding to the colonisation of urban theory and practice. This chapter will address them by drawing on relevant literature and exploring the views and experience of participants in co-creative practices gathered in a series of in-depth interviews with four local stakeholders directly involved in the H2020 Co-Creation case studies in Brazil and Mexico, and with three additional academics from these countries working in related fields. The questions are aimed at capturing the implications of differing contexts and local conceptualisations, exploring co-creation as an emerging concept in conversation with the partners of the project beyond the term Co-Creation as defined in the introduction of this book (Chapter 1). It also brings in material and discussions held at three conferences organised by the project in Berlin, Rio and Mexico City. The discussion is, therefore, largely restricted to the countries participating in the project but the authors hope that this will raise debates and issues with a wider remit.

Seeing from the South

The phrase 'seeing from the South' was popularised in a 2009 article by South African planner Vanessa Watson (Watson, 2009). The article was part of a growing body of work which questioned the ability of the urban theory 'canon' to fully understand and explain the urban experience in the Global South, given such theory was based largely on the experience of major Western cities such as Chicago and Los Angeles. Not only is this seen as an example, for some, of the colonisation of knowledge and the exclusion of some voices in favour of others, but also as resulting in theory which cannot explain Southern cities, much less support calls for interventions within them. Watson was joined by other writers such as Ananya Roy (2011) (writing largely about the Asian experience) and Jennifer Robinson (2013) (Africa) in calling for urban studies and urban theory to be reoriented and transformed by taking on board the knowledge and experiences of the Global South. This, they asserted, would produce different arguments and concepts, and include voices different from traditional hegemonic theory, which, as a result, can be seen as provincial rather than global. There are other dimensions than the geopolitics of North–South distinctions to these critiques, particularly articulations with relations of race, gender and sexuality (Lugones, 2007). However, the focus here is on 'seeing from the South'. The implications of this for a concept such as Co-Creation are twofold: first, is it merely yet another example of a concept from the North, which is imposed on the South, or second (and from a more nuanced perspective) what are the implications of the differing contexts in which Co-Creation occurs for how the concept can be theorised and understood?

What/where is the Global South?

Before exploring these questions further, it is important to understand what is meant by the term 'the Global South'. Like 'co-creation', the term is itself contested. Its origins lie in the Brandt report of 1980 (Brandt and Sampson, 1980), which sought to move away from the 'Third World' label and shift global debates from a focus on East/West. Nevertheless, Roy (2014) has questioned the subsequent construction of the Global South as the location of underdevelopment. She notes that initiatives such as participatory action research (PAR), movements for rights to the city, participatory budgeting, and so on show that new formations are occurring in Southern cities meaning the South cannot be seen as a 'stable ontological category symbolising subalternity' (p 15) but instead should be seen as a source of innovation. Previously (Roy, 2005), she has called for informality to be recognised as a form of urbanisation in its own right, rather as something apart from the formal; in other words, as real urbanisation. Miraftab and Kudva (2015) recognise the dangers of essentialism and hierarchies associated with the term the Global South, but argue for an understanding of the term that 'emphasise(s) a shared heritage of recent colonial histories in the global peripheries … combined with Post WWII experience of development to "alleviate" poverty' (p 4).

Mabin (2014) (also writing from South Africa) sees a dual situation of postcoloniality and a particular political economic situation in which there is a condition of scarcity for the majority as Southern conditions. It is above all, he argues, a relational not a geographical term. However, he also cautions against a focus on 'seeing from the South' which sets up new dichotomies and hierarchies and could potentially repeat the exclusion it is trying to overcome. He and others have questioned the usefulness of the term 'South' itself. He also suggests that some theoretical tools may have value in understanding the global urban experience despite their provenance. The issue then becomes one of conducting research which tests rather than assumes the theoretical efficacy of such tools.

Policy mobility: a new form of colonisation?

It is not just theory which is critiqued from this perspective, but also practice. Vainer (2014), writing from the Brazilian perspective, questions the notion of best practice in policy and the rise of globally circulating city-models (see also McCann and Ward, 2011). These are, he argues, also rooted in colonial history and he details, for example, how urban planning in Rio adopted European models from the Portuguese colonialists through to the French Beaux-Arts and the 'Barcelona effect'. Mabin (2014) also challenges the tendency to export modernity as the aim of city building, which has an underlying assumption that the Western city is somehow 'better'. Vainer argues that this practice has been cemented in more recent years through multilateral development agencies and research which 'reflects particular conceptions and goals' (Vainer, 2014: 51) under the guise of international collaboration. This, he argues, is another form of colonialisation, not the same as the cathedral and squares of the Portuguese but one which nevertheless demonstrates relations of power, domination and exclusion in similar ways to debates about the colonisation of knowledge.

The rise of global research agendas and the search for ways of addressing global challenges such as the United Nations' Millennium Development Goals, imperatives that to a certain extent have driven this project, can be seen as part of these debates. As Izzi points out in an auto-critique of one such project, these agendas set up expectations that research projects will produce cutting-edge results, be interdisciplinary, collaborative and participatory, and achieve impact and equitable North–South relations all at the same time (Izzy, nd). There are dangers that from such practices new forms of knowledge colonialisation will occur and tokenistic practices will emerge, which do not fundamentally alter research agendas in the West unless attention is paid to the difficulties and politics of such projects. For example, she argues that space should be found to reframe questions as a result of participatory research as projects progress. This critique also raises questions about the micro-politics of Co-Creation projects, in particular, the extent that 'experts' and 'outsiders' frame debates, lead activities and present results.

Against this, Vainer (2014) and others argue that practice and knowledge should be decolonised. 'Decoloniality is an intentional act a process of "de-linking" knowledge, theory and praxis from Euro-centric Western structures and systems' (Fernandez, 2019; see also Mignolo, 2009). Vainer argues this is a dual process; recognising how the cities (and theories) of the West were themselves built upon colonialism (trade and slavery) – in other words modernity and colonialisation are linked – and also imagining a 'different world' not by replacing one set of theories with other Southern ones but through pluri-versalism, dialogues and research which is specific to context (Vainer, 2014).

Moving forward: beyond dichotomies

The implications of these debates in terms of future urban research are varied. For some (Roy and Watson), the current challenge is that of replacing many existing concepts and theories with new forms of knowledge and new concepts and theories – 'Southern theory'. However, others (Mabin and Vainer) argue against this, seeing it as replacing one set of limited theories with another. Instead, they say, there is a need to move beyond critique and dichotomies to think about how research and policy mobility can be framed to avoid exclusion and the resulting partial theorisation. This implies more dialogue, reflexivity and hybridity in research. This would include recognition of the diversity of experiences and knowledge, and a commitment to theorising from this plurality/diversity. This is accompanied by an appreciation of the power relations of colonising knowledge and an intent to 'trouble methodological paradigms and knowledge constructions' (Fernandez, 2019) while also paying attention to power dynamics within research processes (Gaventa, 1993).

Robinson (2013) and others, for example, call for a new form of comparative research which is not about comparing or transferring best practice but about understandings emerging out of a deep appreciation of each context. In this vein, Vainer (2014) calls for a dialogical approach based on a borderless, free and fair trade of ideas, an appreciation of the condition of production of the knowledge that is being submitted to the dialogues, a questioning of taken for granted assumptions, and a recognition of the difficulties of translating ideas and practices from one place to another. In short, these seem to be about replacing the North/South dichotomy with a transformed research process and a search for pluralistic/hybrid theorising.

The chapter turns now to look at the implications of these debates for the concept and practice of Co-Creation, as experienced on this project.

Co-creation: a colonising concept?

Major reviews of co-creation and related concepts already exist (see for example Voorberg et al, 2015; Horner, 2016). These indicate that co-creation is a diffuse and contested concept. Leaving aside these debates, this chapter focuses on the question raised in the introduction about whether co-creation is an example of a colonialising concept or whether it could be explored conceptually and methodologically in different contexts in a way that moves beyond dichotomies of North and South. First, the evolution of the term co-creation is explored and, second, the understandings and uses of it from the perspective of respondents are explored in more depth.

Through carrying out a literature review for the project, it became clear that most recent writing and discussion on the concept of co-creation has largely come from and is related to the Global North (Colini and Brownill, 2018). Nevertheless, noting Vainer's (2014) calls for scholars to reveal the interplay between North and South in the formation of theories and ideas is one way of challenging such silences. Such an exercise reveals a pattern of North/South interaction which is arguably underplayed in many accounts. As shown elsewhere (Colini and Brownill, 2018 , and in Chapter 1) co-creation is not a new concept. It initially gained traction in the business world in the 1990s referring to the active involvement of customers in the co-creation of the products they would consume in the future (Vargo and Lusch, 2004). Significantly, the term then migrated to the world of social and economic development through the work of Elinor Ostrom (1990), which stressed the value of cooperation and co-creation in resource development and management, particularly in the Global South. Practices such as participatory rapid appraisal (PRA), which focused on the participation of people in the formation of development programmes and initiatives developed around this, went on to influence community development activities in the North. However, this incorporation into international aid and development practice could be seen as supporting arguments around colonialisation and co-creation.

Another example of North/South interactions is the work of theorists such as Freire (1993), who established a strong base in theory and practice in the South, which then influenced thinking in the North. Crystallised in his work *Pedagogy of the Oppressed* (1993), Freire addressed one of the key concerns that co-creation and related concepts are addressing, that of knowledge and whose knowledge should be used in the basis of action and decisions, seeking to establish an epistemology based on challenging dominant discourses, decentring exclusionary knowledge, and acknowledging the value of multiple forms of knowledge. His theorisation of knowledge based on Brazilian society is a clear example of how the South has impacted theories in the North, as his pedagogic values and theories can now be found through most Anglo-Saxon education systems. In a similar way, but more recently, Mike Davis popularised the term 'favela' (Davis, 2015) in contrast to the English concept 'slum' to acknowledge differences across territories of poverty across the globe. Such a recent conceptualisation may still result in a dichotomy between 'slums' and 'favelas', but it has the potential of promoting the hybrid conceptualisation this chapter is exploring for the term 'co-creation' itself.

Considering the nature of the Co-Creation project, in which knowledge exchange is promoted between partners in Europe and the Global South (Brazil and Mexico), the views of these 'Southern' partners, as expressed in their interviews with the researchers, is of significance here. First, at the level of terminology, most felt that the concept was yet to be commonly used in both the policy and academic literature in their countries. The prior arrival of other 'co-' terms, especially around social and economic development and also participatory arts movements, may have arguably led to the elision of the idea of 'co-creation' with related terms such as 'co-production', a recurrent point raised by the project's informants. Second, there was some support for seeing co-creation as another 'idea from elsewhere' (McCann and Ward, 2011) moving from North to South. On the rare occasions the researchers were told that the term co-creation *was* used, it tended to be by non-government organisations (NGOs) reliant on international funds and therefore linked to the global agenda of cooperation and development discussed earlier in this chapter. In this way, such NGOs become agents of policy mobility.

However, in a comment on why such mobility occurs, a respondent from one such NGO claimed that imported concepts like 'co-production' or 'co-creation' are sometimes imposed not only by the North but also by governments themselves, cementing what he called "the relationship between the centre and periphery". This is an acknowledgement of the relations of power and domination not just potentially between the North and South but also the dominant view in cities of the South, 'the centre', and those voices from historically marginalised communities, the 'periphery'. Nevertheless, while conscious of these relations, the organisation was also attempting to develop its own approaches under the co-creation heading which could challenge them, once again showing the complexities that exist.

Related to this, in the words of one respondent, "the proximity of co-creation to innovation is dangerous; there is a danger that (practices and theorisations) will be lost in the search or fashion for new words and ideas". For some respondents, this raised the danger that the use of a term such as co-creation could obscure long traditions of social thought and action in particular places, while others felt there was an opportunity for co-creation to learn from existing bodies of work pursuing similar goals. Some mentioned the work of theorists such as Freire already discussed. Additionally, several respondents called attention to the long and proud history of popular movements in the South, a long fight for a more meaningful involvement whenever external stakeholders come to work in their territories. This fight has sparked a conceptualisation of what popular movements in Brazil call 'effective participation', while in Mexico it has resulted in advocacy for participative development and horizontally constructed public policies. In both cases, respondents felt these practices, which have existed and matured in their countries over decades, are addressing what Co-Creation is ultimately aiming for. Therefore, arguing not only for continuity of social movements and activism in popular territories but also for a conversation between foreign concepts with local experiences, some respondents insisted on incorporating local traditions to the conceptualisation of Co-Creation when working in their territories.

Third, however, despite the dangers of uncritically adopting concepts from elsewhere, and even though co-creation is not part of the theoretical discourses of these respondents, some commented on the usefulness of a new concept in bringing in fresh ideas and discussions, not only among academics but also policy makers: "Could Co-Creation be a weapon to recognise agency and elevate claims and demands?" asked one. Respondents recognised the importance of having a space for dialogue, a space in which the different participating stakeholders openly acknowledge their interests, knowledge and preconceived ideas. Co-Creation could be a way of opening up such spaces and acknowledging different forms of knowledge and debate. However, interviewees pointed out that Co-Creation "may change the way we look at a situation, the way we describe, analyse and discuss it, but it won't directly change the root of the problem …".

Finally, Co-Creation, by definition focuses on the co-elaboration of objects. Some interviewees recognised the value of focusing on the production of an artefact or output, rather than becoming trapped in the discussion of intangible processes, the search for effective participation or trying to influence wider policy processes. This can open up new ways of influencing debates when other routes are blocked. This also led to discussion around the role of arts, culture and/or citizenship more broadly in the discussions of Co-Creation. For instance, Brazilian respondents advocated a broader role for culture instead of focusing only on arts, as it encompasses popular processes of knowledge production more broadly.

Therefore, it would be too easy to conclude that co-creation is a concept only relevant to the Global North, making its usage in the South questionable, or that an inevitable process of colonisation was occurring. However, while the label 'co-creation' may not be applied by the partners in the Co-Creation project, the process of 'co-creation' may well be occurring under a different name: 'effective participation' in Brazil or 'participatory development' in Mexico being some of them. There is also evidence of an awareness of how terms such as 'co-creation' could be adapted, made and remade as they circulate globally.

Bearing in mind the calls of Watson (2009) and Robinson (2013) for more comparative research, this provides scope for exploring the different meanings, definitions and practices of co-creation in a variety of different contexts in both the Global North and South. The aim here is not to develop conceptual clarity or to reach an overarching definition of co-creation, but to show the complexity, variation and potential of the concept. To do this, the argument focuses on a key aspect of the theory and practice of co-creation: the role of the state and state–citizen relations that are embodied within it. Therefore, in order to reflect on the sociopolitical particularities of these contexts, the following section explores the role of the state in Brazil and Mexico, relating it to Western liberal democracies.

Co-Creation and the state: North and South

Co-Creation as an activity, certainly within this project, tends to focus on the actions of communities attempting to make their voices heard, change conditions or address marginalisation and stigmatisation. In many contexts, this brings the Co-Creation process into contact with the state. Yet if definitions of co-creation are contested, then so is the relation between co-creation, people, and the state. In addition, the spaces of co-creation created by the dynamics between these elements can vary greatly from place to place. Therefore, this becomes fertile ground to explore further debates regarding North and South based on the experiences in the different countries in the project.

The role of the state and the relationship between the state and its publics is a key focus of debates on 'seeing from the South'. As previously indicated, such debates include calls for an awareness of how governance forms part of the 'southern condition' (Mabin, 2014) and the need to avoid imposing theories developed in the context of liberal Westernised democracies, with their emphasis on consensus-building, on the South. Within this, this chapter focuses on two areas: different rationalities of state–society relations and different spaces of participation. In terms of different state rationalities, Parnell and Robinson (2012) for example caution against seeing the state as monolithic and of assuming that neoliberalising trends evident in the Global North are universal. Writing about South Africa, they see the state as having an important role in, for example, anti-poverty programmes which need not follow the coopting logic of neoliberalism. This suggests the need for an awareness of different rationalities of state intervention, which again, this chapter would argue, can transcend North/South distinctions. De Satgé and Watson (2018) extend this to look at state–society relations. They use the term 'conflicting rationality' to describe state–society relations in highly conflictual Southern contexts, where consensus-building or collaborative participatory processes are unlikely to be effective. For example, they write about attempts by the state to 'formalise' informal settlements, which are met with resistance by those who feel their livelihoods and ways of life are being threatened as a result. Even practices such as Co-Creation, aimed at recognising diversity within territories, may be based on universal assumptions of inclusion that would fail to recognise the conflicting rationalities (Watson, 2003) within a sociopolitical context.

The recognition of the complexities of state–society relations is extended when looking at participation. Cornwall (2004), for example, distinguishes between invited and claimed spaces. Invited spaces are those in which participants are asked to participate, such as those linked to public policy. Claimed spaces are those that are created and taken by citizens themselves, either in opposition to or in the absence of formal policies. This inevitably raises questions about power. American planner Sherry Arnstein summed these relations up 50 years ago in her famous ladder of participation, with differing degrees of citizen power represented as different 'rungs' on the ladder. Notable in the ladder are the bottom rungs: these depict attempts at participation without changes in power dynamics, which instead can be used by those with power to legitimate their (unchanged) roles/ decisions and manipulate participants (Arnstein, 1969). It is this sort of manipulation which prompted Cooke and Kothari (2001) to label participation as a new tyranny, linking it to the spread of neoliberal governance forms and development aid agendas (including practices such as PRA) around the world.

Miraftab (2009), writing from the context of the Global South, discusses the role of insurgent planning here. These are practices which are counter-hegemonic, transgressive and imaginative: that is, they create spaces which challenge the status quo (and for Miraftab that includes the transfer of policy objectives from North to South) and aim for more inclusive and just outcomes. Such debates, while intersecting with North/South distinctions, nevertheless ultimately transcend them. There can be no simple reading off of particular participatory spaces being linked to particular geographies. Instead they can coexist or conflict within the same city or even initiative. However, the context in which these practices occur needs to be fully appreciated and taken into account in ways that are aware of North/South dynamics.

Such arguments suggest that the state can take different forms in different places and over time and, as a result, there are complexities in the relationship between co-creation and the state which may or may not correlate with North/South distinctions. This chapter illustrates this with an overview of the context of Co-Creation actions in the different locations within which the project is engaged. Later chapters discuss particular neighbourhoods in detail; here the focus is on broad trends in state–civil society relations around Co-Creation, drawing on ideas of differing and conflicting rationalities and spaces of participation.

In Western Europe, normative assumptions about 'co-creation' as a 'good thing' have led to it being increasingly adopted within policy programmes, such as those of the EU. Many area-based schemes see the democratic deficit as being part of the causes of neighbourhood disadvantage along with related issues such as the lack of social capital. Ways of overcoming this could be through collaborative planning, community involvement and the use of art projects to empower and to build social capital. This will then contribute to the redirection of resources to areas/groups and the building of a consensus around future actions. Co-creation, in this way, is seen as a way of bringing together policy makers, residents and other actors to 'co-create' solutions to particular issues/problems. Such approaches become further embedded through funding programmes on the national and global scales.

The role of culture and artistic practices in addressing urban deprivation and marginalisation has received increased attention in recent years. As Pruvot's chapter in this volume (Chapter 9) shows in the case of Saint Denis, Paris, at the macro level, culture is seen as a way of promoting economic growth and attracting inward investment and, at the micro level, a cultural strategy looks to involve young people in theatre, music and the arts to promote inclusion. Participatory practices are also labelled as 'co-creation' or 'co-production' with consultancies and agencies being employed to implement programmes. One such example is the co-creation with artists and designers of open spaces and art works linked to a major new rail link. In this context, 'co-creation' as a term and a process often implies the complex 'complicity' (to use the phrase from the project's Berlin conference) of state and non-state actors.

Critiques of such actions argue that they can be coopted by the state and constitute 'governance through community' (Rose, 1996) with the state adopting 'co-creative' policies in order to use inclusivity and participation to its own ends. An example in the UK is the Big Society of the 2010–15 Coalition Government, when then Prime Minister David Cameron's political agenda to create a more participatory democracy and devolve responsibility to the local level came at a time of public sector cuts. As a result, the public was being asked to take on the role of co-creators/co-deliverers of services, either instead of the state or as unpaid volunteers for it. Others (for example Swyngedouw, 1997) argue these actions fundamentally ignore the conflict and the inequality in power that exists between participants and naively assume consensus can be built.

Focusing briefly in the role of arts, as the focus on Co-Creation within this project intends, it is important to highlight that similar critiques have been made of 'art-washing' (Pritchard, 2017) as a process by which artists and creative practices are used to literally 'paint over' both the incorporation of communities through participation, but also the continued existence of major socioeconomic divisions which remain unaltered by the regeneration or other policies targeted at 'deprived' communities. The role of artists in the processes of gentrification is a particularly relevant issue here, both in terms of their role in the potential incorporation of community energy and also the micro-politics of 'co-creative' practices (Ley, 2003).

Such examples and experiences highlight the dangers of entering the invited spaces of participation. This does not mean, however, that there are no spaces being claimed by and through Co-Creation in the Western European context. Throughout the European cities involved in the project it is possible to see examples where land is being used to create cultural spaces which celebrate local culture rather than promote economic development, and which use artistic practices to challenge and disrupt dominate narratives about people and places.

In the case of Brazil, by contrast, there has been a dramatic change in state–society relations as a result of the election of a popularist Right-wing government. This has closed down spaces of co-creation and policy opened in previous years and lead to state responses in low-income areas being characterised largely by military interventions and an absence of social programmes. This is particularly the case in Rio, where over the previous two decades, political narratives advocated terms such as community participation and social inclusion (for example the discourse behind Favela Bairro), enabling communities to co-design urban interventions. In the words of respondents, these approached "true co-creation" or "effective participation". In the current political scenario, however, the Western policy ideal of all stakeholders (particularly state and non-state actors) 'co-creating' solutions appears both distant and naïve. Nowadays, the reality for many low-income areas is that the presence of the state is largely characterised though police pacification units, a militarised and controlling form of "poverty management", and an example of "anti-politics" according to the project's partners. As a result, and in a clash of rationalities, favelas are subordinated and remade within public policy not as a space where the state and civil society can work together but as a space to be 'pacified' and occupied.

Therefore, in the face of a militarised state looking to restrict rights and resources to low-income areas, culture and 'co-creation' become both highly constrained and highly politicised. It is here that the discussion of insurgent spaces becomes significant. Cultural practices such as poetry, graffiti, music and dance were seen as challenging such images, bringing different people and communities together and as practices of resistance. As one interviewee said, "Cultural movements have the possibility of reconfiguring the city … . We do politics through culture." But they were also mindful that, "We are not able to change wider structures of power and inequality in society" even though they were able to enact a different notion of community politics which defies the state's positioning.

Within this context, some see the potential of co-creation as a way of opening new spaces of dialogue, sharing knowledge, and legitimising the claims of marginalised groups. An example here is the Popular Plan for Vila Autodromo, a favela threatened with demolition to make way for the Olympic Park in Barra da Tijuca. Pressure groups, residents, universities and others came together to create an alternative plan which was partially successful in ensuring 20 families remained on the site. Such activities, as well as giving support and sharing knowledge, can be useful in legitimising campaigns and validating the claims of marginalised groups. In other cities in Brazil, for example Salvador, where the local state is more open to working with communities, work between universities and community groups has been welcomed as a way of bringing the municipality and professionals into the arena to enable their demands to be implemented. Therefore, there could be hope for co-creation as a form of autonomous practice beyond the state, or which links with parts of the state that are more sympathetic. However, in recognition of the significance of the micro-politics of co-creative practices, respondents were clear that this had to be from the perspective of the community reaching out, not NGOs, universities or artists reaching in. In the Brazilian context, therefore, Co-Creation could be seen as a potential insurgent practice formed in the face of a very different form of state intervention both from the ideals of consensus-building and from the contexts in other partner countries to the project.

The value of making South-South comparisons as part of the attempt to break down rigid North/South dichotomies is underlined when exploring the third partner country. State–society relations in Mexico appear very different from the Brazilian experience. The foundations for the current Mexican state rationality can be traced to the early 1990s. The adoption of a neoliberal model in 1988 increased socioeconomic polarisation, which resulted in a crisis of political legitimacy (see Chapters 4 and 7 for more details on the neoliberal shift in the Global South and in Mexico City respectively). During this political crisis, governmental research on marginality (CONAPO, 1994) acknowledged the 'emergence of an active civil society that claimed new terms of political coexistence, as well as spaces for participation ... specially in the political and social institutions of the State' (CONAPO, 1994, p9). This document not only established an Index of Municipal Marginality (IMM) still used today to locate the most vulnerable neighbourhoods, but also shifted the role of marginalised groups from being purely passive beneficiaries to active agents in urban programmes. Under such a rationality, the state provided multiple invited spaces for participation over the last two decades, including the Neighbourhood Improvement Programme since 2006 (see Chapter 8). However, in practice, questions exist about whether some of these are coopted by the state as in European examples.

The election of a Left-wing government in 2018, which expressly challenges neoliberalism, has intensified the discourse on opening more spaces of participation and social justice. For example, a new programme, PILARES (points of innovation, freedom, arts, education and knowledge) establishes innovation points to provide skills and training aimed at developing economic opportunities together with the community which, while not using the term 'co-creation', suggests a similar approach of bringing together multiple stakeholders and experiences, including artists, to address urban issues. However, it is too soon to see whether this will lead to any changes in outcomes.

There has also been a long history within Mexico on the use of murals as a form of political expression (see Chapters 4 and 7). However, one respondent said, "... sometimes tools from public and community art are appropriated by the state for regeneration purposes", which acknowledges the risk of Co-Creative spaces being coopted by the state as has happened in Western Europe. Therefore, the Mexican example, while not denying the differences between North and South, reveals how rationalities of state intervention and configurations of participatory spaces can cross the boundaries of North and South.

Conclusion

This chapter has shown the significance of 'seeing from the South' to understanding and characterising the theory and practice of co-creation. Not only is it clear that there is a need to highlight the interplay of theorisations between North and South which underpins such concepts (decolonialisation), but it is also apparent that co-creation is constituted and enacted in different ways in different contexts. This underlines Robinson's (2013) call for context-rich research and Vainer's (2014) 'pluri-versatilism' to help break down North/South dichotomies and to generate new forms of understanding. Later chapters in this volume add to these rich understandings of how co-creation is constituted and experienced in a variety of contexts.

It has also shown how the spaces of co-creation, particularly those linked with state activity, vary over time and space, not only between North and South but also within different places. This underlines the need to avoid a one-size-fits-all view of co-creation, and instead see it as a contingent and complex practice which has multiple possibilities and limitations partly dependent on place and context. Practitioners and academics need to be alive to these differences and to take them into account in both theorisation and action.

Finally, the experience of co-creation in some parts of the Global South also underlines its potential in creating autonomous, insurgent and alternative spaces leading to the conception of Co-Creation as set out in Chapter 1. Such spaces can challenge not only the transfer of 'ideas from elsewhere', but also related attempts to impose from the centre/top/powerful on the peripheral and marginalised. Despite the contrasts in the relationship between co-creation and the state in different contexts, this experience can speak to universal debates about cooption, empowerment and 'art-washing'.

Therefore, Co-Creation and Co-Creators need not inevitably be agents of 'colonisation' but *can* be a way of changing relations both between North and South and within individual cities. However, it is equally clear that such potential depends on an awareness of context and micro-politics; such an awareness is deepened and intensified through 'seeing from the South'.

Note

[1]   The authors use 'co-creation' in the context of discussing broader debates in the literature around this concept, and 'Co-Creation' to refer to the definition and use given in this project as outlined in the previous chapter.

References

Arnstein, S. (1969) 'A ladder of citizen participation', *Journal of the American Institute of Planners*, 35(4): 216–24.

Brandt, W. and Sampson, A. (1980). *Brandt Report North-South: A Programme for Survival: Report of the Independent Commission on International Development Issues*, Cambridge: MIT.

Colini, L. and Brownill, S. (2018) *Literature Review*, H2020 EU Co-creation Project, available from https://co-creation-network.org/.

CONAPO – Consejo Nacional de Poblacion (1994) *Desigualdad Regional y Marginación Municipal en México, 1990*, Mexico City.

Cooke, B. and Kothari, U. (eds) (2001) *Participation: The New Tyranny*, London: Zed Books.

Cornwall, A. (2004) 'New democratic spaces? The politics and dynamics of institutionalised participation', *IDS Bulletin*, 35(2): 1–10.

Davis, M. (2015) *Planeta Favela*, São Paulo: Boitempo Editorial.

de Satgé, R. and Watson, V. (2018) *Urban Planning in the Global South: Conflicting Rationalities in Contested Urban Space*, London: Palgrave Macmillan.

Fernandez (2019) 'Decolonizing Participatory Action Research (PAR) in community psychology: tales of tension toward transformation for liberation, presentation to SPSSI webinar', *Toward a Decolonial Psychology*, 22 Feb 2019, available from https://youtube.com/watch?v=IVUgdCmianU&t=8s.

Freire, P. (1993) *Pedagogy of the Oppressed*, London: Penguin.

Gaventa, J. (1993) 'The powerful, the powerless and the experts: knowledge struggles in an information age', in P. Park, M. Brydon-Miller, B. Hall and T. Jackson (eds) *Voices of Change: Participatory Research in the United States and Canada*, Toronto: OISE Press, pp 21–40.

Horner, L. (2016) *Co-Constructing Research; A Critical Literature Review*, available from https://connected-communities.org/wp-content/uploads/2016/04/16019-Co-constructing-Research-Lit-Review-dev-06.pdf.

Izzi, V. (ND) 'Can we have it all? Navigating trade-offs between research excellence, development impact, and collaborative research processes', available from https://blogs.lse.ac.uk/impactofsocialsciences/2018/10/17/can-we-have-it-all-navigating-trade-offs-between-research-excellence-development-impact-and-collaborative-research-processes/.

Ley, D. (2003) 'Artists, aestheticisation and the field of gentrification', *Urban Studies*, 40(12): 2527–44.

Lugones, M. (2007) 'Heterosexualism and the colonial/modern gender system', *Hypatia*, 22(1): 186–209.

Mabin, A. (2014) 'Grounding Southern city theory', in S. Oldfield and J. Robinson (eds) *The Routledge Companion to Cities of the Global South*, Abingdon: Routledge.

McCann, E. and Ward, K. (2011) *Mobile Urbanism*, Minneapolis: University of Minnesota Press.

Mignolo, W. (2000) 'The geopolitics of knowledge and the colonial difference', *South Atlantic Quarterly*, 101(1): 57–96.

Mignolo, W. (2009) 'Epistemic disobedience, independent thought and de-colonial freedom', *Theory, Culture and Society*, 26(7–8): 1–23.

Miraftab, F. (2009) 'Insurgent planning: situating radical planning in the Global South', *Planning Theory*, 8(1): 32–50.

Miraftab, F. and Kudva, N. (2015) *Cities of the Global South: A Reader*, London: Routledge.

Ostrom, E. (1990) *Governing the Commons: The Evolution of Institutions for Collective Action*, Cambridge: Cambridge University Press.

Parnell, S. and Robinson, J. (2012) '(Re)theorising cities from the global south: looking beyond neoliberalism', *Urban Geography*, 33(4): 593–617.

Pritchard, S. (2017) 'Rethinking the role of artists in urban regeneration context', available from https://colouringinculture.org/blog/rethin kingartistsinurbanregen.

Quijano, A. (2007) 'Coloniality and modernity/rationality', *Cultural Studies* 21(2): 168–78.

Robinson, J. (2013) 'The urban now: theorising cities beyond the new', *European Journal of Cultural Studies*, 16(6): 659–77.

Rose, N. (1996) 'The death of the social? Re-figuring the territory of government', *Economy and Society*, 25: 327–56.

Roy, A. (2005) 'Urban informality', *Journal of the American Planning Association*, 71(2): 147–58.

Roy, A. (2011) 'Urbanisms, worlding practices and the theory of planning', *Planning Theory*, 10(1): 6–15.

Roy, A. (2014) 'Worlding the south toward a post-colonial urban theory', in S. Oldfield and J. Robinson (eds) *The Routledge Companion to Cities of the Global South*, Abingdon: Routledge, pp 9–20.

Swyngedouw, E. (1997) *Neither Global nor Local: 'Glocalization' and the Politics of Scale*, New York: Guilford Press.

Vargo, S.L. and Lusch, R.F. (2004) 'Evolving to a new dominant logic for marketing', *Journal of Marketing*, 68(1): 1–17.

Voorberg, W.H., Bekkers, V.J.J.M. and Tummers, L.G. (2015) 'A systematic review of co-creation and co-production: embarking on the social innovation journey', *Public Management Review*, 17(9): 1333–57.

Watson, V. (2003) 'Conflicting rationalities: implications for planning theory and ethics', *Planning Theory & Practice*, 4(4): 395–407.

Watson, V. (2009) 'Seeing from the South: refocusing urban planning on the globe's central urban issues', *Urban Studies*, 46(11): 2259–75.

Vainer, C. (2014) 'Disseminating "best practice"? The coloniality of urban knowledge and city models', in S. Parnell and S. Oldfield (eds) *The Routledge Handbook on Cities of the Global South*, Abingdon: Routledge, pp 48–56.

3

Fostering artistic citizenship: how Co-Creation can awaken civil imagination

María José Pantoja Peschard

Introduction

One of the many spheres from which marginalised and deprived communities have been constantly excluded is that of culture and the arts. Indeed, as Moore (1998) and many others have documented, people living under precarious conditions have very limited access or no access at all to museums, galleries, cinemas and other cultural and artistic venues. The methodology of Co-Creation discussed throughout this book engages researchers, community workers, artists, policy makers and, most importantly, members of a particular neighbourhood or urban community as participants in creative projects and other inclusive artistic practices.

The central idea behind Co-Creation is that, through collaboration where all participants contribute as equals, knowledge is both shared and co-produced and new synergies are fostered. By promoting equal participation through projects that make different art forms and creative practices available to marginalised communities, Co-Creation has the potential to counter segregation and build relations based on solidarity, respect and collaboration. The role of art and creativity within Co-Creation projects is crucial insofar as these practices function as bridges that connect the different participants: researchers, artists, activists, policy makers and residents or community members. Although it is important not to romanticise the extent to which arts-based projects can bring about significant social change, as Rosie Meade and Mae Shaw (2007) have argued 'clearly the arts cannot transcend socioeconomic contexts by the force and will of their craft alone', socially engaged arts do have the potential to 'awaken people to both the negative and positive spaces which it opens up' (Meade and Shaw, 2007: 416).

The aim of this chapter is to explore how and to what extent the collaborative art and creative projects that are essential to Co-Creation can help to make visible the conditions of marginalisation within and beyond the communities in which they take place. The discussion here will be theoretical, as there are other chapters in this book that analyse specific Co-Creation projects and their outcomes. Rather than focusing on any particular case study, this chapter will claim that these projects contribute to awaken what Ariella Azoulay (2012) calls 'civil imagination', and hence also take part in the construction of 'artistic citizenship'.

In order to demonstrate this, the chapter first discusses what 'civil imagination' means for Azoulay. She defines this notion as the potential capacity to build relations of solidarity, partnership and sharing between people within marginalised communities, as well as between the latter and people living outside of them. Such relationships serve to unearth and reflect critically upon the structures, hierarchies and relations of power that are the causes underpinning the flaws, social disparities and injustices existing in our societies. Azoulay's proposal of 'civil imagination' as an ability required for the understanding of photography as a practice (rather than just a product, the photograph), and one which involves spectators, the photographer and the individual photographed, implies that 'civil imagination' is a skill. This chapter will argue that this skill can be – and actually seems to be – put into practice through Co-Creation projects, and not just in photography. Second, this chapter will claim that this 'civil imagination' is necessarily linked with an exercise in 'artistic citizenship', which can be understood as the commitment to engaging in collaborative art projects that stimulate positive interactions and exchanges among participants, and that can thereby improve communal well-being (Elliot et al, 2016).

Finally, the chapter argues that Co-Creation, insofar as it involves a collaborative process based on the sharing of creative and artistic skills, promotes among the participants a sense of community in which their opinions are heard and counted. This sense of community and belonging is crucial, this chapter claims, in the construction of more cohesive and thriving communities.

The potential of a civil imagination

In *Civil Imagination: A Political Ontology of Photography* (2012), Azoulay critically examines issues of visual culture; in particular, she discusses the political aspects of photography, the roles of both spectators and critics (of photography), the body politics, as well as the concept of citizenship. She argues that the boundaries of 'the aesthetic', 'the political', and 'the civil' perpetuate power relations both within the nation-states and among them, which also produce and maintain exclusions and abuses upon certain populations. Following up the arguments advanced in her previous publication *The Civil Contract of Photography* (2008), Azoulay constructs her argument by using the example of the Palestinian struggle and other populations that are vulnerable because they have been displaced or are stateless. In particular, she points to the classification of Palestinians as non-citizens, and the oppression and injustices they endure because of this exclusion from the category of citizenship. In what follows, the author will present how Azoulay constructs her concept of 'civil imagination' and what she means by it so as to explain later how this skill is exercised through Co-Creation.

Azoulay begins her argument by questioning the dichotomy between the realm of aesthetics and the realm of politics, especially as this distinction has been applied to photography. Whenever photographs are qualified as 'aestheticising' what they portray, what is meant is that they are not 'political' enough; and conversely, whenever photographs are said to be 'too political', it is meant that they are not 'aesthetic' enough. Azoulay criticises Walter Benjamin for articulating and institutionalising a relation of mutual exclusion between the political and the aesthetic; she claims instead that the political and the aesthetic are beyond the either/or dichotomy. Her argument is, first, that the fact that an image belongs to the realm of the aesthetic does not depend on the choice of a particular individual or set of individuals (the artist or the critic); rather the image falls under the domain of the aesthetic simply because it is an object that presents itself to the senses, it can be perceived through the senses:

> ... the aesthetic configuration associated with a given object or image may be appraised and evaluated in a variety of ways, but it is impossible to negate its existence. The aesthetic exists there as a consequence of the very fact that an object or an image is given to the senses. (Azoulay, 2012: 48)

The aesthetic is thus a necessary component of any image. The second thing that Azoulay argues is that the political, like the aesthetic, is not a quality attributed to the image by an artist or a critic; the political is not the result of the intention of the artist. Instead, the quality of the political cannot 'be attributed to a single person or thing but involves the relations between human beings in the plural' (Azoulay, 2012: 49).

These two arguments allow Azoulay to affirm that a photograph is always the result of an event, the event of photography, which is necessarily a collective practice insofar as the photographer makes some choices that determine the final product of the event of photography but she or he can never have full control over the photographed subjects nor over the meaning that the spectators may draw out of the photograph. The event of photography thus implies an encounter between people, which remains open and never completely determined by one single person. This means that the event of photography configures a political space, 'a space of relations between people who are exposed to one another in public' (Azoulay, 2012: 52):

> Once the presence of photographed subjects is brought into consideration, it is hard not to see that the space where the image is created, like the space from which it is viewed, is indeed a plural one. ... Whereas the space within which people act is ... always a political one, the photograph is not political in itself except to the extent that people make it exist among themselves, in plurality, in public. (Azoulay, 2012: 54)

Co-Creation, as collaborative creative and artistic ventures, also configures – this chapter will claim – a space of relations that are political in the sense that these projects advocate plurality and are based on the principle of respect and equality of all participants.

The implications that Azoulay draws from all of this are, on the one hand, that photographs (and all images) belong ontologically to the realm of the aesthetic since the images are given to us by way of our senses and, on the other hand, that photographs constitute a political space because they result 'from the actions of multiple participants who play various roles in [their] production and dissemination' (Azoulay, 2012: 55). This explains in what sense she thinks that the political and the aesthetic are not two mutually excluding domains: a photograph can be political and aesthetic at the same time.

Azoulay continues and expands on her theses defended in *The Civil Contract of Photography* (2008), where she claims that photography has the potential to create a space of political relations between the photographer, the photographed subjects and the spectators, which are not regulated or sanctioned by the sovereign rule of the nation-state. These are relationships of solidarity, partnership and responsibility between the three partakers (photographer, photographed subjects and spectators) in the event of photography that escape the sovereign sanction but are, nonetheless, political relations that configure the citizenry of photography (Azoulay, 2008: 23–4). For Azoulay, everyone is already or can become a citizen in the citizenry of photography to the extent that all the participants in the event of photography can address others and make claims through photographs. Even a stateless person can become a citizen in the citizenry of photography, addressing claims to the other members of this citizenry. As Azoulay explains:

> The theory of photography [the one Azoulay proposes] takes into account all the participants in photographic acts – camera, photographer, photographed subject, and spectator – approaching the photograph (and its meaning) as an unintentional effect of the encounter between all of these. None of these have the capacity to seal off this effect and determine its sole meaning. The civil contract of photography assumes that, at least in principle, the governed possess a certain power to suspend the gesture of the sovereign power seeking to totally dominate the relations between us, dividing us as governed into citizens and noncitizens thus making disappear the violation of *our* citizenship. (Azoulay, 2008: 23)

The lines dividing all the governed into two categories, citizens and non-citizens, configure an unfair and flawed conception of citizenship. Such structures of exclusion, Azoulay argues, can be subverted and resisted through photography because it is a practice that constitutes a space that functions without a single unique authority, a space that is also borderless, ownerless and public (Azoulay, 2012: 243). It is in this space of photography that everyone becomes a citizen, and where private spaces and public spaces become one, thereby dismantling the distinctions between citizens and non-citizens as much as those existing between spaces (Azoulay, 2012: 244).

Here it is possible to begin to see more clearly the links between what Azoulay is defending about the practice of photography and the principles underlying Co-Creation, since the latter fosters bottom-up approaches, a plurality of points of view and the equality of all partakers. The hierarchies dissolved, or at least suspended, through the civil contract of photography can also be suspended within the space of relations formed in Co-Creation projects, where participants are equal collaborators with a role and a voice that counts.

The emergence of relationships beyond the sanction of the nation-state through the photograph entails the exercise of a particular kind of gaze, what Azoulay calls the 'civil gaze' (Azoulay 2012: 70–1). This civil gaze differs from the expert or professional gaze (but does not exclude it) because, instead of focusing only on the photograph as a finished product belonging to the photographer (who is the one who determines its meaning), it is a gaze that is aware of the whole picture, of all the relationships, the conditions and all the steps that lead to the photograph. The civil gaze takes into account not just the elements that the photographer intended to be captured within the frame, but also all the participants in the event of photography, including those outside of the frame, as much as all those elements that were not intended by the photographer but that play a part within the photograph. Thereby, the civil gaze conforms an open, collective and public space, a civil space where everyone is (equally) responsible and active.

What Azoulay's argument is pointing at is that all partakers in the event of photography, but specially the spectators, have to 'see themselves as citizens' who have 'the ability to imagine a political state of being that deviates significantly from the prevailing state of affairs' (Azoulay, 2012: 3). This ability is no other than what she calls the skill of 'civil imagination'. According to Azoulay, an essential part of the skill of civil imagination is precisely the activation of the civil gaze. For this reason, civil imagination, she says, is 'the interest that citizens display in themselves, in others, in their shared forms of coexistence, as well as in the world that they create and nurture' (Azoulay, 2012: 5). In this sense, 'civil imagination' constitutes the capacity to see those divisive lines between citizens and non-citizens as blurred, and even as non-existent.

In the case of the practice of Co-Creation, something similar occurs to the extent that participants are encouraged to see themselves and others as equal contributors to the project. In this sense Co-Creation participants are also able to imagine (and even actualise) a state of affairs where their individual voices, actions and contributions are as relevant as those of others. Through imagining and configuring a space of relations where there is no one unique leading figure, a non-hierarchical space of relations, they also help to make visible and think critically about the power relations and structures that sustain the social disparities and exclusions present in their communities.

Azoulay is particularly concerned with spectators' potential to activate the skill of civil imagination and, hence, the civil gaze, because she believes that within the event of photography it is the spectators who, unlike the photographed subjects such as those portrayed in photographs of the Palestinian population, tend to be privileged due to their status as citizens of a particular nation-state. Their status as citizens precludes them from imagining 'what it is not to be a citizen or what it is to be a second class citizen', but this is not a failure of their own particular imagination, rather this is 'a structural failure that expresses the inversion of the relations between the citizen and power that is a feature of democratic sovereignty' (Azoulay, 2012: 9). According to Azoulay, spectators both have the potential and the moral duty to activate their civil imagination and refuse to accept, in the first place, the discourse that separates the governed between a category of citizens and one of non-citizens and, in the second place, the identification of disaster as the defining characteristic of populations that have been denied citizenship by a certain regime. In this sense, civil imagination does not only allow us to make visible the intolerable conditions and the rights violations endured by populations excluded from citizenship, but also this exercise of civil imagination has the potential to 'help the privileged citizens to identify and acknowledge the inherent flaw in their citizenship, a flaw that makes them accomplices to the crimes of a regime that does everything in its power to keep from appearing to be criminal' (Azoulay, 2012: 245).

This is an overview of the main arguments presented by Azoulay in her two books. A more detailed and thorough discussion of the topics and problems that she presents would be necessary in order to fully grasp the nuances and the theoretical assumptions upon which her political theory of photography and the concept of citizenship that is implied by such a theory rely. Such a discussion would extend beyond the scope of this chapter. However, one of the things that is worth pondering as regards Azoulay's theses of the civil contract of photography and the skill of 'civil imagination' is the question of whether her proposal is utopic and never entirely realisable, in the sense that it endorses the existence of political relations that are not sanctioned by the sovereign power of the nation-state (the citizenry of photography), but that nevertheless are able to negotiate with this power and direct claims towards it. It is the author's view that qualifying Azoulay's theory as utopic is not necessarily an objection to her political theory of photography, because a state of affairs and/or a theory that appear utopic open up horizons of possibility; that is, they open up prospects towards which we can work even if we would never fully reach them. It is in this sense that Azoulay's proposal is relevant: it is pointing towards the important fact that we do have obligations towards those worse off, those without citizenship or with a second-class citizenship. Her account also makes evident the fact that the practice of photography and the exercise of the civil gaze have the potential to make visible the conditions under which these populations live, and thus to start shifting some of those conditions. She makes the case that it is necessary to reconsider the importance of the civil as that aspect that allows us to relate to others in ways that are not regulated by the nation-state. The civil dimension allows us to see, relate and participate with others beyond the divisions between citizens and non-citizens.

Azoulay's proposal of a 'civil imagination' can be extended beyond the field of photography to the other arts and, in particular, to community and socially engaged arts such as Co-Creation projects. Her concept of 'civil imagination' as a skill that leads us to take interest in, solidarity with and responsibility towards others and our coexistence implies that there is no clear-cut distinction between the realms of politics, of ethics and the arts. This blurring of the dividing lines between ethics, politics and the artistic is one of the central ideas guiding all Co-Creation projects. The next section argues how Azoulay's 'civil imagination' relates to what some scholars in the area of community and socially engaged arts and activism call 'artistic citizenship', which is the commitment to collaborative artistic ventures that aim to create positive synergies among participants, such as the projects adhering to the principles of Co-Creation seek to produce.

Civil imagination and artistic citizenship

In their book *Artistic Citizenship: Artistry, Social Activism and Ethical Practice* (2016), Elliot et al maintain that the idea that art has intrinsic value regardless of its social, political or ethical implications is a misled one that has its origin in the 18th century European thesis that art should only be concerned with art, that is, the notion of 'art for art's sake'. According to these authors, this notion 'is implausible and irresponsible, leading us to trivialize or marginalize some of art's most powerful contributions to our shared humanity. Social/ethical responsibility lies at the heart of responsible artistic practice' (Elliot et al, 2016: 3). For them, it is important to recognise art's role in improving people's lives at local levels but also at regional and international levels, because from its beginnings this has been art's purpose and the source of its value. Music and musical practices, for instance, have proven to be crucial in promoting bonding and social cohesion. They then conclude that the value of art 'is a function of what it is good *for* the uses to which it is put' (Elliot et al, 2016: 6). This view entails a utilitarian conception of art, which is clearly at odds with the view that art is valuable for its own sake, that art is intrinsically valuable. This debate is not pursued here, but the view advanced by Elliot et al is useful in understanding the role that art plays in society and, especially important for the argument here, the civil dimension that all the arts have.

Alongside this utilitarian position about what makes art valuable, the authors hold three assumptions concerning the nature of art. First, that art is a social and collective venture: 'the arts are made by and for people, living in real worlds, involving conflicts … As such, the arts are also invariably embodiments of people's political and ideological beliefs; understandings and values, both personal and collective' (Elliot et al, 2016: 5). It is for this reason, the authors say, that artistic enterprises involve a particular kind of civil commitment, which entails actively taking part in them with a focus on the social goods they foster. This connects with the second assumption regarding art's nature: since the arts are linked to collective life and founded on social experience, and since they cultivate social goods, the value and importance of the arts stems from how effectively they attain the goods they intended to achieve. Finally, the third assumption is that given that the arts are social practices that make significant contributions on the political, cultural, ideological, spiritual and economic areas of human lives, they should be conceptualised and practised as exemplifications of an 'ethically guided citizenship' (Elliot et al, 2016: 6).

Following from the thesis that the arts are forms of an ethically guided citizenship, the authors propose the concept of 'artistic citizenship', by which they mean an artistic practice that is inextricably linked with a set of social, civic, humanitarian and emancipatory responsibilities, and with a general commitment to the promotion of social goods. This artistic practice is inclusive and non-elitist in the sense that all participants (young or old, professional or amateur) are considered artists making a contribution within an art project where the main purpose is bringing positive changes to people's lives:

> Whereas artistic proficiency entails myriad skills and understandings, artistic citizenship implicates additional commitments to act in ways that move people – both emotionally and in the sense of mobilizing them as agents of positive change. Artistic citizens are committed to engaging in artistic actions in ways that can bring people together, enhance communal well-being, and contribute substantially to human thriving. (Elliot et al, 2016: 7)

The concept of artistic citizenship requires that there is no separation between the realms of politics, the aesthetics and also the realm of ethics insofar as this artistic practice is aimed at promoting social goods and communal improvement, and it is open to everyone regardless of their technical skills or artistic experience. This artistic practice involves interactions and exchanges through collective art projects that seek to make changes in social realities for the benefit of all. As Bowman puts it:

> [New] forms of cooperation, community, or citizenship need to [emerge]. Chief among these ... may be artistic practices, shaped by and devoted to civic responsibility: ethical resources that benefit not just artists but all who acknowledge the need for such resources and engage with them seriously. It is vital to the well-being of any social collective that members care about and commit to the well-being of that community – that there be a strong sense of belonging ... . The arts are potent influences for shaping character, identity, membership, and belonging. Artistic citizens acknowledge those influences and seek to use them responsibly. (Bowman, 2016: 77)

Thus, 'artistic citizenship' implies a capacity to imagine a different state of affairs as well as a commitment to actively contributing to the betterment of the community. This capacity is no different from the skill of 'civil imagination' of which Azoulay speaks, which involves the creation of political and ethical relations beyond those sanctioned by nation-state. In this sense, 'civil imagination' and 'artistic citizenship' are concepts that are deeply connected and require each other to be understood and conceptualised.

The civil skill of imagining a completely different sociopolitical order implies dissenting from a social order that establishes inclusions and exclusions and seeks to maintain them, and this is something that the artistic citizen aims to do. The implications of what this civil skill means might be clearer if we turn to the work of Jacques Rancière. He affirms that the social order, which he calls the 'order of the police' (Rancière, 2010: 139), constitutes a set of conventions and implicit rules that divide a community into groups, assign the positions and functions that each individual within a society must occupy and fulfil, and hence separate 'those who take part from those who are excluded' (Rockhill, 2004: 3). It is worth noting here that what Rancière means by the notion of 'the order of the police' or the 'police' is thus different from what we ordinarily refer to by this term since for him 'the police' is not a social function, nor is it concerned with controlling or repressing the population, but rather 'the police' is a symbolic configuration of the social. The assignation of roles and functions to individuals in the society – and hence, their separation – in turn presupposes a certain 'distribution of the sensible', 'a prior aesthetic division between the visible and the invisible, the audible and the inaudible, the sayable and the unsayable' (Rockhill, 2004: 3). According to Rancière, politics essentially constitutes opposition to and subversion of the order of the police by those who have been excluded, with the intention of producing equality and a reconfiguration of the distribution of the sensible, that is, a new partition of the sensible: 'politics invents new forms of collective enunciation; it reframes the given by inventing new ways of making sense of the sensible, new configurations between the visible and the invisible ... new distributions of space and time – in short, new bodily capacities' (Rancière, 2010: 139). Politics in this sense involves an understanding that the current sociopolitical order is not necessary but arbitrary, and that the exclusions and inclusions that this order establishes can therefore be challenged by those who have been excluded.

It is important to say here that both Rancière and Azoulay think that the realms of aesthetics and politics are not mutually exclusive, and that therefore art can be political. The difference between these two thinkers resides in what Azoulay understands as the 'political' and what Rancière calls 'politics'. Whereas for Azoulay all of our engagements and exchanges with others are public and thus political, for Rancière politics only takes place at the very specific moment and event when there is a redistribution of the sensible, when there is a disruption of the current social order. 'Civil imagination', therefore, as presented by Azoulay, constitutes a skill that can lead to a new distribution of the sensible. Understood in Rancière's way, politics as the effort to reconfigure the partition of the sensible in the name of equality, politics as resistance to the established social order of exclusions and inclusions, coincides with the skill of 'civil imagination', which outlines a new horizon of civil relations that blur the dividing lines between those who take part and those who have no part. It is in this sense that is possible to affirm that 'civil imagination' and 'artistic citizenship' have the potential to lead to a new partition of the sensible. This chapter now explains in what sense Co-Creation fosters 'civil imagination' and 'artistic citizenship'.

Co-Creation as key to promoting civil imagination

As a collaborative arts-based and creative practice aimed at creating synergies among equal participants and thereby promoting more cohesive urban spaces, Co-Creation is a methodology that puts into practice both the exercise of 'civil imagination' and the formation of 'artistic citizenship'. The active participation of academics, artists, policy makers and community members in such projects as equals, without a single leading or authoritative figure, allows for a platform where everyone makes a significant contribution to the collective work regardless of their particular artistic or technical skills, but also regardless of their actual citizenship status. This means that Co-Creation facilitates the formation of relationships based on respect, trust, solidarity and partnership, with a view towards producing a creative or artistic piece which will contribute to making visible the participants' conditions of exclusion and eventually, through this process, start making positive changes within the community. In this sense, Co-Creation practices promote the construction of 'artistic citizenship'. The question of whether the artistic quality of the outcome produced is relevant or even necessary for Co-Creation seems to be beyond the point because, as mentioned before, what is at stake for all Co-Creation projects is the opening of a space where all voices are equally heard and valued, where there is no one single participant that takes prevalence over others or that can claim exclusive ownership of or benefit from the artistic-creative outcome generated. Furthermore, if Co-Creation entails the activation of the skill of civil imagination and the exercise of the civil gaze, then the expert artist gaze or the professional gaze is displaced, and instead what acquires relevance is the gaze that is centred on the creative process as a whole, on the connections developed through it and on the steps that led to the final outcome. Hence, what is at stake for Co-Creation is the configuration of a platform where relationships of solidarity and respect are built, and not so much the artistic value of the work produced.

Similarly, through sharing knowledge, skills and through producing collective artworks or creative products, Co-Creation also provides participants with opportunities to create their own stories and narratives, as well as to become aware of their potential to reappropriate their own space and thus, eventually, claim rights as a community. The involvement of members of a community in a creative or artistic project following the principles of Co-Creation allows them not only to develop a certain artistic-creative skill but also to become aware that they too can tell their own narratives that differ from and contest official discourses and stereotypes. By resourcing their creative potential and configuring a space where participants are encouraged to construct their own narratives through inclusive artistic-creative practices, the potential for agency of these people and their communities is enhanced. In formulating their own narratives and refusing the discourses that have been imposed from outside, by the ruling social order, Co-Creation projects constitute exercises of civil imagination and can as well become the stepping stone towards the reconfiguration of the distribution of the sensible, as understood by Rancière. Indeed, being able to tell their own narratives and histories enables the stakeholders to express their claims and interests in their own terms and, in turn, this leads these communities to build strong bonds and a sense of community that could ultimately help them resist and fight against their oppressed conditions. Therefore, the methodology of Co-Creation fosters civil imagination, and ultimately contributes to the creation of an artistic citizenry.

One could question here if this understanding of Co-Creation is not too idealistic or utopic. However, it is worth noting that the claim is not that Co-Creation projects are able to dissolve all social disparities, destroy hierarchies and eliminate injustices. Instead, the view presented is that Co-Creation opens up a horizon of possibilities that operate as a guideline, a blueprint, towards which we can direct our efforts. Producing the conditions of possibility for the skill of civil imagination to be put into action and an artistic citizenship to be configured constitutes the first step towards questioning and shifting the conditions of inequality. It is this first step that Co-Creation aims to achieve. As other chapters in this book will discuss, Co-Creation projects can be more or less successful at attaining this first step. But by setting the conditions for the equal contribution of all participants and by encouraging the constant discussion and assessment of the artistic-creative outcomes to be produced, Co-Creation projects always remain open to adjustments and improvements.

References

Azoulay, A. (2008) *The Civil Contract of Photography*, translated by R. Mazali and R. Danieli, Brooklyn, NY: Zone Books.

Azoulay, A. (2012) *Civil Imagination: A Political Ontology of Photography*, translated by L. Bethlehem, London and New York: Verso.

Bowman, W.D. (2016) 'Artistry, ethics and citizenship', in D.J. Elliot, M. Silverman and W.D. Bowman (eds) *Artistic Citizenship: Artistry, Social Responsibility and Ethical Practice,* New York: Oxford University Press, pp 59–80.

Elliot, D.J., Silverman, M. and Bowman, W.D. (2016) 'Artistic citizenship: introduction, aims and overview', in D.J. Elliot, M. Silverman and W.D. Bowman (eds) *Artistic Citizenship: Artistry, Social Responsibility and Ethical Practice,* New York: Oxford University Press, pp 3–21.

Meade, R. and Shaw, M. (2007) 'Editorial: Community development and the arts: reviving the democratic imagination', *Community Development Journal*, 42(4): 413–21.

Moore, J. (1998) 'Poverty and access to the arts: inequalities in arts attendance', *Cultural Trends*, 8(31): 53–73.

Rancière, J. (2010) 'The paradoxes of political art', in J. Rancière (ed) *Dissensus: On Politics and Aesthetics*, translated by S. Corcoran, London and New York: Continuum, pp 134–51.

Rockhill, G. (2004) 'Translator's introduction: Jacques Rancière's politics of perception', in J. Rancière *The Politics of Aesthetics: The Distribution of the Sensible,* translated with an introduction by G. Rockhill, London and New York: Continuum, pp 1–6.

4

Global North-South tensions in international Co-Creation projects

José Luis Gázquez Iglesias

Introduction

Co-Creation as a collaborative approach to knowledge production brings together a diverse range of participants and uses art to drive out knowledge and challenge existing hierarchies and preconceptions. While some Co-Creation practices can remain entirely local, many involve North-South encounters either occurring between participants of international workshops or taking the form of conflicts between different traditions of knowledge production specific to the 'Global North' and the 'Global South'. In addition, hegemonic representational practices inherited from colonisation may be present in Co-Creation practices involving marginalised urban populations stigmatised for originating from the Global South.

It is possible to trace processes of predominant knowledge production (those of the Global North) back to the 15th century when Spanish and Portuguese explorers 'discovered' new geographies and peoples that were to be subjected by military force. This subjection was largely justified by the emerging Enlightenment reasoning as the main discourse establishing the right of European nations to dispose of societies considered backward, pre-modern or unable to produce their own knowledge. It has been argued for instance that the rise of colonial anthropology both preceded and coincided with the expansion of European colonisation of Africa (Moore, 1993 and Gruffydd, 2013). Since then, Western knowledge about non-European societies has been characterised mainly by creating hierarchical, dichotomising and classificatory categories in order to justify attempts to control and dominate them. In this sense, the Global North-South divide is the result of evolving categories according to changing historical contexts (the terminological shift from 'uncivilised world' to 'Third World' and more recently to 'Global South' illustrates well this 'evolution') without seriously questioning the processes that produced and naturalised these kinds of representations of the world and the structures of inequality that they imply.

This chapter seeks to address the challenges that Co-Creation, as a methodology that aspires to be empowering and emancipating, is likely to encounter in contexts of urban exclusion in cities of both the 'Global South and North'. In fact, social exclusion linked to the colonial experiences of the past is not limited to urban spaces pertaining to formerly colonised countries but is also strongly related to contemporary migration and integration processes of their populations into former metropolitan cities.

While not all Co-Creation workshops are international – several chapters in this book actually deal with cases that only involve participants from the same context – an important challenge specific to international Co-Creation workshops is the asymmetric relation between the actors involved. International researchers (of both Northern or Southern countries) and members of non-governmental organisations (NGOs) mostly based in the North are often more mobile and therefore able to participate in multiple contexts and activities held in Northern and Southern cities. While one may think that being born in a 'Southern' country like Mexico and working as a scholar at the National Autonomous University would automatically place the author of this chapter in a 'Southern' role within the workshop framework, this is not necessarily the case. National universities are in fact institutional products of Northern knowledge and scientific systems and cosmopolitan spaces rather than communitarian ones. This is important because even if the resources for mobility are more limited for researchers coming from these universities, they allow scholars to travel and participate in more activities of the project than people from local communities where interventions take place. Actors representing marginalised communities on the contrary seem to play leading roles at the local level only, since their participation remains very limited or even non-existent in Co-Creation activities organised outside their home countries. This chapter argues that while international Co-Creation workshops can produce empowering experiences that allow certain members of marginalised communities in global cities to challenge stigmatising representations made of them, they also run the risk of producing only ephemeral results and of failing to disrupt representational hegemonic practices in the long term due to the unequal relationships between participants.

The Global North-South paradigm and the Co-Creation framework

The Global North-South paradigm, which divides and classifies countries of the world in terms of their economic development, is the result of colonisation and the evolution of economic and political thought that emerged to explain and justify it (Said, 1978). While this theoretical development accounts mainly for the 19th century processes of subjection of non-Western societies by European powers and the dichotomising structures of knowledge that it produced, it is possible to track the path leading to the creation of the North-South divide to the decade of the 1960s, when most of the countries of the former colonial world gained political independence and the question of their future development was posed in the first place.

This was the context out of which modernisation theory emerged, claiming both to diagnose the situation of these countries and to provide them with a blueprint towards progress (Cohn, 2011). Promoting liberal principles, modernisation theory suggested that the adoption of open markets and liberal economic policies would allow emerging and poor countries to 'catch up' with the more developed ones. Another important tenet of this theory was the belief that the elimination of backward 'traditional' elements in these societies was also necessary for achieving modernisation.

When economic development did not occur after the implementation of these policies, theoretical thought concerning the development of poor countries was reoriented toward the elaboration of the 'dependency theory'. Given the historical context that gave birth to postcolonial states and the vulnerability of most of them when they obtained formal political independence, the dependency theory argued that the underdevelopment of 'peripheral' countries is a product of the development of 'central' ones (Frank, 1967). It is also important to note that a decade before the emergence of dependency theory, a new category had emerged for referring to poor countries: the concept of the 'Third World'. At the end of the Cold War in the early 1990s, economic theory and thought had to redefine their conceptual apparatus to adapt it to the new world order dominated exclusively by capitalism. This is how categories such as the Global North and Global South and the divide between them rose at this juncture, trying to produce a new framework suitable to describe this new world order. Nevertheless, the North-South paradigm inherited much of the structural character of its predecessors such as the dependency theory and the 'world-system theory' in terms of the binary world view they proposed.

In fact, what must be stressed about these theorising processes describing international structures since the colonisation of the Americas and later of Asian and African societies is not only their Eurocentric nature but also the constitutive and productive character of such representations. More recently, it has been argued that the Global South perspective is a more enabling one than previous categorisations like 'Third World' or 'developing countries' and better suited to resist hegemonic forces (Duck, 2016).

In this sense, it is important to focus on the intellectual mechanisms that have not only created the categories of Global North and South and the system of classifications that determines which countries belong to which category, but which has also configured the nature of these categories and rules the way they interact with other categories within and between themselves. As numerous authors have shown (Chakrabarty, 2000; de Sousa Santos and Meneses, 2009; Seth, 2013; Mignolo and Walsh, 2018), there has been a direct implication of Western science, knowledge systems and institutions not only in the development of theories and paradigms of international relations to which the creation of these categories has been attributed but also in the production of international society itself. As Doty states:

> Arguably one of the most consequential elements present in all of the encounters between the North and the South has been the practice(s) of *representation* by the North of the South. By representation I mean the ways in which the South has been discursively represented by policy makers, scholars, journalists, and others in the North.
>
> Thinking of North-South relations in terms of representation reorients and complicates the way we understand this particular aspect of global politics. North-South relations become more than an area of theory and practice in which various policies have been enacted and theories formulated; they become a realm of politics wherein the very identities of peoples, states, and regions are constructed through representational practices. Thinking in terms of representational practices calls our attention to an economy of abstract binary oppositions that we routinely draw upon and

that frame our thinking. Developed/underdeveloped, 'first world'/'third world,' core/periphery, metropolis/satellite, advanced industrialized/less developed, modern/traditional, and real states/quasi states are just a few that readily come to mind. While there is nothing natural, inevitable, or arguably even useful about these divisions, they remain widely circulated and accepted as legitimate ways to categorize regions and peoples of the world. (Doty, 1996: 2)

A central feature of this domination by reference to hegemonic discursive and representational practices is the idea of the South not being able or not being capable of autonomous development without the assistance or guidance of the North (Doty, 1996).

Of course, as stated before, authors belonging to the 'postcolonial theory' tradition have engaged since the 1980s with a theorising process of deconstructing and contextualising the categories through which international society has been built. There have been, however, since the last decade important developments around this issue. Not only has postcolonial theory demonstrated the 'provincial' origin of the discipline but has also posited that:

Postcolonial theory has at its heart an epistemological concern, namely to question the universality of the categories of modern social scientific thought, and of the disciplines into which it is divided; it is an epistemological challenge to, and a critique of existing disciplines including IR [international relations]. For the insistence upon centrality of colonialism in the making of the modern world has, as its theoretical correlate, a call for rethinking the categories through which we have hitherto narrated and understood that history. The categories of civil society, state, nation, sovereignty, individual, subjectivity, development and so on, emerged in the course of seeking to think through and understand a particular slice of history, that of the region of the world we now know as 'Europe'. (Seth, 2013:2)

Nevertheless, this effort has remained astonishingly shy with respect to the construction of the 'international relations (IR)' mainstream theoretical body, which remains largely a Eurocentric, Anglo-Saxon product.

Assuming as a point of departure continuity in the existence of representational hegemonic practices at the local level of international relations whether occurring in Global North or Global South cities, this chapter questions the potential of the artistic-led/mediated approach that the Co-Creation methodology proposes in different contexts of socioeconomic exclusion. In other words, the goal of this chapter is to explore whether this kind of intervention helps to break or mitigate stigmatising representations based on binaries or if, on the contrary, they contribute to reproducing or reinforcing them in spite of their stated objectives.

In order to understand the issue of contemporary urban exclusion in large metropolises in the Global South, it is necessary first to situate it in the particular histories of colonisation of those countries. Whether in Latin America, Africa or Asia, the presence of Europeans implied the construction of dual urban development projects, consisting of a neat separation between the residential and bureaucratic buildings of the representatives of the colonial power and administrations and the space reserved for the 'natives'.

The crucial question here is whether Co-Creation initiatives intervening in contexts of social exclusion or stigmatisation are different from previous altruistic practices, most noticeably that of international cooperation carried out by Western actors claiming to contribute to the 'development' of less advanced nations. It is important to acknowledge that one of the most important legacies of the Enlightenment and Western 'rational' thought is this hierarchical classification of non-European populations and societies. The work of the late Palestinian scholar Edward Said (1978), who argued that the construction of Orientalist knowledge was more an issue of creating a cultural other in the process of construction of the Western identity, represents a good example of how these representational structures have been put to work since then. In this sense, while it is necessary to take into consideration the diversity of historical contexts derived from the colonial experience in Latin America, Asia or Africa, 'the racial signifier was always an essential and even constitutive structure of what would become the imperial project' (Mbembe, 2017: 62).

Challenging stigmatisation: Santa Marta and Co-Creation

According to Diouf (2013), the study of urban processes in zones of social exclusion and stigmatisation is dominated by two contradictory conceptions. On the one hand, pessimistic conceptions focus on socioeconomic crises and the dysfunctional character of cities and neighbourhoods while, on the other hand, optimistic studies celebrate popular creativity in informal urban practices. While the former approaches focus on capitalist development, political analysis and state intervention, the latter are committed largely to studying the ongoing effects of colonialism and to explore how urban spaces are constantly being recreated or reshaped by a diversity of practices and actors that contest and redefine the public space moving away from official administrative and nationalist narratives (Diouf, 2013). Adopting the latter view of urban processes, the goal in this section is to reflect on the interaction between actors (and their changing roles or hierarchy status) taking part in a Co-Creation intervention in a global urban context of social exclusion. The underlying assumption here is that the framework proposed by Co-Creation engages participants in interaction and creative activities and enables them to express different perspectives about the most pressing local issues. By doing this, it challenges negative representations about the community and its exclusion from the rest of the city and produces empowering or emancipatory effects.

In order to be able to discuss whether (local and international) actors involved in Co-Creation international workshops can produce alternative perceptions of marginalised communities through their interaction, some background information about the Co-Creation project's pilot case study in Rio de Janeiro needs to be provided first (see also Chapters 2, 5 and 15).

The workshop took place over five consecutive days in August 2019 in Santa Marta, a favela of 4–6,000 inhabitants located in the Botafogo neighbourhood in southern Rio de Janeiro. As with many other informal urban communities, it was founded during the first half of the 20th century by migrants coming from the interior of Brazil and, since then, has undergone a process of insertion (both formal and informal) into the urban landscape of Rio de Janeiro (Duarte Aquistapace, 2018; Perlman, 2010). Even if the quality of life and services has improved over the last decades, Santa Marta and other favelas are still experiencing urban exclusion and social inequalities with respect to the city as a whole.

As for the Co-Creation workshop, it consisted of a five-day programme addressing several topics related to urban inequalities and stigmatisation such as tourism in the favela, public policies, cultural and artistic representations, sports and leisure activities. Actors participating in the workshop included international researchers from both Northern and Southern universities, NGOs from the Global North, as well as members of local NGOs and associations and some other members of the community. Although the programme of activities was set up and designed by a local community leader, Itamar Silva (see Chapter 15), the principles guiding the collective activities were suggested by European researchers and NGOs, as well as Latin American academics. These principles included equality, respect, ethics, and engagement to produce shared meanings and collective knowledge about urban development and representations of the favela. While these were the main issues discussed between participants of the workshop, the Co-Creation tools employed to materialise the shared knowledge were 'photovoice' and 'affective mapping' (Flatley, 2008). Both activities were carried out collectively between the researchers, NGO members from the Global North, and the local association (Eco). The photovoice activity was designed by a young researcher from the local university who was familiar with this method.

Photovoice methodology has been in use since the middle of the 1990s in social research for enhancing representations of actors in a specific context (Nykiforuk et al, 2011). It was originally proposed as a research technique mixing narrative and image. The main goals were 'enabling people to record and reflect their community's strengths and concerns, to promote critical dialogue and knowledge about important issues through large and small group discussion of photographs and to reach policymakers' (Wang and Burris, 1997). Since then, photovoice has gradually increased its validity as a social research tool (especially in community-based participatory research, CBPR) to reveal community perceptions. In fact, the main value of photovoice could be found in the blurring effect that is produced in the role of actors participating in a Co-Creation intervention context. From the community members' perspective, active engagement with the intervention allows them to think of themselves as valuable members of the research team and, from the researcher perspective, it can allow the detection of alternative voices and narratives that could help to break or to mitigate stereotyped binary or negative representations of the community and its members.

In fact, it is possible to argue that one of the most noticeable results of employing photovoice is the detection of the ambiguous and changing roles played by the ensemble of actors participating in the Co-Creation interventions and the possibility of developing alternative ways of producing shared knowledge during the running of the workshop. Thus, photovoice enables the expression of a plurality of expressions about the meaning of inclusion in urban landscapes divided by spatial and symbolic borders.

In the case of the photovoice and mapping activities, it could be said that both work as complements to the other. In fact, while the mapping dynamic was present during the visit of the favela with the tourist guides allowing the emergence of an interactive collective dialogue about places in the favela, in the case of the photovoice the mapping dynamic was a prerequisite for the creation of a shared understanding of certain problematic issues and spaces of the favela, such as garbage collection or incomplete urban projects undertaken by the state but abandoned due to political cycles and changes in office.

As a result of carrying out collective activities using these two techniques along with political listening (Bassel, 2017), it could be argued that they allow for a better understanding of the community and its social dynamics beyond common places and stereotypes. The case of political listening is particularly significant because of the great subversive potential it carries as it demands an inversion of roles between the usual speaker and the usual listener and thus enables more participation of the usual subaltern voices of marginalised communities. However, it must be stated that these views do not represent an overall homogeneous vision of the community itself but only of the local stakeholders and organisations such as Escola Bola (the tourist guide collective), Brasilidade (the residents' association), the samba squad and Grupo Eco, or more precisely of their leaders. In this sense it would be misleading to think that methodologies such as Co-Creation automatically enable channels of participation for all the members of the particular community where it is deployed. While collective Co-Creative outcomes are achievements in themselves, providing a better understanding of conditions and factors of exclusion, it could be argued that they are limited in terms of representation of the diversity of social actors of a given community because local participants were mainly community leaders and stakeholders, like the tourist guides association or the key local partner of the project, Grupo Eco.

As mentioned before, Co-Creation workshops contemplate several kinds of actors: researchers from Northern and Southern universities, representatives from NGOs of the North, members of local NGOs representing communities targeted for intervention, and artists from both the North and the South. For the purposes of this chapter, these actors could be grouped together into two groups: 'international participants' and 'local participants'. The first would be composed of researchers, representatives of Northern NGOs, and Northern artists, while the second group would be composed of local artists and members of local NGOs representing the communities of intervention.

While all actors involved in the Co-Creation workshop were supposed to participate in their initial roles, all of them had to adapt their visions and particular interests to the principles of the methodology. In this sense, all participants had to live the duality inherent to adopting the group's agenda and their individual interests and thus also becoming a parameter through which it could become possible to evaluate Co-Creation by posing the question of whether there is a degree of subversion of dominant narratives and representations or not.

Finally, to become an innovative methodology generating a specific kind of knowledge with measurable impact across countries, cities and populations, Co-Creation has to accomplish a central task, which involves the narrowing down of its own definition. In this sense, the question that arises is whether Co-Creation workshops should be standardised in terms of the actors involved and methodologies deployed or if they should allow more flexibility in their design and more room for improvisation during its execution. While mapping and photovoice were the privileged collective techniques of producing participatory knowledge, other artistic and creative tools could and should have been integrated into the framework of Co-Creation, such as poetry, graffiti, digital art, and so on. While these were present during the Santa Marta workshop, they were limited to illustrations of the themes discussed and the artists involved were not all from the local community. Related to this, a still-unresolved issue in the definition of Co-Creation parameters concerns the number of actors involved in each category of participant. As the identities and roles of the participants tend to become blurred during the Co-Creation workshop, new questions could arise about the number and kind of actors participating in it. Ann equal number of international and local actors might seem preferable but, if one of the central aims of Co-Creation is levelling the interaction between international and local marginalised communities, a greater number of the latter could imply a more equitable interaction.

The most burning question that remains to be answered is less concerned with whether Co-Creation leads to fairer representations and the inclusion of subaltern social actors, and more whether this methodology empowers the whole community or only the actors involved in the intervention. Are collective perceptions really constructed in a bottom–up fashion, synthesising multiple and diverse visions or perspectives, or is the process since its inception conditioned and undermined by the traditionally vertical models of North-South cooperation and various other hierarchies, including the agendas of some community leaders rather than those of the community as a whole? In other words, does Co-Creation become a vehicle of community empowerment or actor empowerment? While photovoice and affective mapping are useful tools allowing the expression of multiple perspectives or viewpoints, it remains an issue to verify if the themes and issues discussed through this kind of collective exercise are really a result of bottom-up processes rather than representations of the particular interests of the most prominent local stakeholders (Nykiforuk et al, 2011).

While theoretical and empirical links between artistic practice and urban development are not new, what could be considered innovative in Co-Creation methodology and interventions compared with other practices and methods derived from CBPR projects is the emphasis given to the ethical and equitable principles and dimensions. Of course, the success of the future of Co-Creation interventions in global cities will depend on the long-term engagement of all participants – local or international – with the Co-Creation principles acting as a vehicle for countering misperception of disadvantaged neighbourhoods and stimulating social integration and cohesion in global cities of the 21st century.

Overall, it is not clear however whether this kind of collective creative practice will result in the reproduction of the dominant knowledge structures (that is, the predominance of the epistemology of the North) or, on the contrary, in the emergence of alternative narratives representative of the agency of local participants. While the hybrid character of narratives emerging from this kind of creative exercise is undeniable, measuring their impact beyond their temporal and geographical limits is one of the most problematic issues of the Co-Creation project at large (this will be addressed in Chapter 17).

Actors' identities and the Co-Creation experience

As an emancipatory methodology, a key benefit Co-Creation offers to marginalised communities lies in its capacity to provide these populations with opportunities for enlarging their world views, horizons and networks beyond their secluded urban spaces. As recorded by Clift, Silva and Telles in Chapter 15, the main challenge that residents of the favela working in the tourism industry are faced with are the stereotypes they try to disrupt. They have done this primarily by establishing connections with actors involved in developing community tourism in other favelas in Rio. While the local activists, and in particular the leader of Grupo Eco, designed the programme for the Co-Creation workshop at Santa Marta, the participation of these actors in other contexts comprised in the project H2020 remains limited. In this sense, it is possible to identify a highly mobile group of international researchers and members of European NGOs that can participate in Co-Creation activities in multiple contexts, while the role of local actors belonging to marginalised communities is seriously limited by the lack of economic resources that translates into lack of international mobility. Even if participation of local actors is not limited to the activities of the workshop (the leader of Grupo Eco co-authored Chapter 15), the fact that the great majority of residents of target communities do not travel to other cities and countries where Co-Creation workshops and methodologies are deployed restrains the impact the collectively produced knowledge could have had on them and their communities in a broader context of cultural exchange.

Another ambivalent aspect of the Co-Creation workshop in Santa Marta in relation to the interaction between local and international participants and the opportunities provided for overcoming dichotomising identities and the predominance of Northern epistemologies is the language issue. On the one hand, local participants had to adapt to the fact that most of the international participants were not fluent in Portuguese and translation to English was needed during all the activities of the programme. While this could be considered as proof of the continued predominance of Northern epistemological frameworks, in this context of interaction it is important to mention that, on the other hand, local participants were able to express their opinions and perspectives in their mother tongue (Portuguese) and therefore were not restrained by their capacity to express themselves in a foreign language, even if the workshop provided the context for improving their skills in English.

Conclusion

This chapter intended in the first place to contextualise the theoretical model of the Global North-South divide and the implications it has in terms of the relational structure between countries assigned to each category and as a hegemonic representational practice that reproduces asymmetry and domination. Given this context of interaction, the Co-Creation methodology is proposed as an innovative approach, with the aim of constructing alternative representational structures that build on a world view of human co-belonging to the world rather than insisting in the reproduction of asymmetric differences that provide the discursive context where the Global South is always subject of intervention by the Global North.

Second, the analysis of the international workshop held at the favela of Santa Marta, Rio de Janeiro, was an opportunity to illustrate the basic Co-Creation principles and provide examples of potential methodological tools, including the techniques of photovoice and affective mapping. It addressed Co-Creation's capacity to use these techniques for building shared meanings and collective knowledge with the main goal of disrupting misperceptions and stereotypes that produce stigma and exclusion of marginalised communities.

Finally, the chapter examined the roles and identities of participants in this kind of workshop and explored whether or not the methodology empowers local actors or communities in the process of producing shared collective, participatory knowledge.

As for possible recommendations that could enhance Co-Creation methodology and workshops in the future, first and foremost it is important that project funding considers a greater implication of local actors in the multiple international contexts where interventions are carried out. While it could be argued that outcomes of individual Co-Creation experiences can open new perspectives on collective knowledge production and effectively challenge misperceptions and negative visions of urban spaces of exclusion or relegation in the short term and at the local level, impacts beyond these dimensions remain limited. In fact, by promoting increased mobility among the local participants of workshops, communitarian knowledge expressed during these events could be transformed into a cosmopolitan one, creating connections between members of stigmatised communities across borders. This could, in turn, allow them to identify common problems and possible solutions on a greater scale and participate in the process of knowledge production on a more equal basis. In other words, what would be needed is for favela knowledge to be taken out of the favela by its own producers.

In fact, if Co-Creation projects do not consider the problem of increasing the mobility of marginalised communities with the objective of enlarging their participation in them, they run the risk not only of not being able to achieve their stated goals of reducing inequalities but would actually participate in reinforcing them. In this sense, even if the workshops commit to the ethical principles that guide their implementation, failure to include members of the neighbourhoods or communities within the international dimension of the project would (re)produce hegemonic representational practices that preclude the effective emergence of alternative epistemologies to the dominant North-South paradigm. In other words, what Co-Creation needs to do in order to develop its full potential to reduce inequalities – at least at the knowledge production level – is to foster international participation in local communities to deprovincialise communitarian knowledge, while at the same time provincialising Western dominant paradigms through which reality has been studied and constituted.

References

Bassel, L. (2017) *The Politics of Listening: Possibilities and Challenges for Democratic Life*, London: Palgrave Macmillan.

Chakrabarty, D. (2000) *Provincializing Europe: Postcolonial Thought and Historical Difference*, Princeton: Princeton University Press.

Cohn, T. (2011) *Global Political Economy*, New York: Routledge.

de Sousa Santos, B. and Meneses, M-P. (2014) *Epistemologías del Sur*, Madrid: Ediciones Akal.

Diouf, M. (2013) *Les Arts de la Citoyenneté au Sénégal: Espaces Contestés et Civilités Urbaines*, Paris: Karthala.

Doty, R. (1996) *Imperial Encounters: The Politics of Representation in North-South Relations*, Minneapolis: University of Minnesota Press.

Duarte Aquistapace, M. (2018) 'Prácticas políticas de los sectores populares en Rio de Janeiro: urbanización de la favela de Santa Marta', *Iconos: Revista de Ciencias Sociales*, FLACSO-Ecuador, 61: 203–22.

Duck, L. (2016) 'The Global South via the U.S. South', *Concepts of the Global South – Voices from Around the World*, University of Cologne: Global South Studies Center, available from https://kups.ub.uni-koeln.de/6399/1/voices012015_concepts_of_the_global_south.pdf.

Flatley, J. (2008) *Affective Mapping: Melancholia and the Politics of Modernism*, Cambridge: Harvard University Press.

Frank, A. (1967) *Capitalism and Underdevelopment in Latin America*, New York: NYU Press.

Gruffydd, B. (2013) 'Slavery, finance and international political economy: postcolonial reflections', in S. Seth (ed) *Postcolonial Theory and International Relations*, New York: Routledge, pp 49–69.

Mbembe, A. (2017) *Critique of Black Reason*, Durham: Duke University Press.

Mignolo, W. and Walsh, C. (2018) *On Decoloniality: Concepts, Analytics, Praxis*, Durham: Duke University Press.

Moore, S.F. (1993) 'Changing perspectives on a changing Africa', in R.H. Bates, V.Y. Mudimbe and J.F. O'Barr (eds) *Africa and the Disciplines: The Contributions of Research in Africa to the Social Sciences and Humanities*, Chicago: The University of Chicago Press, pp 4–58.

Nykiforuk, C.I.J., Vallianatos, H. and Nieuwendyk, L.M. (2011) 'Photo-voice as a method for revealing community perceptions of the built and social environment', *International Journal of Qualitative Methods*, 10(2): 103–24.

Perlman, J. (2010) *Favela: Four Decades of Living on the Edge in Rio de Janeiro*, Oxford: Oxford University Press.

Said, E. (1978) *Orientalism*, New York: Vintage.

Seth, S. (2013) *Postcolonial Theory and International Relations: A Critical Introduction*, New York: Routledge.

Wang, C. and Burris, A. (1997) 'Photovoice: concept, methodology, and use for participatory needs assessment', *Health, Education & Behavior*, 24: 369.

5

Doing politics in uncertain times: Co-Creation, agency and the ontology of the city

Niccolò Milanese

Introduction

When and where is Co-Creation a useful strategy? While the term comes originally from marketing and business studies, it has been developed as a strategy in diverse economic, administrative, governmental and artistic contexts, as part of what more generally has been called the 'usological' turn (Wright, 2013). Each of these spheres into which Co-Creation is deployed has its own discursive grammars, embedded teleologies, power struggles, and institutional dynamics; part of the point of introducing Co-Creation as a method in these spheres is to displace, challenge or transform these. What happens, then, if we deploy Co-Creation as a strategy or *mot d'ordre* for urban research? In a Co-Creation methodology, the individuals who could have been conceived as the objects of research (through interviews, surveys, observation) are repositioned instead as its Co-Creators. Together with this shift in authorship and authority, the form of knowledge produced is also displaced and multiplied: the outputs of Co-Creation research may include written articles, presentations, policy proposals and similar paradigmatic forms of knowledge, but they would also include several 'embedded' forms of knowledge such as artworks that remain in the urban setting under study, the interpersonal connections and networks created, the group dynamic and the empowerment of participants. These forms seem to be further from theoretical knowledge, and closer to the kind of knowledge involved in what has been called the 'imaginative dimension of society', or 'social imaginaries' by authors like Cornelius Castoriadis (1987) and more recently Charles Taylor (2003). If we understand the city not only as a material space of constructions but also as a lived symbolic space of relationships, it is plausible to suggest that the Co-Creation methodology in an urban setting is involved in both restaging the interactions that partly produce the city itself and revealing forms of knowledge at the same time as recreating the city through what aims to be a more egalitarian and empowering process. Co-Creation thus intervenes in what Engin Isin (2002) has called the 'political space' of the city, which arises from and mediates the material and symbolic spaces.

This chapter will suggest that Co-Creation is a useful methodology in contexts of political and social uncertainty, and specifically in contexts where urban rescaling combined with geopolitical reordering in a context of risk and unpredictability leads to the unity of the city itself coming into question. Co-Creation is a useful strategy for research in such scenarios because it potentially recuperates a civic capacity, allowing participants to act as agents involved in the creation of the city, even when formal kinds of political agency are weak or non-existent, without ignoring or foreclosing the ambiguity, complexity and uncertainty of political outcomes and futures.

The strategic hypothesis of Co-Creation

The vision of the city as an *oeuvre* of citizens, intellectuals and artists has an obvious precursor in the work of Henri Lefebvre, along with his attempt to reassert use-value in a context of the dominance of exchange value (Lefebvre, 1996). Co-Creation as a research methodology could go somewhat naturally in this direction, putting a stronger emphasis on the autonomy of 'creation' than has become associated with Lefebvre's slogan 'right to the city', which perhaps lends itself to legalistic and stato-centric interpretations (see Holston, 2008 and 2009, and Lopes de Souza, 2010 for critical views). Seen in this way, using Co-Creation would imply making several strong claims of different kinds: an *epistemological* claim that the city can be known through a process of interactions between individuals; an *ontological* claim that the city is in some sense produced by these relations; and *normative political* claims that the production of the city has become alienated, and this alienation should be overcome by a specific form of practice which combines intellectual, creative and practical collective work. The strength of these claims would depend on how much we think can be explained, known or transformed using the methodology. After all, even if social scientists are pressured into pretending that their methods can explain everything, there is no need for any methodology to claim exclusivity and completeness.

Deploying Co-Creation as a slogan in an international comparative research context ostensibly calls into question some of those presuppositions we have just identified as natural to it. First, the comparative question: if the city is an *oeuvre*, is each city produced in broadly the same way, or are there radically different creations of the city? This comparative question cannot be asked today without also raising the issue of the interrelations *between* cities in a global context. This leads inevitably to the question: if the city itself is an *oeuvre*, what about the (international) relationships between cities? Do the relationships between cities – those relationships of spaces – have the same kind of meaning as urban spaces? Are they created in the same way? Are they knowable in the same ways? By asking these questions, we appear to be faced with the disjunction between the 'everyday' subjective experience of urban space and its more impersonal 'structural' processes and determinants: what is the articulation between these ways of approaching and understanding the city? Variants of this question are familiar to all social sciences. Co-Creation as a methodology does not so much avoid these dilemmas as reposition them as a practical reflexive consideration of participants: 'what common space are we at once creating and creating in (or being created by)?' and 'is there a discordance between these spaces?' are two questions participants in Co-Creation need to ask.

Here again, a comparison with Lefebvre is useful. Lefebvre (1996: 187) positions his theory of social space, *The Production of Space*, precisely as encompassing, 'on the one hand the critical analysis of urban reality and on the other that of everyday life'. He says that this 'analysis of the whole of practico-social activities' shows an ensemble which 'has nothing to do with a system or synthesis in the usual sense' but rather seeks:

> … by trial and error where can be located in time and space the point of no return and of no recourse – not on an individual or group scale, but on a global scale … . It would be the moment when the reproduction of existing relations of production would cease either because degradation and dissolution sweep it away, or because new relations are produced displacing and replacing old ones. The possibility of such a moment (a perspective which does not coincide exactly with the usual theory of revolution) defines a strategic hypothesis. It is not an indisputable and positively established certainty. It does not exclude other possibilities (for example, the destruction of the planet). (Lefebvre, 1996: 186)

In this dense paragraph are encapsulated several of Lefebvre's most insightful conjectures, which position the 'right to the city' firmly in a revolutionary perspective.

As Neil Brenner (1999 and 2000) has emphasised, *The Production of Space* explores the 'superimposition and interpenetration of social spaces' (Lefebvre, 1996: 342) in contemporary cities, in a context of global urban rescaling driven by capitalist restructuring as capital seeks to free itself from constraint or friction ('the annihilation of space through time', as Marx famously put it in the *Grundrisse* [Marx, 1973, see Harvey 1990 for the classic urban theory exposition of this notion]) and states struggle to attract, fix and reterritorialise it. As Lefebvre says (1991: 86-7), 'social spaces interpenetrate one another and/or superimpose themselves upon one another. They are not things, which have mutually limiting boundaries'. This suggests that the 'global' does not intrude upon or crush the 'local' but rather that hierarchies and relationships shift and recompose. The urban space becomes at once what Lefebvre (1991: 386) calls the 'milieu' and the 'enjeu' (stake) of contemporary sociopolitical struggle because the city is both the site and target of rescaling processes, due to its historical centrality in the development of capitalism and the density of connections and institutions concentrated in it. Lefebvre's strategic hypothesis is that, at some point soon, the production model will no longer be tenable, and a systemic change will take place.

This hypothesis is only partly sustainable today for us, even withholding judgement on its Marxist character. On the one hand, the processes of scalar recomposition and the politics of space which Lefebvre identified have accelerated to a point he most likely would have thought untenable. Whereas in the 1970s, at least in the 'first world', the Fordist model of production was still based on the nation-state's capacity to organise production, alleviate sociospatial polarisation and preserve social cohesion, today's highly financialised and multi-polar post-Fordist economy has led to a situation in which single nation-states often struggle to stabilise or fix *any* spatial scale in which to contain, regulate or direct global circulations; rather they constantly adapt, resize and rescale territorial policies, priorities and geopolitical alliances as a function of circumstances largely out of their control. If we continue to use Marxist terms, we could say that the mode of production has changed, or is in the process of changing, and has yet to find a settled new form, unless that new form is precisely one of constant upheaval. This sense of constant upheaval is surely part of what is referred to as 'globalisation' in everyday vernacular conversation.

On the other hand, against what Lefebvre may have predicted and hoped, the movements of urban sociopolitical struggle 'from below' have not yet shown a capacity to reappropriate the means of spatial production on anything other than a localised and temporary scale. Networks of some cities may be taking a lead in terms of environmental policies, refugee welcome or housing policies, but we are still far away from a situation where 'mayors rule the world' (to use the title of Benjamin Barber's [2014] provocative book), or where cities challenge either the dominance of global capital or the security prerogative of the nation-state.

Into this context of accelerated processes of global spatial reorganisation, what is the 'strategic hypothesis' of Co-Creation as a methodology of urban research? It cannot be the announcing of an alternative system, let alone anything about how that alternative might look, but rather that the unity of the urban space is constantly in doubt and in some sense our common sharing of space in the city is thereby constantly under threat; further, that the Co-Creation methodology can modestly open up temporary spaces of collaboration in which the shifting shape and time of the urban can be discerned and made accessible to knowledge. Another way of putting this is that the questions 'who are we, Co-Creators?' and 'what common space(s) do we Co-Create (in)?' are both unavoidable, with at best temporary and provisional answers acutely sensitive to their own limits (which means to say that the questions imply their inverse: 'who is not here, not part of Co-Creation?', 'what space are we in which we do not Co-Create, over which we do not have agency?' and 'which discontinuous spaces are we in? which spaces are we unable to make common?'). The experimental conjecture that needs to be tested is that by asking these questions in a specific kind of way, practically and creatively as much as theoretically, we can gain agency rather than inertia.

A comparative urban research with an international dimension (as in the case of the Co-Creation project) only accentuates the pertinence of these questions, but the questions would need to be asked in any setting or scale, not so much because the economy or politics has become more 'global' recently but because economy and politics everywhere is going through a global reorganisation which shows no signs of settling down into a stable form. In the next section of this chapter, we will see how the deployment of Co-Creation as a strategic hypothesis in a specific sociohistoric configuration leads unavoidably to the posing of these questions.

Co-Creation in a context of uncertainty

The practical experience and application of Co-Creation as a methodology which this chapter builds upon comes from fieldwork looking into processes of urban marginalisation between mid-2018 and early 2019 in four 'world-cities': London, Paris, Rio de Janeiro, and Mexico City. The choice of these four cities comes partly from the author's own research interests, partly from the Co-Creation project funded by the European Union – itself one of the most important actors involved in both urban rescaling and geopolitical reordering processes – which connected partners based in these cities and their respective zones of influence. In all four of the cities, during this timeframe, the everyday experience of space of many urban dwellers could not be disassociated from anxiety concerning the future shape and place of the city, and therefore from wider concerns about changing geopolitical contexts. Headline news in each of the cities in the research period touched directly on questions of urban centrality, mobility, scale and change. Urban scholars have been talking about urban rescaling in a context of geopolitical change for over three decades, but rarely have such questions been so pervasive in the news cycles of multiple countries and in the everyday concerns of residents. It is perhaps useful to recite some of these stories to emphasise the sentiment not only of the return of history but of the acceleration of history that it provokes, and to attempt to bring out at least some family resemblances in terms of the kind of change taking place between the different cities.

In London during this timeframe, public discussion was dominated by the relationship of the United Kingdom to the European Union, following the referendum to leave the European Union in 2016 and in the context of the ongoing negotiations as to the nature of this separation ('Brexit') where the outcomes were highly uncertain. It became an unavoidable subject to which all social and political issues were related. Brexit was seen to have potentially enormous implications for the centrality of the city of London to the regional economy of the European Union. To give examples as indications of what seemed to be much more systematic processes of the relegation of London's normative power on a regional scale, the European Medicines Agency was relocated from London to Amsterdam during this period, and the European Banking Authority from London to Paris. Simultaneously, discussions about whether London might reposition itself as a different kind of global centre, with less regulation and taxes on capital, were underway. Aside from these uncertainties concerning London's place in the world, everyone living in the country and UK citizens living in the European Union had reason to be uncertain of the future of their rights to move, to reside and to politically express themselves.

Paris, during this same period, in part as a historic rival to London, was seeking to reinforce itself as a regional and global centre, but it simultaneously found itself beset by sociopolitical conflict manifested in the *gilets jaunes* movement from November 2018 onwards. This attracted global media attention to the city, notably when violent clashes with the police broke out on the famous Champs Elysées. This movement positioned itself as the uprising of those excluded from the metropolitan centre, and the public debate over the legitimacy and limits of the movement was intense. Through an astonishing coincidence, the Presidential response to a process of popular consultation organised by the government to resecure social cohesion was postponed and overtaken by the fire at Notre-Dame Cathedral on 15 April 2019, at 'kilometre zero', in the very centre of Paris historically and geographically, the day before President Macron was due to make his announcements. This fire, followed live through broadcast and social media throughout the world, led to a renewed sense of fragility over the historical relationship between Paris as a national and global centre and its peripheries.

Rio de Janeiro, during the same period, was experiencing high political uncertainty running up to the October 2018 Presidential elections, with highly popular former President Lula attempting to run as a candidate from prison but ultimately being disqualified, and then further uncertainty following the election of hard-Right nationalist Jair Bolsonaro. This change dramatically influenced the prospects and outlook for those most at risk of social exclusion in Rio de Janeiro: notably those living in favelas, Afro-descendants and indigenous populations, women and LGBTQI communities, all of whom were explicit targets of violent hate speech. In the run-up to the elections, the supporters of Bolsonaro attacked rallies held at universities in opposition to his candidacy. Since its election, the government of Bolsonaro has undermined universities through cutting funding and continues to verbally attack the importance of scientific knowledge, particularly in the humanities. The life and death of Marielle Franco, the murdered Rio councillor – favela-born, educated at university, a lesbian and a campaigner for the rights of minorities and against the clientelism, corruption and violence – became during this time a myth or parable by which many in Rio could interpret their historical circumstances. This parable was dramatically represented in several of the Rio Carnival parades in March 2019, most notably that of the samba school Mangueira, which won the competition. As in Paris, fire was again an internationally visible image of the country: the burning of the National Museum in Rio in August 2018, and the burning of the Amazon rainforest both highly mediatised and politicised events globally.

During this same period in Mexico City, uncertainty over the direction in which newly elected President Andrés Manuel Lópes Obrador would take the country was significant. Elected in July 2018 and taking office on 1 December 2018, Obrador promised a 'fourth transformation' of the Mexican state, coming after Mexican independence, reform and revolution: the natural question many people were asking was what direction and implications this transformation would have. In the months preceding his formal investiture as President, Obrador announced that plans for a new international airport for Mexico City would be scrapped, following a referendum. This decision had implications in terms of the international profile of Mexico City, both as a transport hub and a place of investment, and in the manner in which the decision was taken, which led to a debate about government by direct democracy, its implications and risks of instrumentalisation. During this period, an intense rhetorical attack on both Mexicans and, specifically, on migrants crossing the Mexican border into the US was being conducted by US President Donald Trump, while a trade deal between Mexico and the US was being negotiated. Simultaneously, the US military was touting the possibilities for intervention in Venezuela, possibly using the Brazilian military as proxies, and sustained comparisons between Obrador's anti-neoliberal rhetoric and that of the failed Chávez regime in Venezuela were being made both by domestic opponents of Obrador and by Right-wing US media, stoking anxiety both about the course of action of President Obrador and about how international neighbours might react to it.

This necessarily incomplete and unsatisfactory run-through of some of the main news stories of the period of research in the countries and cities under study is intended on the one hand to illustrate the thickness of the context in which any process of Co-Creation will take place, but also to make some general points about this particular configuration of cities at this time.

First, the sense of historical uncertainty was common to all cities, albeit for different reasons. In each city, there was a sense of the changing of an epoch, and this uncertain temporal horizon inevitably has an influence on the way space is experienced. Second, the internationalised character of each of the megacities under study – three of which are national capitals and one of which is a former capital city – implied that the sense of space of their inhabitants was in a complex tension between 'national' framing and 'international' framing: the meaning of living in Paris, for example, was affected by the *gilets jaunes* protests, not just for reasons which concern national politics and social cohesion, but inextricably also because of the international implications of the visibility of the protests and what it might imply for the future development of Paris. Flames and fire – symbolically an antithesis and risk of urbanity – were internationally visible images and symbols of both Paris and Brazil during the period.

Third, the sense of crisis in the European cities under study was sufficiently visible internationally that, to some extent, Europe was at once provincialised, made less dominant as a role-model, and brought nearer to non-European cities: often in the exchanges not only with other researchers but with regular inhabitants in Rio de Janeiro and Mexico City, there was a sense that, for all the enormous differences and inequalities, some similar problems were being experienced in metropolitan Europe to those experienced in Brazil and Mexico, and that some similar processes of political reorganisation were taking place (for recent context on Mexico City see Parnreiter, 2015, and on Brazil see Barcellos de Souza, 2016). Analyses of globalising cities show network patterns of global centres, which cut across North/ South divides, and in this network of global centrality cities may experience promotion or demotion in various sectors and domains (for empirical analysis, see Taylor et al, 2011). The trajectory of London specifically in these globalised networks is of significance at once for urban theory, for the social imaginary of its inhabitants and for the social imaginary of citizens of other cities across the world: London has been so central historically to processes of globalisation and the spatial politics of capitalism that it is a paradigm city for urban studies in this area (see, for example, Brenner, 1999, and Sassen, 1991), as well as being known by people across the world as a centre, meaning that the risk of its peripheralisation or demotion in capital centrality in the context of Brexit creates novel historical circumstances.

Fourth, while travelling between these cities and conducting Co-Creation workshops, discussions and collaborations, the participating researchers were inevitably carrying this context with them: most intensely that context closest to where they normally live (including Paris), but as the project went forward and researchers travelled from one city to the next, increasingly as messengers and representatives of the contexts they were coming from and Co-Creating in. This last point implies ethical and political responsibilities for the researcher, who by having the freedom and privilege to travel between these contexts in a symbolic way could be said to hold the 'keys to the cities' (much like honorary citizens are sometimes ceremoniously given keys to the city). The inequality of mobility rights and possibilities of different Co-Creation participants, and the risk of imperial behaviours and epistemologies of those closest to centrality, power and capital, need to be at the forefront of every researcher's mind, most importantly those in privileged positions.

This rich world-historical and political context becomes an inescapable part of interpreting some of the acts and exchanges experienced in the process of Co-Creation: those approaching the questions of 'who are we Co-Creators?' and 'what common space do we Co-Create in?' must be aware of this context and the geopolitically uncertainty of everyday local city life. In order to give a specific example, this chapter lastly considers one episode that took place within a Co-Creation workshop to articulate the ways in which the methodology can concentrate ambiguities and vulnerabilities, is sensitive to the fluid transformations in togetherness and otherness, and thereby can act as a deep imaginative source of common cause or agency.

Urban space, threat space and common space

The episode occurred in the context of a workshop organised in the favela of Santa Marta, near to the wealthy and embassy-lined streets of Botafogo in Rio de Janeiro in August 2018. The favela has until recently had relatively low levels of violence as the first favela to undergo 'pacification' in 2008, in advance of the global events hosted by the city: the football World Cup in 2014 and the Olympics in 2016. Santa Marta is a case study in the spatiality of the 'grey zone' that emerges through the interaction of formal, informal and illegal economies in global-market dynamics, and the ways different state and non-state actors – most notably the police, militias and the drugs barons – attempt to intervene in these dynamics, not so much to eradicate illegality or reinforce legal forms of work, but to rebalance the benefits and profits of these arrangements between different groups and interests, which includes politicians, residents, multinational companies, global financial institutions and transnational crime rings (Valenzuela-Aguilera, 2019).

In the recent months before the workshop, the levels of violent exchange between drugs gangs and the Rio police had intensified. Walking around the favela it was easy to stumble across visibly armed young men, who nevertheless did their best to stay out of sight, particularly of international visitors and tourists. As part of the Co-Creation workshop, a small group of five people – comprising three researchers from the UK and France (of whom the author was one), one Santa Marta resident acting as a translator, and one younger resident involved in a local NGO – explored the streets of the favela, conducting the exercise of taking street photographs which would represent what we understood as representing key local issues ('diagnostic photos') and future opportunities ('possibility photos') in the favela. In parallel, the group endeavoured to have conversations with local inhabitants about how they saw the future of the favela in terms of its development. In such conversations, the end of the Lula era and the uncertainty of what was to come next were constant themes. The group decided to knock on one door in a narrow street and started a conversation with a resident who had recently moved to the area, explaining the overall aims of the research into the future of the favela and where each member of the group had come from. Very soon into the conversation, several young armed men ran past, speaking hurriedly into their walkie-talkies, clearly on manoeuvres which would imply either an armed confrontation with other drugs gangs or, much more likely, a confrontation with the police. Quite naturally, the resident invited the group into her house to take shelter, where the conversation continued, other family members having noted the new entrants to their house but continuing their previous activity. This simple act of humanity, an everyday reflex for inhabitants, and which surely would have been shown to any stranger outside of that door at that moment, no doubt responded to a reinforced sense of care for *international* visitors. The space of Co-Creation thus suddenly changed, from the public street to the private home, from the external city to the internal domestic space, at the initiation of someone who had not been involved in the group or project of Co-Creation at all until that moment, but was now acting at once as a host, a participant and a protector of the research project and those involved in it. The public space suddenly became unsafe as a space for creative collaboration, because of the changed activity of a set of actors who were previously present in the space but until that point not threatening.

The resident who invited the group into her house had already learnt where its members were coming from. She had televisions, an internet connection, and newspapers in her house, and a level of education which would suggest that she would not be totally unaware of the contexts her visitors were from. The short conversation dealt with the favela itself, its cleanliness, her hopes for the future as a new resident, and did not touch on any international matters, but those 'international' contexts were present in the room through the group's presence and through the need for translation from Portuguese into French (the common language of the group). Once an assessment had been made that the sound of gunshots was no longer close, and that danger outside had abated, the group took a decision to take a photograph of the group, the resident – and including the husband of the resident, who had not been involved in the conversation – in the mirror before leaving. Reunited with the larger group of Co-Creation researchers, both local and international, later in the day, it was decided that this photograph would be used as the 'possibilities' photograph representing 'uncertainty but hope' in the favelas for an exhibition.

The significance of this simple episode as part of a Co-Creation investigation is that the self-reflexive nature of Co-Creation obliged a reflection on: the changing space in which Co-Creation was taking place (moving from the street to the home); the changing composition of the group involved in the common project (which came to include, in a stronger way, the resident); the changing roles of those individuals (from interviewee to host, from interviewer to guest); a reflection on the place of individuals and groups external to the project, and the way their actions changed the space and composition of Co-Creation participation (whether it be the drugs gangs encountered, the police they were most likely confronting, or the family members of the resident who welcomed the group into their home and continued their business); and the development of a common project (all of those inside the home were in some sense committed to continuing exchange, research and mutual learning). Each member of the group was more acutely aware of the position of the other: the resident imagining the concerns of 'international' visitors, the international visitors more acutely aware of the meaning of being a resident of that place. Surely in this process of imaginative 'simulation' in understanding others (Heal, 2003), all kinds of stereotypes and misconceptions continued to exist, but the episode started a process in which such misconceptions could be discussed. Finally, the element of 'creation' in the methodology meant that one of the means chosen to record and to make communicable and knowable both the shared experience and the shared space created through the incident was through a collectively composed photograph (a modest artistic product) in which all appeared as a group in a mirror, as if to fix the temporary unity in space created through the conversation.

The episode in Santa Marta favela had all its local specificities, but the actors involved, and the context of Santa Marta itself, all have 'global' relations: the local is not eradicated by the global, it is transformed, and the city as a lived space is transformed each time by actors coming to it and interacting in it with their own histories, contexts and relationships. The episode shows that Co-Creation can be used to make conscious the interaction of these relationships in changing urban scales. If the episode involved a form of danger or risk which is not of the same degree as to be found in other urban settings, this very present form of risk is a more extreme form of the threat of violence, dissolution or lawlessness which is always the alternative to the social unity of the city. What the episode shows is that, in dealing with such risks, we recompose social unities and that these social unities can be, and frequently are, irreducibly 'international' and do not map to state borders. By self-consciously Co-Creating a new urban space, in a context of threat, we recuperate an urban civic agency in contexts where we may have no formal political agency, and where we are physically weaker actors than others. This urban civic agency has a quite different character to the Hobbesian solutions of overbearing sovereignty, which may otherwise be tempting in such a situation of 'stasis' (see Agamben, 2015). By finding ways of recording, drawing, photographing or recounting such encounters which create shared spaces, we are contributing in small ways to the creation of common social imaginaries which are in their way insurgent against the impersonal and structural violence and expulsion which Saskia Sassen (Sassen, 2014 and Kaldor and Sassen, forthcoming) among others has analysed as a major phenomenon of the global economy.

Therefore, in answer to our initial question of where and when Co-Creation is a useful strategy, we can say that it is useful in urban contexts where the dynamics of change and of threat are strong and disruptive, where multiplicities of different actors are involved in these dynamics, as a way of small groups of researchers, inhabitants, artists and others becoming consciously aware of their own individual and collective involvement in these dynamics, to collectively produce forms of knowledge which recall the memory, the present and the future possibility of spaces of their common civic agency.

References

Agamben, G. (2015) *Stasis: Civil War as Political Paradigm*, translated by N. Heron, New York: Columbia University Press.

Barber, B. (2014) *If Mayors Ruled the World: Dysfunctional Nations, Rising Cities*, New Haven: Yale University Press.

Barcellos de Souza, M. (2016) 'The spatial rescaling of the developmental state in Brazil', *Mercator (Fortaleza)*, 15(4): 27–46.

Brenner, N. (1999) 'Globalisation as reterritorialisation: the re-scaling of urban governance in the European Union', *Urban Studies*, 36(3): 431–51.

Brenner, N. (2000) 'The urban question as scale question: reflections on Henri Lefebvre, urban theory and the politics of scale', *International Journal of Urban and Regional Research*, 24(2): 361–78.

Castoriadis, C. (1987) *The Imaginary Institution of Society*, translated by K. Blamey, Oxford: Blackwell.

Harvey, D. (1990) *The Condition of Postmodernity*, Oxford: Blackwell.

Heal, J. (2003) *Mind, Reason and Imagination*, Cambridge: Cambridge University Press.

Holston, J. (2008) *Insurgent Citizenship: Disjunctions of Democracy and Modernity in Brazil*, Princeton: Princeton University Press.

Holston, J. (2009) 'Insurgent citizenship in an era of global urban peripheries', *City and Society*, 21(2): 247–67.

Isin, E. (2003) *Being Political: Genealogies of Citizenship*, Minneapolis: University of Minnesota Press.

Kaldor, M. and Sassen, S. (eds) (2020, forthcoming), *Cities at War: Global Insecurity and Urban Resistance*, New York: Columbia University Press.

Lefebvre, H. (1991) *The Production of Space*, translated by D. Nicholson-Smith, Oxford: Blackwell.

Lefebvre, H. (1996) *Writings on Cities*, translated by E. Kofman and E. Lebas, Oxford: Blackwell.

Lopes de Souza, M. (2010) 'Which right to which city? In defence of political-strategic clarity', *Interface: A Journal For and About Social Movements*, 2(1): 315–33.

Marx, K. (1973) *Grundrisse: Foundations for the Critique of Political Economy*, London: Penguin.

Parnreiter, C. (2015) 'Strategic planning, the real estate economy, and the production of new spaces of centrality: the case of Mexico City', *Erdkunde*, 66(1): 21–31.

Sassen, S. (1991) *The Global City: New York, London, Tokyo*, Princeton: Princeton University Press.

Sassen, S. (2014) *Expulsion: Brutality and Complexity in the Global Economy*, Cambridge: Harvard University Press.

Taylor, C. (2003), *Modern Social Imaginaries*, Durham: Duke University Press.

Taylor, P., Ni, P., Derudder, B., Hoyler, M., Huang, J. and Witlox, F. (eds) (2011) *Global Urban Analysis: A Survey of Cities in Globalization*, London: Earthscan.

Valenzuela-Aguilera, A. (2019) 'The third circuit of the spatial economy: determinants of public policy in Latin America', *Regional Sciences Policy and Practice*, 2019: 1–13.

Wright, S. (2013) *Towards a Lexicon of Usership*, Eindhoven: Van Abbemuseum.

6

Co-Creation and bridging theory-method divides

Annaleise Depper and Simone Fullagar

Introduction

This chapter explores the possibilities and challenges posed by Co-Creation as a knowledge practice that is more than a 'novel method' for addressing urban inequality, disadvantage and territorial stigmatisation. Co-Creation is informed by a diverse range of disciplinary practices, theoretical traditions and ways of collaborating with communities, artists and academics. The chapter draws on examples from the authors' own and others' work that explores the affective relations of stigmatisation, place and urban inequality through Co-Creative, participatory methods. This methodological banner of 'Co-Creation' has been cited across a range of disciplines, such as children's geographies (Stephens et al, 2014), management and business studies (Voorberg et al, 2015), health care research (Gill et al, 2011; Zanetti and Taylor, 2016), urban and culture research (Carpenter and Horvath, 2018), feminist research (Ringrose and Renold, 2014) and educational studies (Bovill et al, 2011). Across these disciplines, Co-Creation is commonly thought of as moving beyond tokenistic participation and guided by fundamental notions of participation, praxis, collective creativity and knowledge exchange between two or more individuals that continues throughout the inquiry and design process.

In this empirical research, the conceptualisation of Co-Creation is supported by an inclusive approach, whereby young people were invited to contribute insights through the relational production of knowledge. Young people contributed their insights throughout the design process – from initially exploring ideas and questions relevant to them in their community to trialling and selecting creative practices to tell their own stories and experiences of moving through everyday spaces. This study involved creative, arts-based practices to explore the social practices that young people enact through the affective and material contexts of their everyday lives (their 'embodied mobility').

In this project there was no 'artist' involved, as both young people and the researcher were understood to be actively Co-Creating knowledge through a range of arts-based research practices.

The authors' particular interest lies in exploring Co-Creation as a new materialist approach to creative, participatory research. This chapter draws upon Depper's empirical PhD research, which used arts-based practice and knowledge exchange to engage with young people (aged ten to 17), families and local practitioners (health, childhood and family services) in the exploration of inequality, affect and embodied mobility in a large town in the South West of England. Co-Creation provided an overarching process that utilised creative participatory methods, such as 'photovoice', peer-led interviewing, mapping, postermaking and film making. These creative artefacts were Co-Created with young people to explore affective relations of leisure, class, gender, space and place. Arts-based methods produced provocations to think differently and intervene in the complexities of power and entanglements of human and nonhuman relations that shaped young peoples' embodied mobility. While the main part of the empirical work involved engaging with young people through creative practices, this inquiry provided further opportunities to engage with young people's parents, carers and local practitioners in this research. For example, at the start of this inquiry, local practitioners were involved through initial meetings to explore their thoughts about the multiple challenges and complexities around young people's lives in Swindon. Later, practitioners were brought together with young people and their families through the exhibition event, which showcased young people's creative outputs and facilitated the exchange of ideas about their everyday challenges. Throughout this chapter, the authors share specific examples from this wider empirical research, turning, in particular, to young people's stories and experiences of embodied mobility through photovoice and poster-making creative practices.

This chapter discusses how the conceptualisation of a 'creative research assemblage' extends traditional ways of Co-Creating and co-constructing research within interpretative traditions that have previously rested upon dualisms of real/representation, self/world, self/other, mind/body. A creative research assemblage brings together different kinds of knowledge, for example, techniques, artefacts, researcher bodies, young bodies, human and nonhuman contexts. Rather than position the humanist subject at the centre of Co-Creation, assemblage models approach 'creativity as *relational*, emerging through human and nonhuman encounters and affects' (Fullagar and Small, 2018: 125). Throughout, this chapter thinks through some of the onto-ethico-epistemological assumptions that underpin the 'doing' of Co-Creation as inventive post-qualitative practice.

The creative research assemblage: thinking through theory and method

Moving beyond a primary concern with a methodological technique and process, Co-Creation was enacted in this study as a material-discursive knowledge practice to 'produce' different ways of knowing and (re)presenting young people's affective stories of stigmatised spaces. New materialist theories pursue a rhizomatic, rather than linear, movement of ideas and practices. Central to new materialist work is disrupting the method/theory binary assumed in interpretative research that seeks to understand and 'capture' lived experiences (Coleman and Ringrose, 2013; Taylor, 2016). Such humanist traditions often reduce 'qualitative methodology to a matter of technique, instrument or toolkit' to represent the 'real' world (Fullagar, 2017: 249). Post-qualitative inquiry refuses a neat separation of theory and methods, and 'encourages researchers to deconstruct what QR [qualitative research] is and destabilize taken for granted assumptions' (Kuby et al, 2016: 141).

In moving beyond humanist assumptions about individual creativity and essentialist categories of identity, Co-Creation can be thought of as a creative research assemblage that brings into relation a range of objects, desires, bodies and contexts to disrupt, reimagine and contest the normative (for example, stigmatising of groups and places, and the invisibility of privileged perspectives). This creative assemblage helped the authors to rethink what research 'does' and the role of creativity in this process, as both the human and nonhuman informed the process of social inquiry. According to Fox and Alldred (2017: 153), new materialist social inquiry 'treats the researcher and research event ... as an assemblage that produces a variety of material capabilities in its human and nonhuman relations'. As Fox (2013: 495) emphasises, 'Creativity is an active, experimenting flow within a network or assemblage of bodies, things, ideas and institutions'. This present study engaged young people in a creative research assemblage that made visible the affective dimensions of inequality, human and nonhuman relations in order to produce change-oriented cultural artefacts. Filming, photographs and a public exhibition were used to produce a social change-oriented 'creative research assemblage'. This was comprised of both nonhuman and human elements and relations (young people, researchers, organisations and charities, parents/carers); research 'tools', methodology and methods (film equipment, photovoice, arts and design materials, recording devices); the spaces and physical locality of research events; and the theoretical frameworks and ideas guiding and informing social inquiry. As this chapter will explore, there were different ways in which meaning materialised through young people's experiences and the texts, images and stories produced through this creative research assemblage.

In contrast to conventional humanist research that often ignores affective relations in the desire to 'represent' people's lives, this post-qualitative inquiry examined flows of affects and emotions as productive of Co-Creative methodologies. The turn towards affect throughout the humanities and social sciences has been particularly inspired by the work of Deleuze and Guattari (1988) and moves beyond individualised emotion to flows of affect as sensations, desires, power relations and embodied becoming (Deleuze, 1995). Affects have been articulated as 'sticky' (Ahmed, 2004); they 'travel as well as stick in points of fixation' (Kofoed and Ringrose, 2012: 5). Affect and emotion, as sensations, are always bound up with discursive frames and cannot be separated (Ahmed, 2004; Kumm and Johnson, 2018). As Ahmed (2004) further emphasises, emotion and affect cannot be divided; emotions become entangled and circulate through the affective economy of everyday social relations (including inequality). Rather than privileging discourse, affect is considered important in terms of the capacity to disrupt, move and rework the social (Massumi, 1995). Affective relations connect young people's bodies and practices through complex assemblages, which are bound up with broader economic, technological and sociological forces and contexts (such as sport and physical culture, see Fullagar and Pavlidis, 2018). As such, young people are moved by the forces of affect within a broader 'affective economy' (Ahmed, 2004), which 'connects bodies in leisure contexts (gyms, sports fields, pools) with power relations that produce social inequities (class, ethnicity, gender, age, sexuality, disability)' (Depper et al, 2018: 7). Thinking *with* theoretical concepts of assemblage and affect was central to this study, in order to enhance a new materialist social inquiry with layers of meaning, nuance and ontological complexity. The authors were interested in exploring what role *affect* plays in the micropolitics of working with different desires, bodies, and techniques to effect change.

Post-qualitative ways of thinking further helped the authors to theorise ideas around 'voice' within Co-Creation processes. Departing from representational approaches to voice that seek a so-called truth (Berbary and Boles, 2014), the authors explored complex and embodied notions of voice within Co-Creation processes. Previous participatory approaches have often relied upon problematic notions of 'giving' 'a voice to those being researched' (Coad, 2012: 12) or attempting to retrieve an authentic voice (St Pierre, 2014). These claims often position young people as a homogenous group, where 'voice' becomes a transparent means through which young people communicate an inner 'truth'. New materialist ideas were central to exploring questions of what claims are made about participatory approaches in voicing issues of marginalisation, and what forms of accountability are evident in the knowledge claims made by Co-Created research in the representation of the lives of others (Barad, 2007).

This inquiry embraced the materiality of embodied voices and experiences that are negotiated through the process of Co-Creation. This notion of embodied voice disrupts binary oppositions between the mind/body, subject/object, method/theory, interior/exterior (Coleman and Ringrose, 2013; St Pierre et al, 2016). New materialist notions of embodied voice are central to understanding human and nonhuman relations as 'complex, co-constitutive, and co-constructive' (Hroch and Stoddart, 2015: 295–6). Voice, therefore, can be understood 'as an assemblage, a complex network of human and nonhuman agents that exceeds the traditional notion of the individual' (Mazzei, 2013: 734). In this way, the research assemblage produced embodied voice in particular ways through the participatory and creative methods. This study thus extends Co-Creation in new directions, by embracing various theoretical perspectives that reconfigure voice, the subject, agency and embodiment.

Co-Creative practices

Through Co-Creation, young people reimagined, intervened and performed critical ideas about the complexities in their everyday lives. Co-Creative, arts-based practices created an embodied space to challenge normative categories of knowing and being 'young and active'. The authors conceptualise Co-Creation as a democratic process, involving multiple partners and voices, including young people, researchers, communities and practitioners who come together through creativity and interaction. In the present study, photovoice, peer-led interviewing, mapping, poster making and film making methodologies were used during and alongside workshops to explore young people's affective relationalities and experiences of everyday, stigmatised spaces. This chapter now turns to these specific creative, participatory methodologies adopted and to Swindon where this inquiry took place.

The project was located in Swindon, a large town in the South West of England and explored young people's affective practices of mobility in low-income areas. Swindon was purposefully selected as a site where the micropolitics of inequality and disparity played out for young people and their families. In comparison to other places in the UK, Swindon has reported relatively high levels of inequality and poverty, with 16 per cent of children living in low-income families (Swindon Borough Council, 2017) and specific communities facing poverty, deprivation, social exclusion and high unemployment rates (Swindon Borough Council, 2016). Poverty can be understood as households with a relative low income, based upon a local measure of 'children in families in receipt of either out of work benefits, or tax credits where their reported income is less than 60% median income' (NHS Swindon, 2011: 5). Particular families living in marginalised and low-income areas of Swindon have been subjected to stigmatising depictions within the media. Swindon has been labelled the 'ugliest town in England' (Grant, 2015) and elsewhere Swindon was once stigmatised as the 'fattest town' in the West of England (Mackley, 2014). Particular communities have been depicted as a 'no-go zone' (Cross, 2015) and 'a run-down sprawling council estate on the outskirts of Swindon, home to hundreds of unemployed lone parents' (McDonald, 2002). Through this research, young people reimagined stigmatising depictions of Swindon and actively performed a different sense of place in highly affective ways.

This qualitative inquiry took place in Swindon over the course of a year and involved three participatory projects with three different groups of young people, an exhibition event and semi-structured interviews with both the young people's parents or carers and practitioners who worked within children and family support services in Swindon. This research engaged with young people through three different organisations; each of the three organisations supported children, young people and their families who have been identified as 'disadvantaged' in multiple ways. These services support children and young people living in Swindon's most vulnerable communities who are faced with significant challenges, including: living in low-income households; experiencing learning and communication difficulties; living in care; and having care responsibilities for family members. As this research involved data collection with young people, who can be defined as a vulnerable group due to their age, formal safeguarding and ethical procedures were followed to ensure that the welfare of young people was supported at all times. All participants received a study information sheet and were required to sign an adult consent or young person's assent form to confirm their willingness to take part. The names of the participants, organisations and any specific locations within Swindon have been replaced with pseudonyms.

Over a period of nine months, Depper facilitated three projects (with the collective title *Your Space, Your Say*), over different durations with young people in the different groups engaging with creative practices in varying ways. The Co-Creation of qualitative data involved participatory photovoice, peer-led interviewing, mapping, poster making and film making to help Co-Create youth-oriented accounts of mobility through stigmatised community spaces. These innovative methods 'on the move' enabled young people to walk through community spaces, while creatively and critically exploring spaces and issues that were important in their everyday lives through visual methodologies. The process of Co-Creation brought into relation a range of affects (fear, shame, pleasure, belonging), produced through relations of stigmatisation that shape experiences of place and urban inequality. Co-Creation became a process of doing, inventing, and creating knowledge together, guided by Depper's focus on questions of inequality.

This chapter draws upon specific examples from the study; in particular, it looks at photovoice and poster-making practices as ways to explore young people's experiences and stories of embodied mobility. Most of these activities took place during the first phase of the project, when young people started to share their ideas and experiences through creative practices. In these particular examples, a group of five young people aged ten to fifteen worked both individually and collectively to explore different places in Swindon, accompanied by the researcher, to take pictures of objects and places that were significant to them. Following these outings, young people then created posters and collages of their printed photographs, adding their own drawings and words to describe their experiences and feelings of these particular places.

At the end of the projects, young people presented their creative and critical artefacts at a public engagement exhibition in Swindon. The aim of the exhibition was to disseminate young people's findings, as well as to highlight ways in which communities can engage with policy discourses to effect social change. The exhibition event emphasised the health and social challenges in Swindon, while inviting local practitioners to consider more responsive and inclusive approaches to address inequality. As part of the creative assemblage, the exhibition mobilised a 'politics of imagination' (Latimer and Skeggs, 2011). Through watching the films, listening to the views of young people on the panel talks, walking through the exhibition spaces to see the posters, and even contributing their own ideas through an interactive exhibit, attendees were invited to imagine and make sense of young people's lives in different ways. The Co-Creative practices of the exhibition invited the attendees to both move through and be *moved by* the affective imaginaries (Dawney, 2011) of the exhibition space. The exhibition invited new conversations about recognising and responding to issues of inequality that manifest in young people's everyday lives. The *Your Space, Your Say* project disrupted the limited notion of agency and encouraged a more critical and creative engagement with young people about the affective relations of leisure spaces in Swindon. Following the exhibition, Depper facilitated semi-structured interviews with the young people's parents, carers, and local practitioners in children and young people's services, to explore their thoughts and ideas about the young people's projects and their perspectives of the complexities of inequalities.

Thinking-making-doing: Mapping young people's spaces

In what follows, the authors draw upon a specific example from this inquiry that explored affective relations of stigmatisation of urban places through specific arts-based practices. Arts-based drawings, poster making and photovoice helped the 'thinking-making-doing' of the banal and often taken for granted moments of young people's everyday, stigmatised spaces. In particular, the photovoice practice helped to evoke the vivid, sensory and embodied nature of these spaces of multiplicity. The photovoice method involved young people visiting specific places in Swindon that were significant to them and taking pictures of objects, people, places and materials in order to visually represent their local environment and then facilitating discussion around their images. After the photovoice outing, young people used their printed pictures to make collages and posters to illustrate the multiple feelings they experienced in these places. Young people were drawn to particular moments of remembering; they spoke to these 'lively' images with an affective intensity. For example, Megan created a poster (see Figure 6.1).

As active 'Co-Creators' of space, young people shared their stories of embodied mobility, voicing those moments that were fearful, risky or pleasurable. Meaning about everyday spaces was produced in both singular and collective ways through this process of photovoice. From moving through the busy spaces of the high street, relaxing at the park, to meeting new people or waiting at stop signs, young people emphasised the complex affects circulating through the urban milieu:

Figure 6.1: Youth organisation, Megan's poster from the photovoice outing.

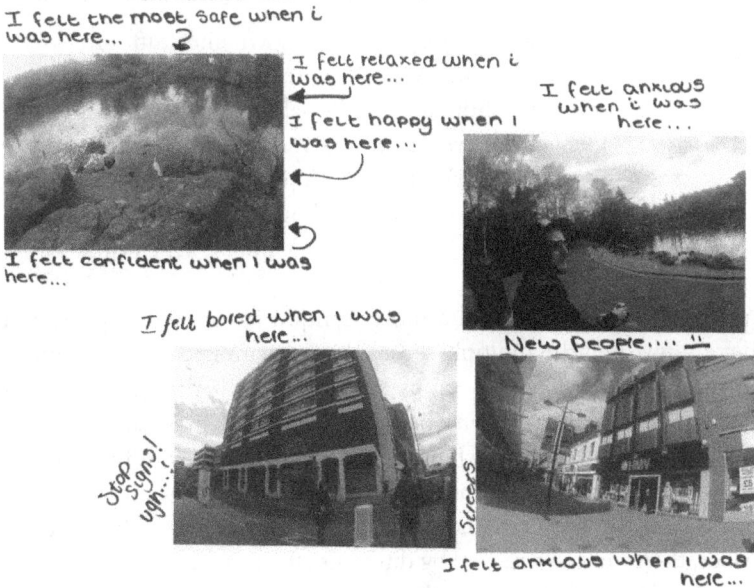

Source: Annaleise Depper.

Researcher:	So Megan, would you say you preferred being in the town centre or being at the park?
Megan:	Park.
Researcher:	Why's that?
Megan:	Because it's calm and chilled and there's no traffic, like constant traffic.
Researcher:	Mmm.
Megan:	And it's a place where you can just sit and relax, it's weird, it's a weird feeling, although it makes me, it's just the looks of it, it just makes you feel calmer, and ... yeah, than like Sports Direct. It's like you're always, even if you're in your favourite shop, you're all constantly ... not nervous or ...
Nicole:	You're always walking.
Megan:	You're just like, it's a weird feeling, cause you're where everyone is and you feel constantly like watched and there's other people there so you go into your favourite shop, still you're not really relaxed, are you?
Researcher:	Mmm.

Megan:	But when you're in parks like this with, like you know, you've got your birds …
Nicole:	And there's teenagers in the town and stuff.
Megan:	Yeah, you're not relaxed, cause like Greggs can be your favourite shop and McDonald's, but there's loads of teenagers there and you never relax so …. But when you're here, it's all calm, it's just nice to sit and chill.

(Extract 1: Youth organisation group, workshop 7, 12 April 2017)

Young people welcomed the more tranquil spaces of the park, and they emphasised the multiple senses that intermingled as they moved through and between the shops and park. Both the materiality of spaces and human relations become entangled in young people's everyday assemblages, which produced significant affects (fear, shame, anxiousness) of seeing, or being seen, by particular groups of people in the busy town centre. As young people moved through mundane spaces, they were also moved by different affects, memories and events connected with them; the park became "a place where you can just sit and relax".

For young people space-time relations were constantly changing and negotiated, as they moved through urban areas in Swindon. Uncertainties, desires and worries coexisted in relation to fears about harassment or shaming. For example, young people articulated how they wanted to escape from the uncertainties, anxieties and business of certain leisure spaces where they constantly felt like they were being "watched". The previous extract evoked the anxious affects and effects of being watched as young people moved through the busy shops, feeling like they were under constant surveillance. Power relations work to produce these affects for young people, who negotiate stereotypical positioning of young bodies as 'trouble'. These multiple relations circulated in young people's everyday spaces as young people feared other groups of young people. They had to constantly negotiate these shifting space-time relations, moving through urban areas and spaces as they felt anxious, or in the case of Laywick Park, a place where they felt safe.

While young people emphasised the affects that circulated in this park to make them feel at ease and relaxed, at the same time there was still ambivalence in their affective responses to Laywick Park. For example, in the following extract, young people reflected on the ubiquity of crime that circulates in multiple spaces in Swindon, even in the idyllic, seemingly 'safe' space of Laywick Park:

Researcher: ... Do you think crime happens in parks though?

Megan: Yeah, obviously, like crime happens everywhere.

Nicole: Yeah.

Megan: No matter how nice or anything, crime happens everywhere.

Nicole: Yeah.

Researcher: Was it that particular park that felt more safe?

Megan: No, it's just that it seems safe, although nowhere's safe if you think about it.

Nicole: Yeah.

Megan: ... like gangs and stuff. Because no matter where you go or how nice the area is, there's always *them* people.

(Extract 2: Youth organisation group,
workshop 7, 12 April 2017)

The Co-Creative methods moved young people in particular ways, as they felt comfortable to take pictures in this space that "seems safe", without the onlooking gaze of other young people or busy spaces of the high street. This emphasised the multiple and highly relational meanings of "safe". For young people, Laywick Park was not just a ubiquitous "safe" space; there were still ambivalences and discursive relations that young people negotiated as they moved through multiple, everyday spaces in Swindon. The fear of crime and "gangs" stayed with young people, even as they moved into the seemingly tranquil spaces of Laywick Park.

The practice of photovoice produced insights into the ways in which young people negotiated the everyday affective flows within these 'risk assemblages', comprised of bodies, class-based discourses and material events such as crime, violence and embodied movement through community spaces. As Megan explained, "no matter where you go or how nice the area is, there's always *them* people". This particular group of young people resided in areas associated with stigmatising discourses around high levels of poverty, crime and limited labels of 'working-class' residents who resided there. Young people navigated their own discursive positioning in relation to "*them* people", as Megan strived to distance herself from the groups of people she was referring to.

Previous literature on health and inequality has highlighted the ways in which people from working-class backgrounds strive to resist and protect themselves from such discourses of stigma and shame (Popay et al, 2003). According to Lamont (2009: 156), resisting spatial stigma can be significant in negotiating social inequalities, as individuals strive to 'draw group boundaries – who is "in" and "out" – and define the meaning they give to their group – who is "us" and "them"'. Elsewhere, Thomas's (2016: 2) study found that, 'Young people produce multiple meanings of place and can resist stigma by Othering certain districts and social groups'. These findings indicate that the stigmatising discourses of spaces have significant consequences for young people, as 'place and identity are inexorably linked' (Thrift, 1997). As Megan emphasised her own positionality as separate to "*them* people", this example is laden with 'sticky affects' (Ahmed, 2004). Both the high street shops and Laywick Park became a complex assemblage of affects, materials and discursive relations which, bound with the dynamics of power and regulatory gaze, constantly shifted within young people's everyday spaces. These relational understandings of power, place and identity speak back to simplistic views of encouraging young people to be more active in public spaces that ignore space-time relations of power.

Conclusion

This chapter has brought together multiple theoretical and methodological ideas that call for alternative ways of thinking about young people's everyday, urban spaces. Through new materialist ideas, the arguments here have reoriented thinking about young people's everyday spaces beyond merely 'containers' for action; they are instead made up of materials, sensations, human and nonhuman relations. This involved enacting a theory-method approach whereby theoretical sensibility was entangled in the process of Co-Creation. This empirical research engaged with young people, their families and practitioners through specific creative practices that enabled ideas to be materialised in ways that conventional research methodologies may not have been able to evoke.

Co-Creation involved a process of challenging and contesting conventional ideas about young people's mobility through low-income communities. The possibilities of Co-Creation with young people have been largely under-theorised and, indeed, still require further attention. In particular, this project turned to the possibilities for arts-based practices and events to become provocations for intervening in the complex power relations of everyday, stigmatised spaces. In moving beyond representational logic and constructionism, this chapter has explored Co-Creation not just as a methodological technique, but also as a material-discursive knowledge practice with young people. Thinking about a 'creative research assemblage' has helped the authors to enact a theory-method approach that reconfigures traditional ways of Co-Creating knowledge within interpretivist approaches.

Co-Creation was both a material means of mobilising change and (re)presenting research, as young people worked individually and collectively to produce creative artefacts that enabled an exploration of the affective relations that entangle leisure, class, gender, space and place. Ripples of change were produced in various ways: the exhibition created a community space for listening-learning with young people to disrupt stereotypes and make issues visible; in turn, the local youth forum pursued key issues and a youth agency incorporated report findings into their strategic discussions. There is a need to intervene in adult-designed spaces to create more youth-friendly spaces, where young people are able to participate in reimagining and creating such spaces through arts-based practices. As class divisions play out in communities, these neglected areas are not just a matter of apolitical aesthetics, they are bound up with an economy of affect that intensifies shame, stigma and exclusion. There was significant value in engaging in aesthetic, artistic creations such as films and poster displays that moved beyond the limitations of language. Carpenter and Horvath (2018: 12) remind us that Co-Creation 'does not consist of a fixed set of tools and techniques', but rather it is a *process* of mutual understanding, Co-Creating ideas and dialogue between individuals. It is thus important to consider the ways in which spaces for Co-Creation can be disruptive, alter relations and produce circulating affects that cannot be separated from the young people's experiences of place and space.

References

Ahmed, S. (2004) *The Cultural Politics of Emotion*, New York: Routledge.

Barad, K. (2007) *Meeting the Universe Halfway: Quantum Physics and the Entanglement of Matter and Meaning*, Durham, NC: Duke University Press.

Berbary, L.A. and Boles, J.C. (2014) 'Eight points for reflection: revisiting scaffolding for improvisational humanist qualitative inquiry', *Leisure Sciences*, 36(5): 401–19.

Bovill, C., Cook-Sather, A. and Felten, P. (2011) 'Students as co-creators of teaching approaches, course design, and curricula: implications for academic developers', *International Journal for Academic Development*, 16(2): 133–45.

Carpenter, J. and Horvath, C. (2018) 'Co-Creation: addressing urban stigmatization, building inclusive cities', Paper presented at the Urban Affairs Association Annual Congress, Toronto, 6 April 2018.

Coad, J. (2012) 'Involving young people as co-researchers in a photography project', *Nurse Researcher*, 19(2): 11–16.

Coleman, R. and Ringrose, J. (2013) 'Introduction: Deleuze and research methodologies' in R. Coleman and J. Ringrose (eds) *Deleuze and Research Methodologies*, Edinburgh: Edinburgh University Press, pp 1–22.

Cross, B. (2015) 'Just back off toffs – Tatler brands Swindon a "no-go zone"', *Swindon Advertiser* [online] 30 September 2015, available from: www.swindonadvertiser.co.uk/news/13792870.just-back-off-toffs-tatler-brands-swindon-a-no-go-zone/ [accessed 13 May 2019].

Dawney, L. (2011) 'Social imaginaries and therapeutic self-work: the ethics of the embodied imagination', *The Sociological Review*, 59(3): 535–52.

Deleuze, G. (1995) *Negotiations*, New York: Columbia University Press.

Deleuze, G. and Guattari, F. (1988) *A Thousand Plateaus*, London: Athlone.

Depper, A., Fullagar, S. and Francombe-Webb, J. (2018) 'This girl can? The limitations of digital Do-It-Yourself empowerment in women's active embodiment campaigns' in D. Parry, C. Johnson and S. Fullagar (eds) *Digital Dilemmas: Transforming Gender Identities and Power Relations in Everyday Life*, London: Palgrave, pp 183–204.

Fox, N.J. (2013) 'Flows of affect in the Olympic stadium', *Sociological Research Online*, 18(2): 1–5.

Fox, N.J. and Alldred, P. (2017) *Sociology and the New Materialism: Theory, Research, Action*, London: Sage.

Fullagar, S. (2017) 'Post-qualitative inquiry and the new materialist turn: implications for sport, health and physical culture research', *Qualitative Research in Sport, Exercise and Health*, 9(2): 247–57.

Fullagar, S. and Pavlidis, A. (2018) 'Emotion, affect and sporting experiences' in B. Wheaton, J. Cauldwell, L. Mansfield and B. Watson (eds) *Handbook of Feminism in Sport, Leisure and Physical Education*, Houndsmills: Palgrave, pp 447–62.

Fullagar, S. and Small, I. (2018) 'Writing recovery from depression through a creative research assemblage: mindshackles, digital mental health and a feminist politics of self-care', in D. Parry, C. Johnson and S. Fullagar (eds) *Digital Dilemmas: Transforming Gender Identities and Power Relations in Everyday Life*, London: Palgrave, pp 121–42.

Gill, L., White, L. and Cameron, I.D. (2011) 'Service co-creation in community-based aged healthcare', *Managing Service Quality: An International Journal*, 21(2): 152–77.

Grant, K. (2015) 'The "ugliest town in England" is getting a makeover', *The Independent* [online] 18 August 2015, available from: www.indy100.com/article/the-ugliest-town-in-england-is-getting-a-makeover--bkecNbdbhEx [accessed 13 May 2019].

Hroch, P. and Stoddart, M.C.J. (2015) 'Mediating environments', *Canadian Journal of Sociology*, 40(3): 295–308.

Kofoed, J. and Ringrose, J. (2012) 'Travelling and sticky affects: exploring teens and sexualized cyberbullying through a Butlerian-Deleuzian-Guattarian lens', *Discourse: Studies in the Cultural Politics of Education*, 33(1): 5–20.

Kuby, C.R., Aguayo, R.C., Holloway, N., Mulligan, J., Shear, S.B. and Ward, A. (2016) 'Teaching, troubling, transgressing: thinking with theory in a post-qualitative inquiry course', *Qualitative Inquiry*, 22(2): 140–8.

Kumm, B.E. and Johnson, C.W. (2018) 'In the garden of domestic dystopia: racial delirium and playful interference', *Leisure Studies*, 37(6): 692–705.

Lamont, M. (2009) 'Racism, health and social inclusion', in P.A. Hall and M. Lamont (eds) *How Institutions and Culture Affect Health*, New York: Cambridge University Press, pp 151–68.

Latimer, J. and Skeggs, B. (2011) 'The politics of imagination: keeping open and critical', *The Sociological Review*, 59(3): 393–410.

Mackley, E. (2014) 'We're the fattest town, figures say', *Swindon Advertiser* [online] 5 February 2014, available from: http://www.swindonadvertiser.co.uk/news/10986620.We___re_the_fattest_town__figures_say/?ref=var_0 [accessed 8 October 2019].

Massumi, B. (1995) 'Politics of affect', *Cultural Critique*, 31: 83–109.

Mazzei, L.A. (2013) 'A voice without organs: interviewing in posthumanist research', *International Journal of Qualitative Studies in Education*, 26(6): 732–40.

McDonald, C. (2002) 'Child's play: helping mothers avoid isolation', *The Guardian* [online] 24 July 2002, available from: www.theguardian.com/society/2002/jul/24/8 [accessed 13 May 2019].

NHS Swindon (2011) *Child Poverty Needs Assessment 2011*, Swindon.

Popay, J., Bennett, S., Thomas, C., Williams, G., Gatrell, A. and Bostock, L. (2003) 'Beyond "beer, fags, egg and chips"? Exploring lay understandings of social inequalities in health', *Sociology of Health & Illness*, 25(1): 1–23.

Ringrose, J. and Renold, E. (2014) ' "F*ck rape!" Exploring affective intensities in a feminist research assemblage', *Qualitative Inquiry*, 20(6): 772–80.

Stephens, L., Ruddick, S. and McKeever, P. (2014) 'Disability and Deleuze: an exploration of becoming and embodiment in children's everyday environments', *Body & Society*, 21(2): 194–220.

St Pierre, E.A. (2014) 'A brief and personal history of post qualitative research: toward "post inquiry"', *Journal of Curriculum Theorizing*, 30(2): 2–19.

St Pierre, E.A., Jackson, A.Y. and Mazzei, L.A. (2016) 'New empiricisms and new materialisms', *Cultural Studies ↔ Critical Methodologies*, 16(2): 99–110.

Swindon Borough Council (2016) *Swindon Inequalities: Research Report*, Swindon.

Swindon Borough Council (2017) *Health and Wellbeing Strategy 2017–2022*, Swindon.

Taylor, C.A. (2016) 'Edu-crafting a cacophonous ecology: posthumanist research practices for education', in C. Taylor and C. Hughes (eds) *Posthuman Research Practices in Education*, Basingstoke: Palgrave Macmillan, pp 5–24.

Thomas, G.M. (2016) ' "It's not that bad": stigma, health, and place in a post-industrial community', *Health and Place*, 38: 1–7.

Thrift, N. (1997) 'The still point: resistance, expressive embodiment and dance' in S. Pile and M. Keith (eds) *Geographies of Resistance*, London: Routledge, pp 124–51.

Voorberg, W.H., Bekkers, V.J.J.M. and Tummers, L.G. (2015) 'A systematic review of co-creation and co-production: embarking on the social innovation journey', *Public Management Review*, 17(9): 1333–57.

Zanetti, C.A. and Taylor, N. (2016) 'Value co-creation in healthcare through positive deviance', *Healthcare*, 4(4): 277–81.

7

Does space matter? Built environments and Co-Creation in Mexico City

Pamela Ileana Castro Suarez and Hector Quiroz Rothe

Introduction

This chapter seeks to understand the role of the built environment in the processes of collaborative projects associated with the concept of Co-Creation. It explores the ways in which space can be not only the product of social and cultural processes developing in a certain area, but also a place as well as a process in which marginalisation and stigmatisation occur through the morphological characteristics of the place itself. What starts as an initiative of a group of residents to improve social cohesion in their neighbourhood, for example, evolves into actions that always happen somewhere: in a square, in a park, a market, in a public building or simply in the street or within the walls of a forgotten alley. Usually, this space factor seems to be ignored by social studies; however, space matters – urban spaces and social interactions cannot be disassociated from one another.

The urban form and architectural dimensions of specific facilities will be explored over other political, organisational or financial aspects that are usually considered in sociological research. It is also important to mention the transcendence of digital platforms in the development of virtual Co-Creative projects; however, these should be studied in further research.

This text considers the authors' experience as both academics and urban planners in Mexico City, enriched with feedback from conferences and workshops organised by the Co-Creation project. Specifically, the authors have deepened the analysis of the case study with an investigation of artistic and cultural venues in Mexico City and with semi-structured interviews with staff members of these facilities.

The approach employed considers the built environment as a useful medium to achieve the social benefits that Co-Creation promoters from the arts sphere are aiming for, through diverse participatory methodologies that are shared with urban planning practice (Miessen and Basar, 2006; Kitao, 2005). In this sense, the definition of Co-Creation here favours the process in which various agents participate to produce information and knowledge about their current situation and expectations about the built environment through the use of arts-based methods to improve their environment, rather than only being interested in producing a collective work of art as a unique goal (Gómez, 2004; Sánchez, 2008, 2015; Palacios, 2009; Bishop, 2012). The authors intend, then, to illuminate the relationships between the location and characteristics of art and cultural venues, social keys for successful Co-Creative projects, and agents involved in these processes. This interest responds to the assumption that these spaces have the potential to implement and improve collective projects based on the principles of Co-Creation that this book suggests.

Conceptual frames: spatial and socially engaged art practices

Several authors agree that public spaces and social interactions cannot be disassociated from one another. These are part of the social structure which helps to develop social interactions but, at the same time, they are the result of these interactions (Giddens, 1984; Shotter, 1984; Krupat, 1985; Soja, 1989; Lefebvre, 1991; Bentley, 1999; Harvey, 2006). Lefebvre (1991: 33, 38) refers to spatial practices as processes that mediate the production and reproduction of particular social formations in different spatial sets. Urban space facilitates the development of social practices and the experimentation of the use of the space in different manners, such as traditional emotional and religious manners (Lefebvre, 1991). According to Giddens (1984: 33, 258), public spaces are a medium of material production and a produced good. This opens the opportunity to think that space intervenes in the production and reproduction of social practices, including artistic practices which influence the space constituted in turn. Participatory and collaborative projects are frequently placed in public open spaces. Squares, parks and the walls of public facilities (schools, markets, social centres, and so on) are the obvious places which enable and enhance participation of diverse agents. These public spaces, however, do not always offer the best conditions to develop long-term projects based on Co-Creation principles.

This chapter focuses on two core elements – first, spaces or places where collaborative processes can take place in better conditions, and second, socially engaged art practices. On the one hand, there are public spaces where some arts practices take place and buildings that offer basic comfort and security conditions to all participants, including those who in their daily life suffer environmental and social risks in their marginalised neighbourhoods. These buildings, public or private, already host creative, and sometimes collaborative, activities based on art methods and their staff have experience of projects that touch on the set of Co-Creation principles.

On the other hand, according to the theory of the 'third place' (Oldenburg, 2002), common spaces in museums and social centres could be ideal locations to host social encounters and build dialogues through Co-Creation principles. How should these spaces be shaped? What are their qualities and limitations that need to be addressed? What kinds of art practices are more common in Mexico? To answer these questions, it is necessary to study the operational conditions of arts and cultural venues. The next section will explore some of these questions.

A long tradition of socially engaged artists

The links between cultural institutions, official and independent aesthetics, artists involved in political activism and diverse collective art experiences throughout the city can be situated along the last century's cultural history in Mexico. Most of them are interwoven and deeply rooted in the marginalised neighbourhoods of Mexico City. Hijar (2007) offers a chronological review of artistic collectives that have had an impact in contemporary Mexican culture, which is used here to explain this sometimes contradictory process. Hijar's (2007) review is concentrated around four moments.

First, during the decade of 1920–30, the social and political post-revolutionary context favoured the creation of popular arts and crafts schools and the participation of young artists to produce a new art for the people. The emblematic expression of this time is the Mural Art that undertook a pedagogical role spreading the national history and values of the Mexican Revolution. In this way, the walls of many public buildings (town halls, markets, libraries and public schools) were covered with mural paintings that today are proudly part of the artistic heritage of many communities. Nowadays, it is not uncommon for communities to still vote for the use of public or common funds to produce such types of artworks (murals), appealing to local history and traditions despite sometimes doubtful narratives.

Second, around 1940, the once revolutionary-inspired art became too official and less provocative. As Hijar (2007) has demonstrated, many artists, dissident or contestant, were finally coopted by the system. In this period, two main national art and culture institutions were founded, the National Institute of Anthropology and History and the National Institute of Fine Arts (INAH and INBA are their acronyms in Spanish). Since then, these institutions have had a strong influence on art and culture projects as the main sponsors and managers of the national art schools, museums and theatres, as well as providing funding and scholarships in any Mexican art domain. Their buildings are landmarks on various scales of the urban landscape and usually noted by people as identity places. There is alternative thinking inside of these institutions that allows experimentation and innovation in artistic practices close to the principles of Co-Creation.

Third, the 1960s were also a period for social contestation against the status quo in Mexico, as in a number of other countries. The 1968 Mexican student movement is considered a turning point for diverse opposition movements, including a new generation of socially engaged artists. During the 1970s, the underground scene was fortified with new individuals and art collectives linked frequently to political opposition parties and creating a new aesthetic in plastic arts, graphics, theatre and even architecture based in deprived urban peripheries. This process still goes on today.

Finally, from 1988, the neoliberal model was adopted by the Mexican government. In the cultural context, subtle assimilation of a mercantilist conceptualisation of the historic and artistic heritage took place. Since 1997, Mexico City has been a national exception, because Left-wing mayors have managed the city favouring – perhaps more in the discourse than in practice – alternative cultural expressions, through long-term programmes and projects. One of the most interesting has been the creation of six schools of arts and crafts called FAROS (acronym in Spanish of arts and crafts factories) located in deprived zones of the city. This innovative cultural project has reversed the location logics of culture and art venues imposed for nearly two decades. However, the current city government is favouring a new programme, called PILARES (Spanish acronym of points for innovation, liberty, art, education, and knowledge). This project is different from FAROS, but both have the same goal of restructuring the social fabric. Out of the planned 300 PILARES facilities, 150 have been put into operation in neighbourhoods with high concentrations of social vulnerability. The programmes focus on sports, basic online education, social economy and culture, offering activities including book and film clubs, collaborative transformations like community work, artistic painting, percussions, and 'pantomime for life' according to the official web page (Gobierno de la Ciudad, 2019).

So, at least since the 1920s, positive examples of public and collective art have been identified that are deeply rooted in official narratives and truly appreciated by local residents. Among them, murals are the most common art form in the official and independent domains of art production. The agents participating in the process include official or independent artists, authorities of different levels, academic and independent researchers, and various local stakeholders. As these collaborative art projects happen over longer time periods that overtake the logics of public authorities or academic timetables, not all the agents participate at the same time. But what they all share is the confidence in the potential of art or arts-based methods to reconstruct positive relationships between stakeholders and new perspectives in the perception of common public spaces (Jiménez, 2016).

Sometimes the resulting artwork transforms the perception of a place in a permanent way and the outcomes include a fresh, collective aesthetic experience based on diverse arts methods. Overall, this is a collective process that produces positive social effects, such as improved communication between agents, acknowledgement and inclusion of others, and awareness about common problems in a shared space. In short, this collective aesthetic process is more valuable than the resulting work of art following the authors' definition of Co-Creation and according to their experience and the evidence found in Mexico City.

About the research

Based on the previous historical review, and to take into account recent artistic and cultural experiences in Mexico City, research was carried out focusing on local collaborative art projects during 2017–19. Between January and May 2017, literature and documentations were conducted, and the authors also undertook informal interviews and fieldwork to identify: individual artist's projects, such as Fe Publica, Carpa orgánica or Casa Refugiados; collective projects, such as Campamentos Unidos, Calmecac Miravalle, ATEA, Galería La Buena Estrella, Green Virus; and official programmes, such as Central de Muros, Lienzo Capital, Ciudad y Palabras.

Analysis of this information made it possible to understand that these practices are pinpointed in time and space and it is difficult to track their social effects in the long run. This is why it was decided that the following phase of the research would focus on the built environment, exploring types of arts and cultural venues that offered the best conditions for the development of participative projects based on the Co-Creation criteria. The geographical analysis, fieldwork and empirical data collection were carried out in 2018–19. A series of 31 semi-structured interviews were recorded with the venues' managers, staff and visitors. Cultural facilities were classified according to their type of management and dimensions. As a result, six categories were established: international cooperations, large public national facilities, large metropolitan and private venues, public universities, local public venues, and small independent private venues. The number of interviews dedicated to each category was determined by various factors, including staff availability. Thus, privately financed institutions such as international cooperations or large private cultural facilities were not included in this phase, while six interviews were recorded with staff from both large national public facilities and public university facilities, 14 with the collaborators of public local facilities, and five with those of independent private centres.

Cultural venues in Mexico City

Data analysis allowed the authors to identify three key components that were relevant to collaborative projects: artistic practices; infrastructure or types of facilities for art and culture; and the types of agents operating facilities. This section will present the characteristics of each of these.

Collaborative artistic practices

Research found that artistic practices corresponding to the authors' definition of Co-Creation have been operated by: groups of professional artists with a permanent place working in public and private spaces; individual artists with projects in public open space; institutional projects of social development with groups of artists and residents and/or volunteers in public facilities; and, groups of self-taught artists together with residents with self-managed cultural projects in low-income neighbourhoods. Examples of these practices are shown in more detail in Table 7.1 and a brief summary of each type is presented as follows.

Collective groups of professional artists with a permanent place

These groups are composed of professional artists and practitioners of other disciplines who usually work in specific neighbourhoods that are their main sphere of action. They have their own stable working place that allows them to develop activities and long-term projects, which implies attachment to and stable relationships with the community. In those places, it is possible to offer courses and workshops to the community. They can have public or private external funding and/or be self-financing. They can also become gentrifying agents; however, this issue cannot be addressed in this chapter. The artists and other professionals are knowledge producers as well, and they work directly with residents of the neighbourhood.

Individual artistic projects in public open space

Professional artists with a regular output mostly use the methodologies of participatory or collaborative art, with major or minor involvement of inhabitants. These are specific interventions in public spaces with the participation of the residents or users of the neighbourhood. The public space is used as a stage or platform, the impact is one-off and of short duration. When dealing with specific events or interventions, it is difficult to measure their impact. These processes include recordings and detailed documentation for formal art media (galleries and associated museums). Funding can be public or private from foundations, through scholarships or prizes.

Institutional social development projects in public facilities

These are publicly funded programmes that use participative arts methods as tools to enhance the townscape and the perception of security through improving public spaces associated with public facilities (schools or markets). Artists or advisers are contracted to develop projects with community participation and the resulting artwork is usually a custom-made mural. Generally, institutions are the initiators of the participation process and they work with the community, landlords or users of the spaces.

Artists and residents with self-managed projects in low-income neighbourhoods

These are projects integrated into self-managed urban planning processes. They accompany the construction and consolidation of popular neighbourhoods of informal origin. The groups are formed of professional and self-taught artists, who participate with partners from other disciplines and are backed by community leaders and political

Table 7.1: Examples of collaborative arts projects in Mexico City

Type of practice	Artistic collective	Project	Description	Reference
Collective groups of professional artists with a permanent place	La Buena Estrella	Memoria 06470	Recuperation of collective memory through digital resources using QR codes, with information widespread through the neighbourhood	http://www.labuenaestrella.info/memoria-06470
Individual artistic projects	Santiago Robles	Carpa orgánica de la Soledad	Shared meals with homeless people and sex workers in public space	https://www.santiagorobles.info/ https://repositorio.unam.mx/contenidos/todos-cocinamos-todos-comemos-proyectos-de-arte-colaborativo-en-el-espacio-publico-de-la-ciudad-de-mexico-68517?c=pNEKoB&d=false&q=santiago_._robles_._bonfil&i=1&v=1&t=search_0&as=0
Institutional projects of social development	Actitivies collectively sponsored by the city Wholesale Market Board and UN 2030 Agenda	Central de muros	Mural to improve the public image of the market	http://centraldemuros.org.mx/ http://www.onunoticias.mx/nuevos-murales-sobre-cambio-climatico-en-la-central-de-abasto/ https://coolhuntermx.com/arte-julio-2018-central-de-muros-central-de-abastos-cdmx/
Collective groups of self-taught artists and residents with self-managed cultural projects	Centro de artes y oficios Escuelita Emiliano Zapata	Diverse workshops and festivals	Independent self-managed social centre in Pedregal de Santo Domingo	https://es-la.facebook.com/pages/category/Community-Organization/Centro-de-Artes-y-Oficios-Escuelita-Emiliano-Zapata-179765332066567/

parties. The artists are usually very attached to the neighbourhood where they are located, and they are well-known among the residents. The project can include the self-production of multipurpose working places, including cultural facilities. These projects combine purposes of community development with artistic training and creativity (plastic arts, dance, theatre, music), as well as creative artistic practices like tools for neighbourhood participation and integration of community. The participation of researchers or academics in the set of mentioned art practices is a constant; sometimes they act as partners, sometimes as observers.

The location of collaborative arts practices

It seems to be a trend for the first two types of collaborative arts practices to be in central areas of the city; in contrast,the other two are mostly located in social or territorial peripheries. Table 7.1 provides examples of each type and their web page for more details.

Characteristics of the culture infrastructure for Co-Creation

The capital city of Mexico has been an emblematic example of a Global South metropolis in Latin America. It was founded by the Aztecs about 700 years ago in a valley already occupied by older human settlements with at least 3,000 years of history. It was later conquered by the Spaniards in the 1500s and became the capital city of the New Spain Viceroyalty for three centuries, remaining the jewel of the Spanish Empire due to the existing rich silver and gold mines. The population of the city remained stable at around 100,000 inhabitants until the end of the 1800s. The Porfiriato period (1880–1910) represents the start of industrialisation and development of modern urban infrastructure financed with foreign investments. The first suburban neighbourhoods appeared around 1860.

During the next decades, the urbanisation process accelerated and reached its peak around 1970. The demographic transition then entered a stabilised stage that defines present-day urban dynamics. Nowadays, Mexico City is a city of eight million inhabitants, the centre of a metropolitan zone containing 22 million inhabitants, governed through a structure of three levels of government, three states and more than 80 municipalities.

In morphological terms, at the metropolitan level, the city is a mix of four main residential types: planned developments of middle and upper class, social housing estates, working-class neighbourhoods of legal and illegal origin, and the remains of conurbated historic towns. It also includes large facilities, industrial parks and green areas that shape a metropolitan puzzle. All areas are connected by corridors of commercial and service uses. Historically, the population with higher incomes have been concentrated mainly to the west and south of the city, which has been fully consolidated with all urban services like running water, street lighting and a sewage system since the early 1900s. The population with lower incomes have been located mostly to the north and east of the metropolitan zone. It is important to mention that the origin of more than 50 per cent of Mexico City's neighbourhoods are illegal urbanisations which have been consolidated over time, reaching acceptable levels of habitability (Abramo, 2011).

Beyond the criticism produced by the hegemonic aesthetics and urbanism discourses, low-income neighbourhoods have been a platform for innovation in social organisation and housing architecture. Without a doubt, the experience of a more sustainable, inclusive and fairer city is found here than in the 'green' certified skyscrapers and shopping malls produced by financial institutions.

Mexico City contains 456 cultural venues: 170 museums, 46 public art galleries and 240 cultural centres (SIC México, 2018). In addition to this universe, 150 out of 300 programmed new PILARES were inaugurated between 2018 and 2019 and added to the cultural infrastructure. Mexico City has the largest offer of cultural facilities in the country per inhabitant. However, there are scarcity and deficiencies in the running of cultural facilities of the city.

The built space is a container of Co-Creative practices and the community that it aims to engage. It is difficult to ensure the continuity of a cultural or artistic project that seeks to improve social relations within and outside of a community, without the guarantee of a limited space that can accommodate its members and its public users with minimum conditions of comfort. However, in the documented cases, the promoters and users consider important spatial aspects as: having a cover that protects their meeting space from the sun or rain, a toilet, and a door or similar that delimits the appropriate space for the members of the collective. The latter is especially important in those marginal neighbourhoods where insecurity and crime determine many activities in public space.

To understand the universe of these facilities in Mexico City, six types have been identified. They are described as follows. In Table 7.2, details and examples of each category are presented.

- *International cooperation cultural venues* have an outstanding presence in the city cultural agenda. The German, French and Spanish embassies lead this offer.

Table 7.2: Examples of art and cultural facilities in Mexico City.

Type and subtype	Name of the venue	Description	Reference
International cooperation cultural venues	Cultural Centre España	The cultural centre of the embassy of Spain. Hosts a very active programme with exhibitions, workshops and projects focused on participative and collaborative art with deprived communities	http://ccemx.org/envia-tu-proyecto/
Large metropolitan private cultural facilities	Children's museum, Papalote	A kind of franchise sponsored by private business conceived as an interactive space for children to learn about science, ecology, art. Also located in the Chapultepec Park, without neighbouring residential areas	https://papalote.org.mx/
Public universities cultural facilities	The Chopo Museum	Managed by the UNAM (university), a reference for alternative art events associated with minorities. A landmark in the neighbouring area	http://www.chopo.unam.mx/
Local public facilities	FARO Oriente	The first FARO created around 1999, a model replicated in other areas of the metropolis offering a wide range of arts and crafts courses, workshops, festivals, and so on	https://www.cultura.cdmx.gob.mx/recintos/faro-oriente https://es-la.facebook.com/faro.deoriente/
Independent venues	ATEA	A pioneer hipster venue located in a deprived area of the Historic Centre	https://www.facebook.com/ateacdmx/
	Calmecac Miravalle	In a self-built building, a complete example of a cultural venue and offering resulting in long-term participatory processes. Located in a highly deprived area of the Iztapalapa borough	https://mivaledor.com/documental/asamblea-comunitaria-miravalle/

- *Large national public cultural facilities* are generally localised in prestigious central areas with appropriate spaces and professional staff for the development of Co-Creative projects.
- *Large metropolitan private cultural facilities* conceived as cultural businesses sponsored by the private sector and sharing the prestige of big national facilities.
- *Public universities' cultural facilities* managed by the National, Metropolitan and the City's autonomous universities and the

National Polytechnic, with diverse locations throughout the metropolitan area, some in deprived areas.

- *Local public facilities* managed and financed, totally or partially, by the government of Mexico City. Includes museums, cultural centres, artistic schools and theatres, all located in the south-west privileged districts of the city. The offer is completed with the FAROS and more than 200 centres and houses of culture that service basically the needs of the neighbouring population. Currently, the PILARES programme is planned by the authorities to double these numbers.
- *Independent private cultural centres* are a heterogeneous category by way of their finance, cultural offer and approach over the social function of art. Created by the initiative or individuals or collectives, sometimes with family ties, that can collaborate with organisations of neighbours to fight for improvement of surroundings at the local level. In some way, they are the heirs to the socially engaged artist tradition (see also Table 7.2).

Urban form and architecture considerations

In spatial terms, the geographical distribution of culture venues is uneven and concentrated in the centre-west of the city. Hundreds of them are distributed following a clear trend of concentration in four main centrally located districts: Historic Centre, Roma Condesa, Coyoacan centre and Chapultepec Park, which all together comes to 136 facilities (around 30 per cent of the total of cultural venues). Accessibility is another morphological condition that relates location of the enclosure in residential or mixed-use areas and public transportation and main avenues. Most of the lines of the underground converge in the centre. This situation ensures the flow of public and users to the central zone of the city from the periphery at low cost. Some facilities managed by local governments have direct access to subway stations.

On the contrary, some other venues are located in isolated peripheral neighbourhoods which struggle to attract the public from remote areas due to the quality and specificity of their cultural offer. This is the case with the FAROS and some independent venues which operate in the same way despite their isolated location. Therefore, one is almost overcrowded while the other presents a lack of users. The explanation of this difference is still not clear but could be related to the quality of their programming and promotion. It should also be recognised that there is a new offer of spaces focused on serving residents and marginalised populations in other locations, continuing the tradition of socially committed artistic creation.

The management of cultural facilities, public or private, has little influence in strengthening the ties between the venue and its surrounding community. It depends mainly on its location. But, there is a strong correlation between cultural venues and built heritage. In every type there are facilities located in prestigious but old buildings. Maintenance of these buildings increases operation costs considerably, which provokes the exclusion of non-profitable groups.

Alternative art practices such as Co-Creation are not only neglected by official budgets but also placed in 'backyard' spaces. Despite the international discourse for the recognition and strengthening of the qualities of public open spaces in neoliberal urbanism in Mexico, nowadays social conflicts and violence cannot be ignored as they restrict the use of streets, parks and public transport for common citizens in the context of Mexican cities.

At the architectural scale, there are two main aspects to be considered: architectural design project and size. In the set of culture venues, morphological differences between public and private independent facilities are considerable; some have a formal architectural project purpose while housed in adapted facilities. The FAROS are the only type of buildings that were specifically designed for art and culture activities. In fact, equipment there has high quality standards that contrast with other shortcomings usually found in low-income neighbourhoods (Secretaría de Cultura, 2015).

The unique self-build and self-managed venue belongs to the independent venue type. Other cases of this type are adapted buildings frequently associated with irregular ownership conditions. The use of historic buildings to house cultural facilities is very common. In federal and public university venues, it is even the main trend. In terms of size, the bigger facilities belong to the public federal type, going from 2,400 m^2 to 20,000 m^2, in contrast to independent venues that occupy buildings of less than 500 m^2.

On the other hand, open spaces are considered important amenities for the functionality and success of art practices among audiences in all types of venues. Plazas and forecourts, included in the original design or adapted, are multipurpose spaces for massive events allowing projects to enlarge the cultural offer beyond the limits of their walls.

Additionally, local cultural managers, who have moved away from doing arts and crafts as part of collaborative social projects in any kind of public spaces, realised that a closed space is a basic requirement to accomplish the objectives. Best intentions can be blocked in the long term by the absence of basic facilities such as a toilet, a storehouse or simply a fence that allows users to see the difference between a common place dominated by violence and insecurity and a delimited 'shelter' where participants can meet and work together. This condition is even more important as children, seniors, women and disabled people have specific requirements that can hardly be fulfilled in public spaces, at least in the current conditions of most Latin American cities.

Although Co-Creation is conceived as a tool to fight social segregation and spatial stigmatisation, the authors believe that in the current context of Mexico City it is first necessary to improve the spatial conditions for participatory activities, at least in the initial stages. Therefore, art and cultural facilities, official or independent, offer alternative locations for the development of projects based on Co-Creation principles in safer conditions because of the security and services they provide.

The impact of cultural agents

As mentioned, to better understand the operational conditions of art and culture venues, managers and staff members of 30 facilities were interviewed. This section briefly summarises the relevant issues.

In most of the analysed facilities, collaborative art projects associated with the Co-Creation concept have been considered in former annual programmes, attending to the needs of residents, minorities or vulnerable groups. Specific spaces or programmes to encourage Co-Creative projects were not identified. In fact, managers and staff members of the venues did not have a precise definition of Co-Creation. In their experience, Co-Creation initiatives were managed by artists, professional or self-taught, who look to promote the participation of residents or vulnerable groups such as indigenous people, LGBT collectives or disabled groups in art projects. There is a generalised acknowledgement about the social value and transformation potential of Co-Creative experiences (Jiménez, 2016).

The positive influence of the FAROS in their communities cannot be denied. However, their impact is not reflected in the statistics regarding social conflicts and violence deeply rooted in the boroughs where they are located. It is clear that art cannot solve complex social problems that affect those deprived communities.

In the case of facilities managed by public universities, their educative and leisure offerings tend to be exclusive, considering the cost and academic requirements. On the other hand, their programmes include the most innovative practices, methodologies and aesthetic subjects generated by highly qualified artists and researchers. Facilities managed by the national government are in most cases museums that may consider spaces to offer some educational or recreational activities. Nevertheless, their offering is restricted to opening time schedules and available staff members. A public budget ensures basic maintenance of their infrastructure and permanent professional staff. Strengthening links with residents or other social groups is not a priority in their annual programmes when they exist. Openness for innovation and the continuity of alternative projects depends on the empathy of managers and the staff more than because of an established policy.

Finally, despite their contributions to the cultural and artistic realm of the city, the legal and financial fragility of the independent venues draw attention. Their staff are oriented to operate in pressurised conditions and the current city government seems not to be interested in supporting them. As previously mentioned, some cases have developed strong links with their resident communities (in particular the self-managed ones).

Conclusion

At the national level, Mexico City has a diverse endowment of cultural facilities that offer good conditions to develop new Co-Creation projects. Different moments and contexts show the relevance that people have found for their involvement in community projects, including cultural or artistic ones. Even superficial interventions, such as the painting of murals on abandoned walls, are positively appreciated by the inhabitants of neighbourhoods mired in the violence associated with organised crime. These are experiences that improve communication between neighbours, training in dialogue and the elaboration of agreements that strengthen essential values for a peaceful coexistence: respect, tolerance and solidarity. It is in the popular neighbourhoods of irregular origin that it is possible to find the most complete and consolidated experiences of participation and collaboration in all types of urban improvement projects, ranging from the organisation of cultural events to the consolidation of venues for the realisation of training activities, recreational and artistic. Formal culture facilities documented in this text are, or should be, the privileged location for the enhancement of these virtuous processes.

Assessing the social impact of these projects is a pending task that requires the construction of indicators and monitoring over time. For the time being, it is just possible to adhere to the conviction that several generations of creators have been guided by the social function of art and its capacity to transform lives and neighbourhoods even though its tangible and quantifiable effects can be short-range and very localised. But also, it has been seen that artists have been employed by the government to consolidate politically oriented narratives using pre-hispanic and colonial values as common ground to build a national identity.

The challenge is more complicated; the existence of facilities is not enough. What is needed is a platform of intertwining relationships between the budget, commitment by the authorities, tangible benefits for the population, continuity of the activities, and the facility to be successful. In this process, premises are very important for continuity in the case of the independent groups; but it seems that the most important element is a policy able to open formal places to Co-Creative initiatives.

References

Abramo, P. (2011) *La Producción de las Ciudades Latinoamericanas: Mercado Inmobiliario y Estructura Urbana*, Olacchi: Quito.

Bentley, I. (1999) *Urban Transformations: Power, People and Urban Design*, London and New York: Routledge.

Bishop, C. (2012) *Artificial Hells: Participatory Art and the Politics of Spectatorship*, London: Verso.

Giddens, A. (1984) *The Constitution of Society: Outline of the Theory of Structuration*, Cambridge: Polity Press.

Gobierno de la Ciudad de México (2019) 'Puntos de innovación, libertad, arte, educación y saberes (PILARES)' [online], available at https://pilares.cdmx.gob.mx.

Gómez, F. (2004) 'Arte, ciudadanía y espacio público' in *On the w@terfront*, 5 (March): 36–51.

Harvey, D. (2006) *Spaces of Global Capitalism*, London: Verso.

Hijar, A. (ed) (2007) 'Presentación' in *Frentes, Coaliciones y Talleres: GruposVisuales en México en el Siglo XX*, México: Conaculta, Fonca, pp 9–26.

Jiménez, L. (ed) (2016) 'Educar en artes y cultura para la convivencia y a paz' in *Arte para la Convivencia y Educación para la Paz*, México: CFE, Conaculta, pp 19–33.

Kitao, Y. (2005) *Collective Urban Design: Shaping the City as a Collaborative Process,* Delft: Delft University Press.

Krupat, E. (1985) *People in Cities: The Urban Environment and its Effects*, Cambridge: Cambridge University Press.

Lefebvre, H. (1991) *The Production of Space*, Oxford: Blackwell.

Miessen, M. and Basar, S. (eds) (2006) *Did Someone Say Participate?*, Cambridge: MIT Press.

Oldenburg, R. (ed) (2002) *Celebrating the Third Place*, Cambridge: De Capo Press.

Palacios, A. (2009) 'El arte comunitario: origen y evolución de las prácticas artísticas colaborativas' in *Arteterapia, Papeles de Arteterapia y Educación Artística para la Inclusión Social*, (4): 197–211.

Sánchez de Serdio, A. (2008) 'Prácticas artísticas colaborativas: el artista y sus socios invisibles' in *Revista Duharte*, 3, July–September, available at https://app.box.com/s/lc7n36xcestq3m21sceyz7y067twcjw9.

Sánchez de Serdio, A. (2015) 'Prácticas artísticas colaborativas: comprender, negociar, reconocer, retornar' in A. Collados and J. Rodrigo (eds) *Transductores 3: Prácticas Artísticas en Contexto*, Granada: Centro José Guerrero, Diputación de Granada, pp 39–44, available at https://app.box.com/s/40qgpahs06t59n14duw551jyga0j69yk.

Secretaría de Cultura (2015) *Fábricas de Artes y Oficios de la Ciudad de México, Quince Años de Navegar el Siglo XXI*, México: Trilce.

SIC México. Sistema de información cultural (2018) 'Espacios culturales' [online], available at https://sic.cultura.gob.mx [accessed 13 April 2019].

Shotter, J. (1984) *Social Accountability and Selfhood*, Oxford: Blackwell.

Soja, E.W. (1989) *Postmodern Geographies: The Reassertion of Space in Critical Social Theory*, London: Verso.

8

Co-Creation, social capital and advocacy: the Neighbourhood and Community Improvement Programme, Mexico City

Karla Valverde Viesca and Dianell Pacheco Gordillo

Introduction

This chapter suggests that community social capital generated in public programmes is one of the key inputs for advocacy actions and therefore is a determining factor that impacts communities, either through the results of its application or via the redesign of policies and programmes. Based on this premise, the authors suggest that a cohesive process in a city should involve participatory action, engaging with communities and making their inclusion in the decision-making process possible. These could include Co-Creation, in two aspects. The first is as a method that, with different actions, can promote a process of cohesion. In this sense, as some contributors to this book analyse it, Co-Creation uses art as a catalyst and involves different actors to promote knowledge production. Through the development of community social capital as described above, the authors believe, however, that Co-Creation has a second sense: that is, as a participatory process that includes distinct actors and distinct actions to have an impact on social cohesion in marginalised communities through the implementation of governmental plans. The core aim of this chapter is to explore this second aspect of Co-Creation, through analysing the experience of the Neighbourhood and Community Improvement Programme in Mexico City. Although the main focus of this book is on the first aspect, this chapter will argue that – given the important benefits that marginalised communities can gain from advocacy resulting from programmes implemented in close collaboration with the state – this second aspect is not to be dismissed.

Currently, the crisis of representative democracy and the weakening of institutions in the world encourages citizens to seek involvement through discussing public problems directly (Mounk, 2017; Martino, 2018). In this context, the idea of involving citizens in making decisions becomes relevant. In terms of participatory democracy, the notion of citizen participation aimed at inclusion, empowerment, articulation and sustained dialogue between multiple and plural actors assumes a fairer distribution of power and the construction of a balance between civil society and the state. Some contributors to this volume consider that one of these options is Co-Creation, understood as a process that includes the participation of civil society to achieve changes in public policies and programmes in public spaces by bringing different stakeholders together and using artistic tools and expressions. That is, in other words, one possible method to advocate for civil society gaining some power and influence over decision makers, ensuring that they really respond to the social interests or dynamics that society needs to resolve.

Some examples of advocacy in Mexico and in other countries of Latin America include community development, participatory citizenship, participatory development, community intervention, citizen's participatory budget and co-production initiatives. Although these processes are not referred to as Co-Creation, they can be found in some political advocacy campaigns in Mexico and could be identified as Co-Creative actions. These processes involve communication and negotiation actions, but also decision making involving different actors. It is crucial for this book to look at, and discuss, experiences like the Neighbourhood and Community Improvement Programme in Mexico City to identify social capital-making processes promoting actions that support the articulation of stakeholders in a community. The core aim of this chapter is to examine whether such advocacy processes can be explored as Co-Creative initiatives on a larger scale of action to generate greater impact.

Participatory citizenship and setting agendas

One of the dichotomies established in philosophical and political traditions is the contrast between the public and private spheres (Bobbio, 1989). Often these adjectives are used, in both common and specialised language, as opposites that refer to property and collective life. According to Nora Rabotnikof (1998), who draws on Habermas' (1987) reflection about the public sphere, there are at least three meanings that refer to what is 'public'. The first, related to the common or the collective, is opposed to private property or the logic of the market. The second is closely linked with an idea of the state authority. The third refers to what is considered to benefit the community.

Knowing what happens in the public sphere and the issues that should be addressed is an important task. A problem, in general, is defined in its own terms and in that sense a public problem would be linked to the idea of the community in which it is defined. In the same way, as a dynamic process, the participation and the definition of public policies depend on that community and their context. Globalisation as part of the current context has modified the forms in which public problems and policies are defined, especially through new interactions between organisations, individuals and the ways of daily life, such as basic infrastructure, social security, health, and public security, among others. Political actors then change the ways and conditions in which they publicly manifest and manage their actions to define public problems and policies.

Therefore, the constantly changing nature of social and political problems today requires new strategies from the actors, whether they are located inside or outside the circles of power, to be able to seize the challenges and opportunities that arise in the public and in the political arenas to move and renew structures of power. One group of these actors is civil society organisations. They can be composed of homogeneous or heterogeneous groups or sums of individuals with specific and differentiated powers, but in general they can act in the political arena and are able to call for action around a specific issue or community.

In Latin America, especially, the history of governments and the transition to democracy has long delayed the understanding of the concept of advocacy and the emergence of civil society organisations. Yet, over the past 30 years, (de Sousa Santos, 2010; Elizalde et al, 2013) these questions have resurfaced with such force that citizens have rethought their own role in the construction and representation of interests, objectives and problems through new channels of participation that question the order, structure and social processes, echoing the dynamic nature of civil society.

What does civil society do? It is very important to determine the actions in which civil society is related to the government. As groups or organisations, civil society forces are constantly working to set the agenda, to increase the benefits of public action, and to make the government listen to their complaints or needs. In the Mexican

Congress there is a specific time to set the agenda and, in order to do so, civil society organisations can protest, advocate, lobby or use institutional mechanisms to exert pressure. The success of their actions can determine to what extent the community will be able access their rights.

Different organisations may use different ways to approach a problem. Sometimes civil society groups are asked to be involved through government initiatives, while in other cases they advocate getting involved. The extent of their participation in political decision-making processes can be an indicator of how well a problem can be resolved through the collaboration of all types of community actors. Faced with institutional crisis and the eclipse of the state (Evans, 2007), some government programmes involve citizens in the solution of social problems. In that sense, they constitute top-down initiatives. One example of these is the Neighbourhood and Community Improvement Programme in Mexico City.

Neighbourhood and Community Improvement Programme in Mexico City

This chapter aims to explore the making of community social capital (Durston, 1999) in the Neighbourhood and Community Improvement Programme, both as an input in the decision-making process and as a Co-Creative process involving different kinds of agents and attempts to get their issues on the agenda. In this context, it is very important to understand the relationships between the wider society, local communities and the government, bearing in mind that 'the community social capital consists of the structures that form the institutionalisation of community cooperation. It resides not only within the set of interpersonal dyadic relationships networks, but also in the sociocultural system of each community, in their legal, administrative, and sanctioning structures' (Durston, 2003: 160) [authors' translation].

The Neighbourhood and Community Improvement Programme or Programa de Mejoramiento Barrial (PCMB) is community driven and since 2007 has been carried out by the Ministry of Social Development of Mexico City's government. The creation of the Programme itself is an interesting example of a great coordination of effort by social movements and civil organisations. The Programme's main aim is to promote citizen participation in disadvantaged, marginalised or vulnerable neighbourhoods. Another important objective is to develop a participatory process of improvement and recovery of the public spaces of the towns and neighbourhoods of Mexico City, especially those that, according to the Marginalisation Index of Mexico City (established by The National Population Council), have a high degree of urban degradation or those suffering from medium, high or very high levels of marginalisation. Over 500 million pesos (US$26 million/€23 million) have been disbursed to date and the Programme is ongoing, with 600 projects completed by 2012. In 2011, PCMB gained international recognition, winning the World Habitat Award sponsored by UN-Habitat (World Habitat, 2011).

Projects within PCMB work on street lighting, paving the streets, sports and recreational facilities, rain collection and sewage systems, parks and recycling, among others. It facilitates social infrastructure projects, for example establishing community centres, houses of culture, parks, recreational and sports areas, improvements of the urban image, museums, ecological projects, skateboarding tracks, service works, expansion or improvement of existing works, among many others, depending on the needs of the community.

The proposals that are funded seek to develop links between people who want to be involved in social actions. After receiving training in financial and project management, the funds are distributed directly to the local communities, who then become fully responsible for delivering the projects selected, together with the support of the municipality. This Programme has funded almost 2,000 projects between 2007 and 2017, with more than 500 million pesos (US$26 million/€23 million) involved (see Table 8.1).

Table 8.2 shows the kind of projects the Programme has funded in ten years. Their comparison allows us to appreciate that most are oriented toward improving the urban image (693), retaining walls (288) and constructing community centres (259). It is important to explain that proposals for these projects come from neighbourhoods with high indexes of marginalisation. In this sense, the infrastructure problems and access to libraries, cultural centres and other community activities are also issues that need to be solved. Also, new topics have been included in the calls for projects. For example, in 2017 urban orchards and the rehabilitation of damage after an earthquake appear as options to choose.

The approved projects have focused on the construction of community centres, and the restoration, renovation, rehabilitation and rebuilding of other centres or public equipment. This does not necessarily mean that they have also resulted in building and reinforcing citizen networks and social capital. The Evaluation Report, however,

Table 8.1: Neighbourhood Improvement Community Programme: number of projects approved, 2007–17.

Year	Proposals	Approved
2007	139	48
2008	273	101
2009	549	183
2010	752	199
2011	750	200
2012	780	249
2013	908	196
2014	999	208
2015	667	169
2016	758	185
2017	877	215
Total	7452	1953

Source: Own elaboration based on Hernández (2012: 77); Report on Internal Evaluation of the Neighbourhood and Community Improvement Programme 2014.

Note: The Evaluation Report 2019 is based on results processed in 2018.

provides some evidence in this sense. For example, in figures it has been reported that almost 40 per cent of beneficiaries consider that the Programme promotes participation in decision-making processes, 80 per cent are considered satisfied, 81 per cent believe it attends to more than half of their needs and they generally give the Programme a score of 7.69 out of 10 (Evaluation Report, SIDESO 2019).

A closer look at some examples such as the 'Chavos Banda' [Youth Band] Sports Centre, also called Consejo Agrarista Mexicano [Mexican Agrarist Council] or the 'Modulo Bosques' [Forest Module] allows for a better appreciation of the Programme's impact. In the first case, the sports centre is located in a marginal area in the Iztapalapa municipality. Local gang members and community members have participated in the Youth Band which asked for space in a wasteland to be turned into a recreation area to contest violence (Mejora tu barrio CDMX, 2017). Members have links with a social organisation that promotes social and cultural activities in different areas of the city. Today, after having obtained resources from the Neighbourhood and Community Improvement Programme, the citizens and the Council for Community Development [Consejo para el Desarrollo Comunitario A.C.] (CODECO) have a space in which to offer sport and music

Table 8.2: Neighbourhood and Community Improvement Programme: type of intervention in community public spaces, 2007–17.

Type of project, according to the intervention of public community space projects	2007	2008	2009	2010	2011	2012	2013	2014	2015	2016	2017	Total
Construction of community centres: libraries, multipurpose rooms and cultural centres	16	22	39	41	17	49	9	11	9	36	10	259
Construction of outdoor forums	1	2	2	5	3	1	0	5	2	1	2	24
Construction of greenhouses	0	1	0	0	0	0	0	0	0	0	0	1
Construction of auditoriums	1	2	0	0	1	7	0	0	0	0	0	11
Retaining walls	3	2	4	31	48	52	58	38	41	11	0	288
Ridges rehabilitation	4	3	3	8	19	11	13	9	4	4	2	80
Public places rehabilitation	3	4	4	7	6	8	22	17	13	19	21	124
Rehabilitation/construction of sports fields	9	6	16	13	11	7	5	2	1	17	32	119
Rehabilitation of common areas, green areas, parks, gardens, play areas	7	27	38	32	27	49	26	31	33	17	25	312
Urban image (fixtures, furniture, arrangement of facades, hallways placement)	4	32	77	62	68	65	63	95	66	74	87	693
Urban orchards	0	0	0	0	0	0	0	0	0	6	2	8
Rehabilitation of damaged spaces after the 2017 earthquake	0	0	0	0	0	0	0	0	0	0	34	34

Source: Author's elaboration based on Hernández (2012: 77), Valverde and Gutiérrez (2018) and data from Gaceta Oficial de la Ciudad de México (2019). Órgano de Difusión del Gobierno de la Ciudad de México, January 18. Ciudad de México: 253–88.

activities, graffiti and aerographic workshops, computer services and a radio station. There is even a drug addiction prevention programme run here.

The second example is a project that was studied by Liliana González (2019) in the framework of a larger study on social innovation in the Neighbourhood and Community Improvement Programme. In her work, she emphasised the project 'Modulo Bosques' [Forest Module] as an initiative funded by the Programme in which we can appreciate how social relations have changed the life of citizens and how the community reports benefits from it. The project is located in the Bosques del Pedregal neighbourhood in the southwestern area of Tlalpan. As the interviews with the beneficiaries of the project quoted here show, what was seen as the major benefits by members of the community included the economic cost of workshops, the services for adults and children, and the offer of activities and events responding to the demands of the residents (González, 2019: 72, 73, 97):

> It helps a lot. There is nothing here of workshops or anything. So, it does help children reinforce some things. For example, in the case of my child [reinforce] English or to do sport so they don't have a sedentary life. The fact of not having to pay private classes helps a lot, because I pay ten pesos … . (Interview with Claudia Hernández in González, 2019)

> Here I give a tattoo workshop. It is very common here for boys to go around in gangs. Let them come to the Module and see that not everything in life is drugs. Let them see that they can do more things and earn some money and be more useful in society. (Interview with Luis Alberto in González, 2019)

> At one point, I used the facilities. They lent them to me so that my daughter could rehearse the dance for her 15th birthday. It is satisfying to see that there is such a place. And just like me, there are several people who request it and lend it to us. That is, it has been for our benefit … . (Interview with Guadalupe Martínez in González, 2019).

In her case study, González (2019) reports on some initiatives that sought to address different types of vulnerability. These built a recreation space and, at the same time, improved the safety of the area and the image of the neighbourhood, as before it was a wasteland that was used as a garbage dump. The activities and services offered at low cost help families on a low income, while some of the activities taught by neighbours generate extra income for the workshop leaders. The activities also bring greater cohesion among the residents of the neighbourhood or, at least, more contact between them.

In relation to the type of dynamics and organisation that arose for and from these initiatives (changes in social relations), as González (2019) observed, leadership was fundamental for the organisation and its operation. Although there was some leadership in the neighbourhood before, this initiative helped to consolidate it and allowed coordination with other neighbourhood leaders in order to access resources and increase their social capital through their new connection with the civil society organisation 'House and City'.

In general, the Programme encourages the participation of community organisations in the decision-making processes, the use of public spaces for community development (accessibility, inclusion, opportunities, motivation for skills improvement), and promotes an improvement in quality of life of the community members who become active participants in the transformation process of their public spaces (Hernández, 2012). The focus here is on social capital, but it is important to mention embeddedness as part of the new relations and networks made by the Programme. In this sense, and as a result of the Programme, a renewal of social embeddedness and a boost to cohesion can be observed. This was not part of the initial objectives of the Programme but rather a welcome, although unexpected, outcome that has transformed the reality of these places.

In a recent evaluation of the Programme (Design Evaluation of the Neighbourhood and Community Improvement Programme, 2014), citizen participation is highlighted as a key factor in linking the social dimension (generating social capital, empowerment, new leadership, sharing identities and ending social conflict) with the architectural dimension of neighbourhood renewal (construction design and neighbourhood reconstruction).

The voice of the community

The evaluations of the Neighbourhood and Community Improvement Programme have shown that community involvement has resulted, among other achievements, in the construction of ties and networks that benefit the community itself and allow it to participate in problem solving. It can require a considerable amount of time for the community to build ties necessary for a stable level of communication with decision makers. This type of communication can be carried out through advocacy actions or campaigns.

Advocacy suggests a series of systematic efforts with specific political objectives. It could be suggested that advocacy is an integral part of politics and that, by not referring to any particular political sphere, it touches on a range of issues such as environment, health, work, religion, rights and democracy. Andrews and Edwards (2004) present advocacy groups as organisations that publicly claim certain interests or demands, either promoting or resisting social change, which, if carried out, may generate conflict with other social, cultural, political or economic interests or values of other constituted groups.

In a 2012 study, Obar et al point out that, 'The advocacy group has distinguished itself from the political party or conspiracy group in the sense that advocacy groups try to influence politics, but do not seek to exercise governmental power' (Obar et al, 2012: 4). This difference helps us to understand the ways of organising, the strategies and the scope of advocacy.

Participation in public challenges may be an engagement exercise if people are organised into an advocacy group or they mobilise through advocacy actions. This type of transformation depends on the human resources, networks, alliances, time and structure that materialise. In that sense, the strengthening of social cohesion is key to understanding how different actors in a community participate.

It is important to consider that advocacy is not the same as influence. The first responds in order to articulate a position and mobilise support towards that position. The second could be direct action and implies immediate power or capacity. If we see it from a practical point of view, influencing a policy can be simpler and faster than ensuring that a wide range of opinions and viewpoints are expressed and considered. Perhaps that is why Jenkins (2006), as a key reference in advocacy studies, defends the idea of distinguishing between advocacy and the influences on an institutional or governmental decision to create and execute a policy.

Jenkins (2006) first refers to advocacy, taking a restricted definition, with reference to Hopkins (1992) as an act of advocating or declaring for or against a cause, as well as being in favour of or recommending a position in relation to the cause (including lobbying in the sense of addressing legislators with the intention of influencing their vote). Later Jenkins also refers to Boris and Mosher-Williams (1998) when they speak of a rights-advocacy that includes legal and court activities, surveillance in government programmes and civic involvement around lobbying, attempts to influence public opinion, processes related to educating and involving the community, and participating politically. Finally, Jenkins turns to Reid (2000) to differentiate a political party from advocacy, saying that while the first version focuses on those who make the governmental decisions, the second attempts to have an impact on public opinion, encourage civic and political participation and influence the policies of private institutions or organisations.

These highlight how advocacy implies multiple meanings depending on the context and the moment in which it is used. For example, if advocacy is referred to in legal terms, it will be related to certain types of activities that are reported and therefore regulated. On the other hand, if used in research, it requires the description of various aspects with regards to the representation, participation or effectiveness of the processes. Or, if it is part of the discourse or the objectives of the organisations themselves, then it will focus on the mobilisation of resources, capacities and influences.

Even recognising that it has multiple understandings, the advocacy concept faces several problems. One of them is measurement. Given the variety of actions that can be undertaken, it is difficult to quantify the intensity or magnitude of the effort that has been made. Another issue turns out to be that of the multiplicity of actors that participate in the same activities and the areas in which these actions are executed. Therefore, determining the direct results of the advocacy undertaken is complicated. Defining the effects of advocacy actions is difficult and, in that sense, evaluating the success of the activities and participating actors can be problematic. In addition, within the dynamics of advocacy, there is the question for an organisation of whether to take direct action or to look for other groups that can represent their interests. This last point is very important in the case of countries with unstable participation structures like Mexico because organisations or groups have limited or unfavourable political contexts to carry out advocacy actions within or through less visible channels than those provided in countries with a democratic society that is stable and regulated. This is why governmental initiatives that seem stable are questioned and inspected more frequently.

In the Neighbourhood and Community Improvement Programme, we clearly see the actions in which organisations and communities mobilise their efforts to advocate for a proposal or to make their project work. For example, they can rebuild a community centre, but their actions continue until the community centre is in constant use. They advocate for problems or issues that they consider important for the neighbourhood and look for solutions. The channels of communication between stakeholders and all the actors in the community are open and stable, and the way in which they interact with the government is demonstrated through the Programme that they themselves have created. In that sense, the Programme has built a unique opportunity to advocate for the interests of the community and has allowed efforts and actions to be taken on a higher scale.

Decision making and agenda building: a Co-Creative process?

In the case of the Neighbourhood and Community Improvement Programme, it has been shown that the Programme has consolidated the networks between neighbours and the community. The social fabric demonstrates greater cohesion and users report benefiting from the Programme. In terms of Co-Creation, this process underlines two fundamental aspects: there is a push from the authorities to create a mechanism in which citizens participate around a problem in their community, and there is a participatory decision-making process.

If Co-Creation means a participatory mechanism, there is no doubt that the Neighbourhood and Community Improvement Programme includes this principle. If Co-Creation means having an open dialogue between the community and the decision makers, the Programme facilitates this by allowing civil society to advocate for their proposals and their needs. And if Co-Creation means a group of actions that involves culture, creativity and social aspects, we can see that the approved projects aim to create a new solution for public issues that involves all perspectives of community life, including creative and cultural dimensions.

In Latin American countries, Co-Creative processes are common, either through governmental programmes/initiatives (top-down) or in participatory exercises promoted by local organisations (bottom-up). The challenge is to install these initiatives in the social fabric so that they transform social interactions, integrate all kinds of actors and solve community problems. In that sense, the Neighbourhood and Community Improvement Programme is an example of such initiatives, which facilitates Co-Creative processes on a larger scale by installing bottom-up processes with lasting dialogue and interventions that depend on a renewed social fabric where all the actors of a community converge.

References

Andrews, K.T. and Edwards, B. (2004) 'Advocacy organizations in the U.S. political process', *Annual Review of Sociology*, 30(1): 479–506.

Bobbio, N. (1989) *Estado, Gobierno y Sociedad: Por una teoría general de la política*, Ciudad de México: Fondo de Cultura Económica.

Boris, E. and Mosher-Williams, R. (1998) 'Nonprofit advocacy organizations: assessing the definitions, classifications, and data', *Nonprofit and Voluntary Sector Quarterly*, 27(4): 488–506.

CODECO-OJR (2011) 'Qué es CODECO? Consejo para el Desarrollo Comunitario AC', CODECO, available at http://codeco-ojr.com/codeco.htm.

Design Evaluation of the Neighbourhood and Community Improvement Programme (2014) 60, available at http://data.evalua.cdmx.gob.mx/docs/evaluaciones/externas/2014/inf_mbarrial_2014.pdf.

de Sousa Santos, B. (2010) *Refundación del Estado en América Latina: Perspectivas desde una Epistemología del Sur*, Lima see: Instituto Internacional de Derecho y Socieda.

Durston, J. (1999) 'Building community social capital', *CEPAL Review* (69): 103–118.

Durston, J. (2003) 'Capital social: parte del problema, parte de la solución, su papel en la persistencia y en la superación de la pobreza en América Latina y el Caribe', in R. Atria, M. Siles, I. Arriagada, L.J. Robison and S. Whiteford (eds) *Capital Social y Reducción de la Pobreza en América Latina y el Caribe: En Busca de un Nuevo Paradigma*, Santiago de Chile: CEPAL Universidad del Estado de Michigan, pp 147–202.

Elizalde, A., Delamaza, G. and Córdova Rivera, M.G. (2013) 'Sociedad civil y democracia en América Latina: desafíos de participación y representación', *Polis*, 36.

Evans, P. (2007). 'El eclipse del estado: reflexiones sobre la estatalidad en la era de la globalización' in *Instituciones y desarrollo en la era de la globalización neoliberal*, Bogotá: ILSA, pp 97–129.

Gaceta Oficial de la Ciudad de México (2019) *Órgano de Difusión del Gobierno de la Ciudad de México*, January (18): 253–88.

González, L.D.V. (2019) 'Políticas para la innovación social: análisis de dos casos en el marco del Programa de Mejoramiento Barrial y Comunitario', Thesis, Gobierno y Asuntos Públicos.

Habermas, J. (1987) *Teoría de la Acción Comunicativa*, Madrid: Taurus.

Hernández Sánchez, J.A. (2012) 'Capital social comunitario: una herramienta útil en la relación gobierno sociedad: Programa de Mejoramiento Barrial del Distrito Federal', Thesis, UNAM, México.

Hopkins, B. (1992) *Charity, Advocacy and the Law*, New York: Wiley.
Jenkins, J.C. (2006) 'Nonprofit organizations and political advocacy', in W.W. Powell and R.S. Steinberg (eds) *The Nonprofit Sector: A Research Handbook* (2nd ed), New Haven, CT: Yale University Press.
Martino, A.A. (2018) 'Crisis de la democracia representativa: alternativas participativas o democracia directa con medios electrónicos', EUNOMÍA. Revista en Cultura de la Legalidad, pp 9–32.
Mejora tu barrio CDMX (2017) [For a better neighbourhood] [Archivo LabCDMX 2013–2018], 27 March 2017, #MEJORATUBARRIO (CONSEJO AGRARISTA MEXICANO, IZTAPALAPA) [video archive] available from https://vimeo.com/210343813.
Mounk, Y. (2017) 'Signs of deconsolidation', *Journal of Democracy*, January.
Obar, J., Zube, P. and Lampe, C. (2012) 'Advocacy 2.0: an analysis of how advocacy groups in the United States perceive and use social media as tools for facilitating civic engagement and collective action', *Journal of Information Policy*, 2: 1–25.
Rabotnikof, N. (1998) 'Público-Privado', *Debate Feminista*, 18: 3–13.
Reid, E.J. (ed) (2000) *Structuring the Inquiry into Advocacy. Volume 1 of the Seminar Series Nonprofit Advocacy and the Policy Process*, Washington, DC: The Urban Institute.
SIDESO (2014) *Evaluación del diseño del Programa Comunitario de Mejoramiento Barrial 2014*, Ciudad de México.
SIDESO (2019) *Evaluación Interna Integral 2016–2018 del Programa Mejoramiento Barrial y Comunitario*, Ciudad de México.
Valverde Viesca, K. and Gutiérrez Márquez, E. (2017) 'The Community Programme for Neighbourhood Improvement in Mexico City', in G. Tonon (ed) *Quality of Life in Communities of Latin Countries*, Phoenix: Springer.
World Habitat (2011) 'World Habitat awards: winners and finalists', available at https://world-habitat.org/world-habitat-awards/winners-and-finalists/community-programme-for-neighbourhood-improvement/#award-content [accessed 12 September 2019].

PART II

Co-Creation in practice

9

A top-down experiment in Co-Creation in Greater Paris

Ségolène Pruvot

Introduction

This chapter explores how Plaine Commune, the local authority in charge of urban development in an area north of Paris, has implemented a 'top-down' arts-based collaborative process, which may be regarded as Co-Creation. The local authority commissioned artists to coordinate a citizen consultation process, via a series of arts-based activities, about a major urban development project. This chapter will analyse whether and how a process initiated by a public authority can be understood as part of the Co-Creation method defined in this book.

This reflection will be anchored within the debates on Creative Cities (Florida, 2002; Landry, 2003), investigating under what conditions Co-Creation could be used as a tool for building (more) just 'Creative Cities'(see the first section for a more detailed explanation). The chapter will look at how the project 'The Football Pitch, the Player and the Consultant', an experiment set within the frame of Plaine Commune's strategy of becoming a 'territory of culture and creation', fits with the ten principles this book suggests for Co-Creation.

The project 'The Football Pitch ...' was a two-year arts-based project, led by the artists' collective GONGLE (2017) and the cultural operator CUESTA in the Pleyel neighbourhood in Saint-Denis, France. The neighbourhood is facing major redevelopment, driven by the construction of a large train hub of metropolitan scale and of the Olympic Village and swimming pool for the 2024 Olympic Games. After the two first stages of the project had been implemented, the author's active involvement took place in its last stage: a participative evaluation process. This analysis is based on qualitative interviews and informal conversations with the artists and curators, civil servants working for the local authority and other researchers, as well as on a review of extensive artistic documentation and local authority policy documents.

The chapter will argue that, beyond its impact on the local community and on the urban development project itself, the Co-Creation experience can be a methodology that local authorities could use within Creative City strategies, as a first step towards innovation and changes in urban development processes.

Co-Creation as a tool for (more) just Creative Cities

This first section will investigate whether and how Creative City strategies can be made inclusive while simultaneously exploring Co-Creation's potential as a method to enforce a more creative relationship between artists and local authorities.

Defining the Creative City

There is extensive criticism within the academic community about Creative City strategies – understood in international urban policy circles as the implementation of the Creative City (Landry and Bianchini, 1995, Landry 2003) and Creative Class (Florida, 2002) concepts within the policy field. Several comprehensive literature reviews (Boren and Young, 2013; Nathan, 2015) have scrutinised different aspects of Creative Cities, drawing attention to the fuzziness of the concept (Evans, 2005; Markusen, 2006; Pratt, 2008) or reproaching it for hiding presuppositions and political conceptions (Evans, 2005; Krätke, 2010) and for being exclusionary, notably when it comes to diversity and gender (Gill and Pratt, 2008; Leslie and Cantugal, 2012; McLean, 2014). Others argue that Creative City policies may have adverse side-effects on creativity (Peck, 2005; Martí-Costa and Pradel i Miquel, 2011) and may create new inequalities (Hutton, 2017).

This chapter takes stock of these criticisms and argues that exploring the concept of the Creative City further is useful, notably since it continues to be highly influential in policy circles (Boren and Young, 2013). Some researchers suggest that the 'Creative City model' (Jakob, 2010) could be revisited and that a new one, which builds on the potential to create (more) sustainable and just cities can be proposed (Kirchberg and Kagan, 2010; Kagan and Hahn, 2011; Pratt, 2011; Ratiu, 2013; Leslie and Catungal, 2012; Boren and Young, 2013).

However, Creative City strategies are more diverse than the initial assessments of it as a mere repackaging of neoliberal policies suggest (Peck, 2005) and the 2008 financial crisis may have pushed local authorities to change their practices due to limited resources available to cities (Vicari-Haddock, 2010; Miles, 2013). This chapter argues that there may even be specific potential for Creative City concepts in stigmatised urban areas, since artistic activity can help reappropriate and rework symbolic representations of place. The term '(more) just cities' is based on the concept of justice developed by Amartya Sen in the *Idea of Justice* (Sen, 2009). In very practical terms, Sen calls for an understanding of justice that goes beyond ideal, and suggests trying to achieve justice means enforcing 'more just' situations, while acknowledging that other conceptions of what is 'just' rationally coexist.

The Creative City in Plaine Commune

Most of the early literature on Creative Cities comes from the US and the UK, countries where the national context can be considered closer to a 'neoliberal' model and which are marked by the withdrawal of the state and cuts in municipal funding as well as by increased reliance on private funds for urban development. Compared with these two countries, a larger state intervention in urban development projects and more public funding for culture are still characteristics of the French context. Creative Cities literature also often focuses on inner city neighbourhoods and creative quarters.

Plaine Commune has developed a complex and inclusive understanding of the Creative City – at least on paper. Plaine Commune is a type of area that is currently under-researched in the literature about Creative Cities. Located within the deprived periphery of a large metropolis, the local authority is a grouping of nine smaller municipalities in the northern 'first ring' around Paris, in one of the poorest areas of the metropolis, the department of Seine-Saint-Denis, which continues to experience impoverishment (IAU, 2019) (see Figure 9.1). Historically a working-class area, it is also known as the Red Belt as it has been characterised by a strong communist presence in local government since the 1920s, which continues today. The area currently acts as an entry point for newly arrived migrants. In the city of Saint-Denis, about 40 per cent of the population was born outside France (against 18 per cent in the whole Ile de France region) and 30 per cent of the population is of foreign nationality (against 13 per cent in the whole Ile de France region) (INSEE, 2013).

The area is complex. Nationally it is highly stigmatised for including some of the poorest housing estates or *cités*, which have experienced civil unrest movements since the 1980s. It is known for drug trafficking, violence in high schools and has more recently been depicted as a

Figure 9.1: Saint Denis, Plaine Commune and the Greater Paris Metropolis.

Source: Olga Suslova, based on Metropolegrandparis.fr.

place where extremist Islam and terrorism develop, as exposed in the controversial book published by two journalists, *Inch'Allah* (Davet and Lhomme, 2018). Culturally, Seine-Saint-Denis is known as the birthplace of some of the most famous French rap bands from the 1990s, as demonstrated by songs such as 'Seine-Saint-Denis Style' by NTM (1998) and 'Saint-Denis' by the slammer Grand Corps Malade (2006).

Economically, the area is changing rapidly. Seine-Saint-Denis is the third biggest area in terms of the concentration of businesses in the Greater Paris metropolitan region. Despite showing high levels of unemployment, it hosts 10 per cent of enterprises and jobs in Ile de France (Lebeau, 2018). In terms of urban development, due to the pressure on land for mega projects within Paris metropolitan area, Saint-Denis is likely to undergo radical change in the coming years. Several projects of metropolitan or national scale have already transformed, or are in the process of transforming, the area significantly. In 1998, driven by the building of the Stade de France, a new neighbourhood hosting tertiary activities grew up around the stations of the suburban metropolitan rail network (RER) in the southern part of Saint-Denis, la Plaine. The area now hosts a new metro station, adjacent to the new University hub named Condorcet. Opening to its first students in September 2019, the latter aims to become an international hub of knowledge generation and exchange.

The two main driving forces for change in the area are now the construction of the Grand Paris Express – the new transport infrastructure of Greater Paris whose main interchange hub in the north of Paris will be located in the Saint-Denis Pleyel neighbourhood – and the Olympic Games, with the construction of two major infrastructure projects both located in the immediate vicinity of Pleyel: the Olympic Village and swimming pool.

Within the new conceptualisation of the Greater Paris metropolis by the state and local public authorities, Plaine Commune has been positioned as a 'territory of culture and creation'. Policy documents suggest that Plaine Commune took up the proposal from the state to concentrate fully on creative industries and turned it into a project that better reflected the political interest of its elected representatives. The start of the process can be situated around 2010. It was boosted by a double movement, initiated simultaneously by the local authority and by the state. Plaine Commune commissioned the 'Mission Nuage' (Cloud Mission), incorporating an artist and a specialist in cultural policies. The objective was to identify cultural places and to make recommendations on how to stimulate arts and creation. Concomitantly, after the creation of Greater Paris metropolis (under the 2010 law) and the finalisation of a transport plan for the metropolitan region (Grand Paris Express), the state proposed to focus on creative industries. The final contract between the state and the local public authority includes a larger conception of creation and uses the terms 'culture and creation':

> From an urban development project limited to perimeters around the train stations, accompanied by the ambition to develop a 'cluster of creative and cultural industries' in the area, the partners have gradually evolved into a much broader project, covering the entire area. ... Culture and creation have been identified as some of the main characteristics of the area but also as tools that have a transversal leverage power to strengthen its development. (Territorial Development Contract 2014, 9) [author's translation]

The area links the objectives of creation and culture with that of social justice: 'the objective is to aim for a city that is more participative, more united and more ecological through culture and creation' and insists on enhancing participation: 'Plaine Commune makes culture and creation a medium to develop the participation of inhabitants and citizens in projects of renewal and urban transformation'. (Call for Tender, 2016: 3) [author's translation]. This objective is closely connected with the issues of sustainability and the implementation of Agenda 21 (the UN action plan on sustainable development) in policy documents.

'The Football Pitch …' and local authority led Co-Creation

The project 'The Football Pitch, the Player and the Consultant' can be understood as an example of Co-Creation initiated by a local authority, with the objective of changing the way urban development is implemented. One can draw from this that Co-Creation is a tool implemented as part of the Creative City strategy of Plaine Commune. This section provides an overview of the project and explains why it can be considered as Co-Creation. The author was actively involved in the participative evaluation process of the project and led qualitative interviews and informal conversations with the artists and curators, public servants working for the local authority and other researchers.

The arts-based project 'The Football Pitch …' was commissioned as part of the urban development project. The originality of the project process lies in the fact that it was supposed to inform and accompany the urban planning of a large area of strategic interest, the Pleyel neighbourhood. The call for proposals asked for an 'artistic and cultural approach for the implication of the inhabitants in the urban project of the sector Pleyel' (Call for Tender, 2016). The project that was selected aimed to make stakeholders' voices heard in a different way using the resources of sports and theatre. For a duration of two years, it was co-managed by the theatre collective GONGLE and an innovative cultural operator, the cultural cooperative CUESTA. All the stakeholders interviewed pointed out that this was a first experiment, in which the local authority was taking risks because it had no clear control of the process, which was left in the hands of the artists. The choice of the cultural operator was not consensual within the administration: it did not receive the support of all elected representatives.

The Pleyel neighbourhood had been earmarked for ambitious development projects of metropolitan and national significance. It is a low occupation area, with some small housing units. Today it hosts 7,200 inhabitants and more than 13,000 employees, including those of large employers such as EDF (an ex-national electricity company that employs 3,000 people) on site. The neighbourhood is to be almost completely redeveloped. The new plans include a new highway interchange and a new train station – to be designed by the Japanese star-architect Kengo Kuma and which will receive an estimated 250,000 users per day. Around the train station the new development project 'Pleyel Lights' will host 143,000 m^2 of offices (45 per cent of new constructions, including 10 per cent for the cluster 'creation'). The nearby Olympic Village will be turned into up to 2,400 housing units and 119,000 m^2 of offices after the Olympic Games.

According to the project website, 'The Football Pitch ...' was 'based on the practice of sports commentaries proposed to use "games" and voices to grasp and invent possibilities for Pleyel' (TUMBLR of 'Le terrain, le joueur et le consultant', translation by author). The project had two objectives, according to the artists: first, to collect narratives on the space and the urban development project from various stakeholders (from residents to architects, from local authority civil servants to social actors), and second, to inform the urban development project.

The project unfolded in three stages, which involved 67 workshops and a major final event called 'Big Encounter'. During the first stage, the artists met with more than 200 local stakeholders in the area. The objective was for them to understand the issues at stake and to meet stakeholders. The second stage was the artistic competition, during which 'football' teams were composed. Co-Creation, in the sense of active and creative involvement of participants, happened at this stage. The football teams reflected the diversity of the area's users and inhabitants: one was composed of employees from EDF, another of young users of the local facility for youngsters. The others included teams of public servants, architects and developers, residents of an area with small detached houses, parents from the school and so forth. Each team created its own song and sports outfit. All teams met at the 'Big Encounter' (see Figure 9.2), a one-day artistic-sports competition. The third stage was an 'after-game' period, in fact, a collaborative evaluation process.

The ten Co-Creation principles and 'The Football Pitch ...'

This section will discuss how Co-Creative this project was, in terms of its fit with the ten Co-Creation principles identified in this book (see Figure 1.1), and will explore whether this project can be regarded

Figure 9.2: La Grande Rencontre (The Big Encounter).

Source: GONGLE.

as an example of a successful Co-Creation process initiated by a local authority.

The fit with the Co-Creation principles is necessarily imperfect since there was no link with the project at the time. The parties involved did not expressly use the term Co-Creation but rather those of co-construction, involvement and participation. Therefore, the analysis focuses on the principles that seem the most relevant among the ten Co-Creation principles outlined here: (1) Equal; (2) Respectful; (3) Ethical; (4) Shared property; (5) Trust-based; (6) Embedded; (7) Aware; (8) Plurivocal; (9) Active; (10) Creative. The chapter also provides an analysis of how the project seemed to score regarding the objectives formulated by the artists and the local authority.

The attention to the inequality (1) of voices (8) between those of the local authority, planners and residents was taken into account from the beginning of the project. As the call for tender states: 'Plaine Commune wishes to implement a co-constructed artistic and cultural project, to involve the inhabitants and users in the definition and implementation of the urban project, as fully-fledged actors. This approach will feed the programming of the future district and some aspects of local life' (Call for Tender, 2016: 3) [author's translation].

The artists were called upon by the local authority to create new participation dynamics, to change power relationships in the preparation of the urban plans, and to give participants a 'fully fledged' role in the process. Thus, the artistic project becomes a medium for the confrontation of ideas on new grounds. According to the main artist-curator, she took on a role as 'mediator' between the different teams. She highlights that being engaged in playful artistic projects allowed ideas to be expressed and to be listened to differently by all parties. The teams take part in the game on equal footing and the dynamics of power are transgressed, at least temporarily, due to the change of setting and the different use of the participants' bodies. The local authority civil servant then in charge of the project highlights that sitting on the floor in a sports facility dressed in sportswear and on an equal footing with the youngsters created for him the opportunity to listen to voices that he would not have been able to hear otherwise. The game allows confrontation and criticism to be expressed and heard.

One of the most informative outcomes of the process is the book of songs. Some of the songs are directly critical of the project, such as the song 'Let's unite, join us' with its lyrics: 'The project proposed by the public authority team destroys classified landscaped areas. The hubbub of the world, chaotic traffic, of all of this our eyes are tired … let's get together, join us, we will change the terms of the debate!' They can also express cynicism: 'How long will it take to wait for Metro line 16? We will see the winners and the losers. … Buildings, a football pitch, barbecues, hotels. Tomorrow, no more problems, we have villas'. Beyond confrontation, the songs also express positive comments: 'There will be dust but for a good cause. Solid, pleasant, beneficial for children'. This was pointed out as unusual by the civil servants. Even the local authority civil servants felt free to express their doubts and hopes: 'Working today to go towards tomorrow, without being overtaken … do we have the means of our ambitions? Associating, consulting and building bridges. Are we all there for this new challenge?' The main artist-curator highlights that the project may have acted as a space for the formation of political ideas, by creating groups that identify and articulate ideas, which are neither in line with that of the local authority nor with the artist-curator's own views.

Even if the number of directly involved participants in the 'players' teams (around 40) may appear limited, there was an ongoing involvement of many actors, which went beyond the 'usual suspects' attending regular consultation meetings about urban planning development projects.

Embeddedness (6) and Awareness (7) are also at the core of the project, thanks to the long preparatory process, the first stage of the project, during which the artists met a large number (200) of stakeholders in the neighbourhood. To ensure embeddedness, many of the events were organised to coincide with usual meetings, such as the traditional start-of-the-year cake-eating celebration in January or the neighbourhood festival, and existing events of local associations. The 'Football Pitch ...' also chose the local facility for youngsters as a home and placed new information there regularly.

The principles of Trust (5), Shared property (4) and Creative outcomes (10) are more problematic. In terms of Trust, the participants did have several occasions to share informal times together, the 'Big Encounter' being a celebration as well as a competition. However, with the artists engaging in the project for two years, their involvement was inevitably limited in time. Discontinuity was bound to happen at the end, once they had finished the project. The curation and animation of the project were largely left to them, even if they benefited from the organisational back-up of Plaine Commune in terms of access to facilities and use of the local authority contact book.

The main Creative outcomes (10) of the project are available for free online on the project's website, including audio postcards, reports, photos, songs. However, some of the content produced within the project, notably during the evaluation, was turned down for the final publication by the local authority. For instance, the use of the concept of 'aestheticisation of public policy' in one of the texts did not please the local authority, a misunderstanding on the meaning of the concept according to its author.

In terms of Ethics (3), from the beginning the expectations for the artistic process sounded quite ambitious for a two-year creative project with a relatively low budget – €76,000 for the whole period. The artistic team had to rely on interns and contributed much of its time for free.

For the local authority, there were:

> ... three objectives for this artistic and cultural process: 1) To tell the story of the neighbourhood and to project oneself into the neighbourhood of tomorrow; 2) To feed the urban project through an experimental in situ approach; and 3) To contribute to strengthen the links between the inhabitants, the users, the actors of the district and to create attachment to the district and the city. (Call for Tender, 2016: 3)

As regards 'telling the story of the neighbourhood', this objective seems to have been achieved: visual (photos and photomontages, maps), audio (audio postcards), and written and digital tools have been used to capture the reality of the neighbourhood at the time of the project.

The songs written by the teams testify to the achievement of helping people to 'project oneself into the neighbourhood of tomorrow'.

However, no measure has been developed to assess the achievement of the third objective, to 'strengthen links ... and to create attachment to the district'. The main limitation here actually relates to the second objective. There was a disconnection in terms of timing between the urban planning study and the artistic process, due to the failure to recruit an artistic team at the end of the first call for tender. There was, in the end, little space for the needs expressed by residents and users to be taken into consideration in the preliminary urban development study.

The urban planner in charge of the development project within the local authority does mention that he gained from the process new elements of understanding of the area, such as the significance of the Pleyel Tower. This old tower – considered an outdated asbestos-filled tower by the local authority – was pinpointed as a landmark in the neighbourhood by residents. "I'm against [destroying the Tower] because it is our emblem, when the young take pictures, there is always the tower in the background; when my children were young and we were coming back from the countryside, they saw the tower, they used to say 'We are home'", reported a resident (quoted in the workshop report #12 (GONGLE, CUESTA, 2017: 112). The urban planner also mentions that, in the short run, the local authorities would be more attentive to the expectations of the resident population during the urban transformation, instead of focusing only on the final output of the urban project. But the artistic team did mention on several occasions that they were doubtful about how much of the process would actually be used in the final development. The local authority says that the documentation of the project will be attached to the documents passed on to the final teams realising the urban projects. Its actual take-up will depend on the interest, intentions and obstacles met by these teams.

The scale of the redevelopment has quite severely constrained the potentialities of the artistic project from the beginning, as has the deadline imposed by the Olympic Games. There was little the artists – and even Plaine Commune – could do to influence a process that involved powerful and complex actors such as the state, the Olympic Games Committee and a major developer.

The final project, Pleyel Lights, as presented on the website of the developer looks closer to a 'neoliberal' Creative City development, focusing on expensive, beautiful landmarks and buildings rather than a space for a (more) just city. Simulations made by the developers show an imagined city that does not cater for the existing population of Saint-Denis but is directed to attracting a new population (mostly young and white). Further contacts with the developers would be needed to explore that issue in more depth.

Co-Creation and innovation in public policy making

This chapter has asked whether the new approach developed by Plaine Commune could lead to a (more) just city. The reference to the 'different' Creative City concepts presented by Plaine Commune in policy documents in the context of this project seems to only have a limited impact on the actual content of urban development. From those public documents available, it appears to be a quite classical neoliberal revenue-making development, in which culture is used as a cool and beautiful accessory. For example, the project includes two glass 'bubbles', one of which is to be used for cultural and artistic events. A group of artistic institutions and collectives is developing an artistic project for the space but no reference is made to the process of Co-Creation or co-construction, despite it being at the core of Plaine Commune's strategy as a 'territory of culture and creation'. Different visions of the Creative City are at play and stakeholders do not have the same power of influence on major urban development projects. The pressure of the Olympic Games and the involvement of powerful and complex stakeholders, such as the state and Grand Paris Express on the development of the new train station, make this particular artistic project one of secondary importance.

To make Co-Creation processes initiated by public authorities a useful methodological tool for policy making means addressing the obstacles that 'The Football Pitch ...' came up against. Within Plaine Commune, there were several obstacles to making the artistic project a full component of the urban development project. A lack of political commitment is one of them. One elected representative came to the 'Big Encounter' but he did not stay for long, nor did he seem to listen to the inhabitants, according to the artists. The relationship with and involvement of other stakeholders is also a key issue. It may have been possible to engage the developers and state actors in more in-depth involvement. The low budget allocated to the project is another limitation. The question of the instrumentalisation of artists is also relevant. In this case, despite low financial return, the project allowed the curator to pursue her own artistic research, so she accepted the terms of the contract. The limited impact of the participatory process on urban development remains an issue, and the legacy and usefulness of such Co-Creation actions must be thought through in the long term.

The willingness of local authority planners to change the way they plan cities in the future may be one of the most interesting prerequisites and outcomes of 'The Football Pitch ...' and of the experiment as part of the local authority's implementation of becoming a 'territory of culture and creation'. With 'The Football Pitch ...', the local administration took a risk. It is process-based and leaves no physical trace – no new artistic space to promote, no new public space installation, no major street level activity. The most interesting outcomes are quite intangible and difficult to measure: the participants from the local authority mention that it changed the way they were now leading urban project development processes, that it gave them the feeling "for once" of being really in touch with the area, of being able to listen to the people. They felt that the process gave "meaning and humanity" to the planning process.

The local authority has tried to address the difficulty of transferring such experience from one person to another and from one project to another. The civil servants involved in the project have made several presentations to their peers to share their learning. The local authority has a team dedicated to the implementation of the strategy transversally and organises regular sectoral training. The objective is to reach out beyond the civil servants who are the most inclined to change their own practices. Plaine Commune has, after this experience, changed and adapted the way it issues calls targeted to artists, and as a result of a call in another area of Saint-Denis, a new collaboration is beginning with the same artists' collective, but with a different planning team. The local authority has started a collective reflection process on these issues, which led it to organise a workshop in the Architecture Biennale in Venice in 2018, which gathered artists, developers, promoters and local authority representatives.

Conclusion

This chapter proposed an understanding of Co-Creation that includes projects initiated by stakeholders other than researchers, as long as the objective is the co-production of knowledge about a deprived and stigmatised area.

This book has defined Co-Creation as a method that brings together different communities in a neighbourhood (researchers, residents, artists and stakeholders) to use arts-based methods to generate creative outputs that are relevant to the local community, and that act as a catalyst for reflection on understanding around urban and neighbourhood challenges, and address these to build more socially just places for the future (see Chapter 1).

The project analysed in this chapter, 'The Football Pitch ...' – an experiment set within the frame of Plaine Commune's strategy of becoming a 'territory of culture and creation' – does not fully comply with this definition, notably in that researchers did not actively take part in all stages of the project. However, 'The Football Pitch ...' did include many of the elements of Co-Creation. Participants from all key groups – local residents, artists, stakeholders involved in decision-making, and researchers – were actively involved at different stages of the project. The main objective was the co-production of knowledge about a deprived and stigmatised area. This chapter has shown that 'The Football Pitch ...' put into practice several of the ten principles this book suggests for Co-Creation, more particularly the following: (1) Safe; (2) Respectful; (3) Ethical; (6) Embedded; (7) Adapted; (8) Voice. The key challenge remains the application of the principles linked to co-ownership and trust.

In this case study, the actual impact of the artistic process on the urban development plan remains uncertain, and the local politicians and most powerful actors, such as the state, have been relatively absent from the project. In many ways, these pitfalls are similar to those of classic residents' consultation and participation in urban planning developments. If Co-Creation was to be used as a tool for building (more) just Creative Cities, the stakeholders should pay specific attention to these principles when implementing artistic and creative projects with residents.

This case study provides an example of how involving artists can change the dynamics of listening to each other in an area, can disrupt – at least temporarily – the relations of power,and how an artists' led project can have a strong impact on local authority civil servants' practices of urban planning. Charles Landry, one of the authors who formulated the Creative Cities theories, suggested that Creative Cities were those able to implement innovative 'organisational structures' and 'creative thinking' (Landry, 1995, 2003). From the experience of 'The Football Pitch ...', it appears that this form of Co-Creation, involving artists and local authorities, could trigger changes in local policy making in the long run, potentially making them more inclusive and sensitive to other 'voices'.

This chapter has shown how artists can act as seeds of innovation and displacement, how they can act as mediators between stakeholders. Co-Creation could be a method for inclusive Creative City strategies by calling in artists to help develop new ways of making the city together, by opening spaces of listening between urban planners and other stakeholders.

References

Boren, T. and Young, C. (2013) 'Getting creative with the "creative city"? Towards new perspectives on creativity in urban policy', *International Journal of Urban and Regional Research*, 37(5): 1799–815.

Call for Tender (2016) 'Cahier des clauses techniques et particulières de la démarche artistique et culturelle pour l'implication des habitants dans le projet urbain du secteur Pleyel', available from https://centraledesmarches.com/marches-publics/Saint-denis-cedex-EPT-Plaine-Commune-Amenagement-du-secteur-Pleyel-lot-3-demarche-artistique-et-culturelle-pour-l-implication-des-habitants-dans-le-projet-urbain-du-secteur-Pleyel-a-Saint-Denis/2045997.

Davet, G. and Lhomme, F. (2018) *Inch'allah: L'Islamisation à Visage Découvert*, Paris: Fayard.

Evans, G. (2005) 'Measure for measure: evaluating the evidence of culture's contribution to regeneration', *Urban Studies*, 42 (5–6): 959–83.

Florida, R. (2002) *The Rise of the Creative Class*, New York: Basic Books.

Gill, R. and Pratt, A.C. (2008) 'In the social factory? immaterial labour, precariousness and cultural work', *Theory, Culture and Society*, 25(7–8): 1–30.

GONGLE, CUESTA (2017) 'Compte-Rendu atelier #12', available from https://cjoint.com/doc/17_04/GDyonIqhPku_170403-CR-ATELIER-12-NB-LD.pdf.

Hutton, T. (2017) 'The cultural economy of the city: pathways to theory and understanding inequality' in *Inequalities in Creative Cities*, New York: Palgrave Macmillan, pp 15–40.

IAU (2019) May, available from https://iau-idf.fr/fileadmin/NewEtudes/Etude_1807/Gentrification_et_pauperisation.pdf.

INSEE (2013) *Statistics*, available from https://insee.fr/fr/statistiques/2106113?geo=COM-93066.

Jakob, D. (2010) 'Constructing the creative neighbourhood: hopes and limitations of creative city policies in Berlin', *City, Culture and Society*, 1(4): 193–8.

Kagan, S. and Hahn, J. (2011) 'Creative cities and (un)sustainability: from creative class to sustainable creative cities', *Culture and Local Governance*, 3(1–2): 11–27.

Kirchberg, V. and Kagan, S. (2013) 'The role of artists in the emergence of creative sustainable cities: theoretical clues and empirical illustrations', *Cities, Culture and Society*, 4: 137–52.

Krätke, S. (2010) '"Creative cities" and the rise of the dealer class: a critique of Richard Florida's approach to urban theory', *International Journal of Urban and Regional Research*, 34(4): 835–53.

Landry, C. (2003) *The Creative City: A Toolkit for Urban Innovators*, London: Earthscan.

Landry, C. and Bianchini, F. (1995) *The Creative City*, London: Demos.

Lebeau, B. (2018) 'Les Jeux Olympiques de 2024: Une Chance pour le Grand Paris?', *EchoGéo* (online), Sur le Vif, available from http://journals.openedition.org/echogeo/15202; DOI: 10.4000/echogeo.15202.

Leslie, D. and Catungal, J.P. (2012) 'Social justice and the creative city: class, gender and racial inequalities', *Geography Compass*, 6(3): 111–22.

Markusen, A. (2006) 'Urban development and the politics of a creative class: evidence from the study of artists', *Environment and Planning*, 38(10): 1921–40.

Martí-Costa, M. and Pradel i Miquel, M. (2011) 'The knowledge city against urban creativity? Artists' workshops and urban regeneration in Barcelona', *European Urban and Regional Studies*, 19(1), 92–108.

McLean, H. (2014) 'Digging into the creative city: a feminist critique', *Antipode*, 46(3): 669–90.

Miles, M. (2013) *A Post-Creative City?*, RCCS Annual Review (online), available from http://journals.openedition.org/rccsar/506; DOI: 10.4000/rccsar.506.

Nathan, M. (2015) 'After Florida: towards an economics of diversity', *European Urban and Regional Studies*, 22(1): 3–19.

Peck, J. (2005) 'Struggling with the creative class', *International Journal of Urban and Regional Research*, 29(4): 740–70.

Pratt, A.C. (2008) 'Creative cities: the cultural industries and the creative class', *Geografiska Annaler, Series B: Human Geography*, 90(2): 107–17.

Pratt, A.C. (2011) 'The cultural contradictions of the creative city', *City, Culture and Society*, 2(3): 123–130.

Ratiu, D. (2013) 'Creative cities and/or sustainable cities: Discourses and practices', *City, Culture and Society*, 4: 125–35.

Sen, A. (2009) *The Idea of Justice*, Cambridge, MA: Harvard University Press.

Territorial Development Contract (2014), available from https://plainecommune.fr/fileadmin/user_upload/Portail_Plaine_Commune/LA_DOC/PROJET_DE_TERRITOIRE/Projet_metropolitain/CDT_2014.pdf

TUMBLR of *Le terrain, le joueur et le consultant*, available from https://leterrain-lejoueur-leconsultant.tumblr.com.

Vicari-Haddock, S. (2010) 'Branding the creative city', in S. Vicari-Haddock (ed) *Brand-building the Creative City: A Critical Look at Current Concepts and Practices*, Firenze: Firenze University Press.

10

Can literary events use Co-Creation to challenge stigmatisation?

Christina Horvath

Introduction

This chapter takes a comparative approach to two initiatives, one from the Global North and one from the South, that have been developed by writers to bring literary events to peripheral neighbourhoods. The Dictée des Cités, a spelling competition organised by Rachid Santaki in French cities since 2013, and the Literary Festival of the Urban Periphery (FLUP), curated by Julio Ludemir and Écio Salles in Rio de Janeiro's favelas since 2012, were not conceived as Co-Creation events but are founded on similar principles and processes, insofar as they promote art and creativity in marginalised urban areas and seek to challenge the perception of these neighbourhoods as places devoid of the production and consumption of literary texts.

The aim of this chapter is therefore to compare the two artist-driven events and explore their respective strategies to engage with local communities and broader audiences. Based on interviews and ongoing dialogue with the organisers of both events, this chapter seeks to tap into their extensive experience of knowledge production with communities to see what Co-Creation can learn from their practices and how it can inspire them in return. A secondary aim is to evaluate how collaborative literary events adapt to specific local challenges in the Global North and South.

Chikako Mori (2012) sees the persistent overlooking of scriptural practices in the urban margin as a deliberate denial of highbrow cultural forms in stigmatised areas. She reminds us that French *banlieues* are often represented in public (political, media and academic) discourses as places that fall short of a written culture recognised and validated by the establishment. According to Mori, the non-recognition of *banlieues* as places of reading and textual production comes from a desire to reaffirm a longstanding divide between high- and lowbrow cultures, based on the understanding that writing is not quite a cultural practice like the others, insofar as it has always been perceived and used to mark the line separating 'us' and 'them', both inside the French Republic (fight against regional languages) and outside (colonial ideology). In this representation some are perceived as 'literate', 'civilised', 'enlightened', 'masters of themselves' and others as 'uneducated', 'barbarians', 'obscure', 'uncontrollable' (Mori, 2012: 75, author's translation). This observation is also confirmed by Bettina Ghio (2016), whose research highlights that French rap artists' complex relationship with and contribution to highbrow literature is generally ignored, or by Keira Maameri, whose 2016 documentary, *Nos Plumes* (*Our Pens*), shows how bestselling French novelists with postcolonial and *banlieue* roots (like Santaki himself) continue to be marginalised by mainstream literary institutions.

Similarly, from the earliest days of samba, Brazilian favelas have consistently been associated with popular musical genres rather than with a vibrant literary scene (Maddox, 2014). In recent years, favela youths have been actively engaged in different musical movements, from hip-hop to AfroReggae. According to Patrocínio (2013), these have contributed to the emergence of an avant-garde literary movement called 'Marginal Literature' in the peripheries of São Paulo and Rio de Janeiro since the 1990s. Hip-hop was also instrumental in providing peripheral youth with alternative identities, feelings of self-affirmation and 'a sense of protest, creating a counter-discourse, erasing hegemonic discourses and producing an interstice between centre and periphery' (Patrocínio, 2013: 107, author's translation). However, in spite of their participation in literary production, favelas just like *banlieues* continue to be referred to as 'primitive' and 'savage' and depicted in opposition to the formal city perceived as 'civilised' (Maddox, 2014: 466).

This chapter will systematically compare the two festivals' attempts to shift the image of peripheral urban areas in France and Brazil from 'zones of non-writing' (Mori, 2012) to places of written culture. The first section will explore their similarities and differences. The second section will place them in the Global North/South divide to shed light on their different participation in knowledge production. The final section will compare the two events' ethos, aims and strategies with those of Co-Creation. The conclusion will discuss how Co-Creation projects and socially engaged literary festivals could learn from each other.

Destigmatisation through art in two literary festivals

La Dictée des Cités (the Dictation of the Periphery) was launched in 2013 by writer and journalist Rachid Santaki, in collaboration with community activist Abdellah Boudour, president of the association Force des Mixités (Strength in Diversity). Santaki, who lives in Saint-Denis, Greater Paris, is a journalist, essayist and novelist, author of several scripts and crime novels set in the area. As an engaged writer, he seeks to "be active beyond writing books, to play a role in society, to take the books outside the library" (Santaki, 2019), using strategies ranging from pasting posters in the street to promote his novels to teaching creative writing in prisons or launching cultural initiatives.

The Literary Festival of the Urban Periphery (then called FLUPP) was also founded by writer, journalist, novelist and cultural producer Julio Ludemir and Écio Salles, a poet, essayist, former Cultural Secretary of the municipality of Novo Iguaçu and one of the coordinators of cultural group AfroReggae. The festival was established in 2012 as a counter-event to Brazil's most prestigious book fair, the International Literary Festival of Paraty (FLIP) which has been held annually since 2003 in the seaside town of Paraty. The FLUP has both challenged and extended the international festival model adopted by the FLIP (Heyward, 2017) by seeking to make literature accessible to all, reaching out to the over one million people living in Rio de Janeiro's favelas (Perlman, 2013: 52).

Both the Dictation and the FLUP are itinerant events with strong community roots, although they both have experienced important mutations over time. The first Dictation was an outdoor event organised in May 2013 in Clichy-sous-Bois (Greater Paris) before spreading to other *banlieues* around Paris. Later it was held in other cities across France and was even exported to Italy, Belgium, Cameroon and Morocco (Boucher, 2019). Its size expanded from an initial average of 40 to 200–400 participants (Dictée Géante website). In May 2017, the event reached its 100th edition in Bagnolet (Brancato, 2017) and earned Rachid Santaki the rank of Knight of the National Order of Merit. The Dictation's 200th edition was celebrated at the Elysée Palace In 2019. A record 1,473 participants were registered in March 2018 when the largest Dictation ever held took place in the iconic sporting venue, Stade de France. According to Santaki "it was something incredible because so many things happened around this simple exercise we all had at school but never outside it" (Santaki, 2019). To reflect its mutations, the event changed its name from La Dictée des Cités to La Dictée pour Tous (Dictation for All) and to La Dictée Géante

(Giant Dictation). For the organisers, this transition meant an increased potential to connect to more diverse audiences but also a shift in focus:

> "In fact, the first version of the dictation was staged in the neighbourhood and was perceived as an event in the periphery. ... It was a way to respond to the clichés, to show that *banlieue* residents liked dictations just as much as people in the centre but as a side-effect it contributed to enclosing participants in the margins and seemed to suggest that people in the periphery had their own dictation. ... Things changed since, as soon as we took the dictation out of the neighbourhoods, it actually allowed people to mix. ... Today, organising a dictation and bringing all the audiences together allows for a neutral meeting ground. I think that the dictation has made it possible to create a bridge between these publics, which do not necessarily meet. But there are so many differences between these audiences that the dictation is just one meeting point, other instances of sharing and transmission need to be invented to go even further." (Santaki, 2019)

Similar to the Dictation, the FLUP is also a nomadic event. The first five iterations took place in different Rio de Janeiro favelas: Morro dos Prazeres in 2012, Vigário Geral in 2013, Mangueira in 2014, Chapéu Mangueira in 2015, Cidade de Deus in 2016, and Vidigal in 2017. Yet in 2018 the festival broke with this tradition by moving to the Valongo Wharf, a UNESCO world heritage site where enslaved Africans were traded, while the 2019 edition was held at the Museum of Art in Rio (MAR). Initially called FLUPP (the Literary Festival of the Pacifying Police Units), the festival progressively distanced itself from the police pacification process that started in 2009 by moving from pacified favelas to an unpacified one in 2013 and by "freeing itself from the UPP [Pacifying Police Unit] brand after the decline of the pacification policy" (Ludemir, 2019) by changing its name to the Literary Festival of the Urban Periphery (FLUP). The change of location from favelas to cultural institutions in the city centre was simultaneously motivated by the difficulty of negotiating with a range of new stakeholders in a different favela every year and the desire to draw attention to racism, sexism, homophobia, the legacies of colonialism and slavery, reminding audiences that 'the idea of the "periphery" in this festival extends beyond the geographical sense to include communities and identities that are marginalized in society' (El Youssef, 2016).

While the two events share similar goals, they use different strategies to reach these. Dictations are one-day events based on classical literary texts which are read out loud and have to be spelled by the participants. This school exercise, traditionally used to test students' spelling skills, has been turned into a game to attract wide audiences to literature, reconcile postcolonial populations with the French Republican school system which they often resent, and demonstrate that "the French language belongs to all and can be enriched by the participation of others and adopt different forms according to the context" (Santaki, 2019). The FLUP's annual programme, on the other hand, unfolds over five consecutive days and includes roundtable discussions, activities for children, performances and other celebratory moments. The festival's main innovation, however, is the ongoing rather than one-off engagement with the host communities; this helps build relationships, involve local actors and stakeholders, create a community of readers, challenge the stigmatisation attached to the urban margins, and ultimately nurture a new Brazilian literature from below through discovering and forming new talents. According to Heyward:

> The FLUP engages a territory in a year-long, bottom-up creative process before conducting tailored writers' and readers' workshops over a series of months. ... The community consultation and co-creation process is key to developing ongoing relationships with residents and integrating a variety of genres and tools in the festival's programming. (Heyward, 2017: 1)

Thus, both the Dictation and the FLUP use artist-initiated events based on literary texts to engage with mixed audiences and dispel preconceptions about peripheral populations. Their differences lie in the varying depth and length of this involvement and its more or less creative nature, as well as in some structural dissimilarities caused by the North-South divide.

Literary festivals in the context of the Global North-South divide

Although France and Brazil occupy different positions in the global economy, their present-day social, educational and cultural inequalities are deeply rooted in the discriminatory practices of colonisation, leading to lasting divides between educated elites and stigmatised postcolonial populations in both countries. Due to the accessibility of books and higher literacy rates, the percentage of regular readers in France is much higher: 91 per cent (Pech, 2017) as opposed to 56 per cent in Brazil (Failla, 2016). According to Mustafa Dikeç (2017), the current stigmatisation of French *banlieues* is shaped by a strong colonial legacy, a persistent imaginary based on distinctions between populations and civilisations believed to be superior or inferior:

> The Republic is at once the product and the producer of racialized social relations through its public policies and official discourses. … The working-class *banlieues* of France bear the weight of this colonial legacy. … Through policies and discourses, the State perpetuates, indeed reproduces, forms of colonial domination in the banlieues. (Dikeç, 2017: 104)

This legacy explains that, in the country that achieved the world's third highest literacy rate in 2002 (0.987 against 0.905 in Brazil, EFA 2002), an important divide persists between the populations of metropolitan centres and the residents of low-income *banlieues*. The latter have distinctively lower literacy rates, higher numbers of non-native speakers of French, weaker school performances and higher concentrations of students experiencing difficulties. A recent study on illiteracy revealed that, in 2011, 27 per cent of the population aged 18–65 in the so-called 'sensitive urban zones' or ZUS experienced difficulties when reading and writing, compared with only 11 per cent of those living outside these areas (Rapport de l'Observatoire national des zones urbaines sensibles, 2013: 133). Since 1981, schools in these areas have received extra support from priority education policies, enabling them to reduce their class sizes, offer higher remuneration for teachers and allocate extra time for small-group activities. A reform in 2017 transformed the so-called ZEPs (Priority Education Zones) into Priority and Reinforced Priority Education Networks (REP and REP+) and extended the scheme to 1,095 geographic areas encompassing 21 per cent of public school students aged 11–15 in about 8,000 schools across France. Yet, according to a government report published in February 2018 (Rosenwald, 2018), both REP and REP+ areas still have a significantly higher percentage of socially disadvantaged students whose parents are either unemployed or manual workers and these students have a considerably lower competency in the French language: 15-year-old students entering the sixth and final year of college tested at the beginning of the 2015–16 academic year scored only 60 per cent against 83 per cent in schools outside REP areas (Rosenwald, 2018: 2).

While these statistics explain why French *banlieues* are seen by some as 'zones of non-writing' (Mori, 2012: 75), other studies (Van Zanten, 2001, Caillet, 2005, Beaud and Mauger, 2017) highlight the existence of a prevalent 'anti-school sentiment' in these areas (Beaud and Mauger, 2017: 35), which explains why during the 2005 riots several schools were torched (Dikeç, 2017).

Banlieue residents' mistrust of the Republican education system is rooted in a complex range of factors: racially and socially biased practices targeting students of postcolonial origin (Beaud, 2002); curricula promoting colonial values; anti-Muslim policies culminating in the banning of the headscarf in French schools since 2004 (Dikeç, 2017); and the orientation of children of immigrant or working-class parents towards vocational training at an early age, which impedes their social mobility while maintaining former hierarchies (Van Zanten, 2001).

Brazil's marginalised urban population is similarly linked with colonial history. The abolishment of slavery in 1888 brought significant numbers of freed slaves from around Brazil to Rio de Janeiro in search of affordable housing (Freire-Medeiros, 2013). Freire Medeiros suggests that 'in the absence of public policies capable of providing-housing for those in need, [favelas] emerged as a solution based mostly on the self-construction of homes in territories where building was formally forbidden – areas beyond the reach of the formal real estate market' (Freire-Medeiros, 2013: 57). From their inception, favelas were configured as the 'space of the poor', both geographically and culturally, and by the 1920s they were durably associated with samba and carnival. Although these products of Afro-Brazilian counter-culture were integrated into the national culture and identity by the regime of Getúlio Vargas in the 1930s (Yúdice, 2003), the economic and social marginalisation of favela residents continued throughout the Brazilian dictatorship from 1964 till 1984, and even after the democratisation that started in 1985. Perlman (2013) notes that the arts have played an important role in the resistance to marginalisation in Brazil too:

> In the wake of the return to democracy, community groups, federations of community groups, and non-profits working in favelas flourished. Some of these promoted the rights of citizenship and attempted to correct past social injustices. Others were organized around cultural activities

such as theatre, dance and filmmaking, sports ... or around reclaiming weak or even lost racial or ethnic practices. (Perlman, 2013: 151–3)

Perlman argues that the distinction between the worthy 'in-group' and the unworthy 'out-group' remains strong in a country where 34 per cent of the population lives below the poverty line and the top ten per cent of the population earn 50 per cent of the national income, while the poorest 20 per cent earn 2.5 per cent of the national income (Perlman, 2013: 48). She suggests that, although racial and spatial stigmatisation remain strongly interlinked, the fact of living in a favela remains more stigmatising than people's skin colour. The criminalisation of favela residents in the fields of the media, local administration and public policies reinforces this stigmatisation (Lacerda, 2015) and the fight against drug trafficking is frequently used as a pretext to justify aggressive policing that denies the residents' human rights.

Ireland (2008) states that the distribution of quality education among the Brazilian population is one of the most unequal in the world and functional illiteracy rates remain high (Ireland, 2008: 718). This mainly affects older people, the indigenous and black populations as well as those living in rural areas and in the North East of Brazil. Besides the important socioeconomic disparities that make books unaffordable for many, the main obstacle to reading is illiteracy. In 2006, Brazil registered over 13 million illiterate youths and adults, representing 10.38 per cent of the country's population (Rodrigues Mello and Marini Braga, 2018). As a result of the ambitious adult literacy programmes introduced under the Lula presidency, this number was reduced to 11.8 million people (7.2 per cent) in 2016 and 11.3 million (6.8 per cent) in 2018 (Indio, 2019). According to Julio Ludemir, the FLUP has capitalised on the success of these education policies to train new readers and authors (Ludemir, 2019).

Despite some similarities regarding the territorial stigmatisation, racial discrimination and educational disadvantages experienced by *banlieue* and favela residents, there are also important structural differences between the Global North and South. While most researchers agree on describing class and race issues in Brazil as a 'social apartheid' (Resende, 2009, Lacerda, 2015), references to a 'postcolonial urban apartheid' in France remain sporadic (Silverstein and Tetreault, 2006, Tchumkam, 2015). In French *banlieues*, governmental, regional and municipal structures are in charge of running schools, community centres, libraries, theatres, houses of culture and cultural events. In Brazil's favelas, most cultural institutions are maintained by the efforts of local and foreign associations, volunteers and non-governmental organisations (NGOs). The neoliberal turn of the 1980s, which in the Global North resulted in the retrenchment of the welfare state and 'the reduction of state-subsidised social services, the lowering of wages and the evisceration of labour rights' (Yúdice, 2003: 82), had a somewhat different effect on the Global South where the welfare state has never been fully developed and unskilled labour has been less affected by unemployment (Perlman, 2013: 159). In both parts of the world, however, it has triggered a turn to civil society, transforming culture into the main arena of progressive struggle led by the most innovative actors (Yúdice, 2003: 88).

North-South differences also prevail in the domain of knowledge production and epistemology understood as the critique and validation of scientific knowledge. As previously argued in Chapter 1, the epistemologies of the North have attracted significant criticism in recent years for their 'pretence to be the planetary centre and the desire and design to homogenise the world to its image and likelihood' (Mignolo and Walsh, 2018: 194). Due to the unequal relations of power, they succeeded in imposing the mirage of their universal validity upon the totality of cultures colonised (Quijano, 2010). However, with the rise of decolonial theory, the embodied and technically and culturally intrinsic social practices of Southern epistemologies born from the struggle against capitalism, colonialism and patriarchy have been increasingly recognised and the necessity of decolonising Eurocentric ways of knowledge production has been gaining ground (Santos, 2018). FLUP's efforts to collect and conserve favela residents' practice-based knowledge and oral memories in events like the 'Feijoada da Memória' (Memory Meal), which will be discussed in the next section, can be considered as part of decolonial strategies aiming to erase hierarchies between Northern and Southern ways of knowledge production.

Finally, the North-South divide is also encapsulated in both events' different access to public funding and national and international institutional validation. The Dictation mainly relies on national and municipal funders, including France Culture, the Centre of National Monuments, municipal and regional councils and ministries (according to La Dictée Géante website), while since the decline of state support, the FLUP receives most of its financial support from private sponsors (such as Ford) and foreign institutions (among others the Open Society Foundation, the French Institute, and the British Council) (Ludemir, 2019). The Global North is also known for concentrating the most prestigious literary institutions, publishing houses and globally known literary prizes (Casanova, 2007) which act as instances of legitimation by validating new writers and introducing them to global audiences. The London Book Fair's International Excellence Award awarded to the FLUP in 2016 is a good example of the international power of legitimation which is still mostly held in the Global North.

The literary festivals through the Co-Creation lens

This final section will assess the two events' aims, ethos and strategies through the lens of Co-Creation. According to the definition championed in this book, Co-Creation is a method of collaborative knowledge production that relies on socially engaged artistic and cultural practices to provide communities with opportunities for self-understanding and resistance to the dominant social imaginary. Co-Creation brings together artists, researchers, residents and stakeholders from disadvantaged neighbourhoods to generate tangible and intangible, creative and intellectual outcomes relevant to the community. Arts practice is embedded in Co-Creation workshops in which all actors are recognised as equal participants actively taking part in both the creative process and the knowledge production which are inseparable from each other. A deeper understanding of different perspectives on the neighbourhood, the divided city and social justice emerges from the process spontaneously as a by-product of this engagement, with art used as a leveller to enable different voices to be heard.

Like Co-Creation, both festivals use literature to destigmatise disadvantaged urban audiences and build capacity by engaging participants in arts-based practices. Co-Creation generally works with small groups of participants and seeks to develop strong, trust-based relationships between them through collectively set goals, discussion and time spent together, shared creative and bodily experiences and communal meals. The two festivals, however, seek to reach out to broader audiences in timeframes that are often too short to establish such solid links. Dictations are one-off events that attract 200–400 participants on average and promote a limited engagement with creativity, insofar as the activity they promote consists of reading and writing out extracts of classical texts. Original texts are only produced on special occasions, such as for World Refugee Day in June 2019 when Rachid Santaki set up a wall "on which each participant wrote words and expressed, in the form of drawings, their ideas but also their feelings" (Santaki, 2019). According to Santaki, the Dictation is less about creativity and capacity building than about bringing together schoolchildren, middle school and high school students, adults, people with disabilities, learners of the French language, and institutions involved in the fields of education, culture and sport who would not meet otherwise. Santaki insists on equality between participants:

> "The Dictation provides means for all participants to be equal when it comes to words. It is above all an event about the French language that can be enriched by the participation of others and adopt different forms according to the context in which it takes place." (Santaki, 2019)

However, participants are unlikely to be equally involved in the literary activities as these are not co-designed by them: the texts that are read are chosen by the organisers without consulting the participants and thus the divide between those who dictate and those who participate in writing out the dictation remains unchallenged.

As a larger-scale event, the FLUP brings together several thousand participants for five days each year. It also includes a series of creative workshops run by artists and academics over a number of months leading up to the festival. Workshops like the 'Laboratory of Black Narratives for the Audiovisual' run in partnership with TV Globo are quite similar to Co-Creation workshops in that they produce creative outputs and help young people from the urban periphery to develop their creative skills and self-esteem. For organiser Julio Ludemir, the FLUP's greatest achievement is having launched over 200 writers from the periphery of Rio, among them bestselling novelist Geovani Martins from Rocinha, poet and cultural producer Vivi Salles from Cidade de Deus, and internationally recognised writer and filmmaker Yasmin Thayná from Nova Iguaçu:

> "The first two editions of the workshops resulted in the creation of 56 original stories for television, several of which have been accepted for screening. In August and October 2018, we organised poetry slam workshops in 14 public high schools in Rio de Janeiro. By 2018, we organised four workshops leading to the publication of five books and 25 original audio-visual documents, a politically engaged fashion show which drew attention to the killing of black youths by the state and a documentary about the first generation of black professionals arriving to the job market after passing through the quotas. Achieving this was a challenging process for which significant human and financial resources were mobilised." (Ludemir, 2019)

Similar to Co-Creation, the FLUP engages academics, artists, communities and stakeholders in collective creative processes and shared bodily experiences by bringing together disadvantaged and more privileged audiences to spend time together in favelas. Its workshops have resulted in the publication of several collective volumes but, unlike Co-Creation, these activities are not co-designed by the participants and researchers are largely absent from the creative process. It is important to note that while scholars have been regularly involved in teaching creative writing and film making on FLUP workshops, they do not contribute to these as researchers.

While research and long-term engagement with the same community are less central to FLUP than Co-Creation, forms of shared understanding may nevertheless arise from the regular workshop activities in which artists, academics and other participants share ideas and work together towards a shared goal. Engagement with communities' local and orally circulating or embodied knowledge has been nevertheless central to FLUP's repeated attempts to reassemble oral history and community memory. For example, the 'Feijoada da Memória' (Memory Meal) introduced in 2015 in Babilônia brought together the favela's founders with the younger generations and resulted in a comic-strip exhibition based on the history of the inhabitants. In Cidade de Deus, FLUP co-produced a book celebrating 50 years of the favela, and in 2017 in Vidigal they staged with local partners a 'Memory Competition' for children and adolescents (Ludemir, 2019). These events are just a few among the many FLUP initiatives that encourage the inclusion of Southern epistemologies through the valorisation of oral narrative modes. Oral culture and spoken word practices inspired by African griots and hip-hop artists from the Northern urban periphery have also been celebrated through the FLUP Slam Battle, which, according to Julio Ludemir (2019), has been offering a platform for youth from Rio de Janeiro's margins to voice their indignation over homicidal security policies and racial and social discrimination. These arts-based practices, aimed at abolishing extant hierarchies between oral and written forms of expression, are strategies that could be adopted by Co-Creation projects seeking to engage with knowledge emerging from social struggle in the Global South (Santos, 2018: 13).

Through arts practice, Co-Creation encourages communities to critically engage in 'questioning unexamined beliefs ..., disarticulating the existing common sense and fostering a variety of agonistic public spaces', as advocated by Chantal Mouffe (2013: 95). Therefore, Co-Creation workshops can be considered as 'agonistic' interventions insofar as they promote democratic processes and encourage political adversaries to respect each other's discordant viewpoints. By bringing together scholarly and embodied 'ways of knowing' arising from academic and non-academic perspectives and from both Northern or Southern epistemologies, a shared Co-Creation develops an agonistic understanding of the city which can be translated into actions that can lead to practical and potentially transformative change. Co-Creation aims to harness participants' capacity to challenge and dismantle multiple stigmas attached to disadvantaged neighbourhoods using 'complicated gestures of rewriting, strategies of decontextualizing' (Rosello, 1998: 18). This aim is shared by the two festivals, although they challenge negative perceptions of the urban periphery to different extents, using different strategies. While both demonstrate that both *banlieues* and favelas are places fit to host highbrow cultural events, only the FLUP seeks to promote new aesthetics emerging from the margins. By focusing on classical texts and spelling rules set by the famously conservative French Academy, the Dictation shows respect to literary conventions, institutions and canons validated by the establishment. On the contrary, by launching and endorsing new writers, the FLUP contributes to shaping alternative canons, while simultaneously establishing itself as an alternative instance of literary validation. The efficiency of this strategy can be measured by the FLUP's recent success of imposing its ethos on other festivals. For example, its efforts to increase the number of female invitees, to include indigenous and black writers, to honour marginal writers such as Lima Barreto in 2016, and to draw attention to racism by introducing FLUP Preta (Black FLUP) in 2019, have been imitated by the more traditional FLIP literary festival and have resulted in the emergence of new national trends (Ludemir, 2019).

Finally, both literary events and Co-Creation seek to promote the inclusion of peripheral populations, although their ambitions in this respect vary. Rachid Santaki admits to being sceptical about the Dictation's potential to challenge negative stereotypes:

> "With the Dictation, I don't think we have changed the image of the *banlieue* and I don't believe that an event can change the image or the stigmas of the periphery. I rather think that I surprised audiences who did not imagine that the French language concerned everyone, including people living in the periphery but I did not change the perception of those who believe in the clichés." (Santaki, 2019)

Julio Ludemir advocates a more radical approach, inspired by affirmative action that promotes the participation of marginalised groups, in particular women, black and indigenous populations and the LGBTQI community. Despite the obvious differences between the French and Brazilian contexts, both festivals aim to bring art and literature closer to underprivileged communities and to open up a space for public participation through active engagement with literary texts. Although Co-Creation is more focused on producing in-depth knowledge at the neighbourhood level, it may struggle to build such extended networks and raise such high levels of media attention due to its limitation to single neighbourhoods.

Conclusion

The literary events promoted by Rachid Santaki and Julio Ludemir are artist-initiated, participative projects that celebrate the margins and promote the inclusion of disadvantaged groups into the mainstream city and society. They highlight the importance of artists as initiators, organisers and promoters of multi-partner events which bring together several Co-Creative elements (being respectful, ethical, plurivocal, and sometimes also embedded, aware and creative) while others (being equal, trust-based, shared, occasionally also embedded, aware and creative) are missing. Just like Co-Creation, these events are founded on the ideal of equality and inclusivity and share Co-Creation's interest in marginality and arts methods. They may, however, lack some other key elements, such as research practices involving academic partners, the explicit focus on knowledge production and dissemination, and the active production of artistic outcomes, which plays a more central role in the FLUP where new literary works are produced, than the Dictation where literary works are mostly consumed.

The comparative analysis of both events showed that, while organising touring events such as the FLUP may be more time-consuming than setting up Co-Creation workshops with a more steady focus on specific small communities, these events may benefit from a greater visibility which enables them to change national canons, pressure institutions into becoming more inclusive, produce new spaces for participation, generate new audiences and enable marginal voices to emerge and to be heard. Such events have the potential to attract significant public attention to urban and social margins and challenge stigmatising discourses about 'the periphery' perceived as areas of 'non-reading', places devoid of high culture. However, arts-based events that are not rooted in a specific community and do not rely on scholarly research and partnerships with academics and community activists are also more vulnerable due to their greater dependence on the organisers' individual efforts, charisma, availability, and commitment. Academic collaborators bring to Co-Creation projects not only symbolic legitimation and knowledge validation but also potential sources of funding and a greater degree of institutionalisation that can be key to make projects sustainable. Co-Creation, in return, needs to learn from the engagement of literature-based events with embodied knowledge and oral forms of expression which have been particularly prominent in FLUP's practice. This can help Co-Creation go further in the inclusion of Southern epistemologies in knowledge production.

Acknowledgments

The author gives her heartfelt thanks to Rachid Santaki (Dictée des Cités, Saint-Denis, France) and Julio Ludemir (FLUP, Rio de Janeiro, Brazil) without whose insight and comments this chapter could not have been completed.

References

Beaud, S. (2002) *80% au Bac ... et Après? Les Enfants de la Démocratisation Scolaire*, Paris: La Découverte.

Beaud, S. and Mauger, G. (2017) *Une Génération Sacrifiée? Jeunes des Classes Populaires dans la France Désindustrialisée*, Paris: Édition rue d'Ulm.

Boucher, A. (2019) 'Née à Argenteuil, la dictée pour tous a fait son entrée à l'Elysée', *Le Parisien*, available from http://www.leparisien.fr/val-d-oise-95/nee-a-argenteuil-la-dictee-pour-tous-a-fait-son-entree-a-l-elysee-26-04-2019-8061024.php [accessed 2 September 2019].

Brancato, R. (2017) 'Une 100ème "dictée des cités" à Bagnolet pour Rachid Santaki, le "Bernard Pivot du ghetto"', *France Bleu Paris*, 12 May 2017, available from https://www.francebleu.fr/infos/education/une-100eme-dictee-des-cites-bagnolet-pour-rachid-santaki-le-bernard-pivot-du-ghetto-1494609828 [accessed 10 August 2019].

Caillet, V. (2005) 'Le sentiment d'injustice chez les jeunes de banlieue' in M-M. Bertucci, and V. Houdart-Merot (eds) *Situations de Banlieue : Enseignement, Langue, Cultures*, Paris: INRP.

Casanova, P. (2007) *The World Republic of Letters*, Harvard: Harvard University Press.

de Sousa Santos, B. (2018) *The End of the Cognitive Empire*, Durham: Duke University Press.

Dictée Géante website, available from http://ladicteegeante.com [accessed 10 August 2019].

Dikeç, M. (2017) *Urban Rage: The Revolt of the Excluded*, New Haven: Yale University Press.

EFA (Education for All) (2002) *Global Education Monitoring Report, 2002*, Paris: UNESCO.

El Youssef, N. (2016) 'FLUPP literary festival for Rio's favelas returns for fifth edition in City of God', *Rio on Watch*, 21 November 2016, available from https://www.rioonwatch.org/?p=34069 [accessed 10 August 2019].

Failla, Z. (2016) *Retratos da Leitura no Brasil 4*, Rio de Janeiro: Instituto Pró-Livro.

Freire-Medeiros, B. (2013) *Touring Poverty*, Abingdon: Routledge.

Ghio, B. (2016) *Sans Fautes de Frappe*, Marseille: Le mot el le reste.

Heyward, E. (2017) 'New territories for literature in contemporary Brazil', *Arts and International Affairs*, 2(2), np, available from doi: 10.18278/aia.2.2.8.

Indio, C. (2019) 'Illiteracy in Brazil sinks to 6.8% in 2018', *Agenciabrasil*, 19 June 2019, available from http://agenciabrasil.ebc.com.br/en/educacao/noticia/2019-06/illiteracy-brazil-sinks-68–2018 [accessed 12 July 2019].

Ireland, T.D. (2008) 'Literacy in Brazil: from rights to reality', *International Review of Education*, 54(5–6): 713–32.

Lacerda, D.S. (2015) 'Rio de Janeiro and the divided state: analysing the political discourse on favelas', *Discourse and Society*, 26(1): 74–94.

Ludemir, J. (2019) Interview with the author, 17 August 2019.

Maameri, K. (2016) *Nos Plumes*, 83 minute documentary, self distributed.

Maddox, J.T. (2014) 'AfroReggae: "Antropofagia", sublimation, and intimate revolt in the "favela"', *Hispania*, 97(3): 463–76.

Mignolo, W. and Walsh, C.E. (2018) *On Decoloniality*, Durham: Duke University Press.

Mori, C. (2012) 'L'archipel invisible : L'écriture dans "les cultures de banlieue"', *Hommes et Migrations*, 1297: 68–76.

Mouffe, C. (2013) *Agonistics: Thinking The World Politically*, London and New York: Verso.

Pech, M.-E. (2017) '91% des Français lisent des livres', *Le Figaro*, 21 March 2017, available from http://www.lefigaro.fr/actualite-france/2017/03/21/01016-20170321ARTFIG00044-91-des-francais-lisent-des-livres.php [accessed 10 August 2019].

Perlman, J. (2013) *Favela: Four Decades of Living on the Edge of Rio de Janeiro*, Oxford: Oxford University Press.

Quijano, A. (2010) 'Coloniality and modernity/rationality', in W. Mignolo, and A. Escobar (eds) *Globalization and the Decolonial Option*, London and New York: Routledge, pp 22–32.

Rapport de l'Observatoire national des zones urbaines sensibles (2013) *Comité Interministériel des Villes*, available from https://www.ladocumentationfrancaise.fr/rapports-publics/134000865/index.shtml [accessed 12 September 2019].

Resende V.D.M. (2009) ' "It's not a matter of inhumanity": a critical discourse analysis of an apartment building circular on "homeless people"', *Discourse & Society*, 20(3): 363–79.

Rodrigues Mello, R. and Marini Braga, F. (2018) 'Schools as learning communities: an effective alternative for education and literacy in Brazil', *Frontiers in Education*, 3(114): 1–17.

Rosello, M. (1998) *Declining the Stereotype: Ethnicity and Representation in French Cultures*, Hanover and London: UP of New England.

Rosenwald, F. (2018) *L'Éducation Prioritaire, État des lieux, Note d'Information 2018/02*, Paris: Direction de l'Évaluation de la Prospective et de la Performance.

Santaki, R. (2019) Interview with the author, 10 August 2019.

Silverstein, P. and Tetreault, C. (2006) 'Postcolonial urban apartheid', *Social Science Research Council*, available from http://riotsfrance.ssrc.org/Silverstein_ Tetreault.

Tchumkam, H. (2015) *State Power, Stigmatization and Youth Resistance Culture in the French Banlieues*, Lanham: Lexington Books.

Tonani do Patrocínio, P.R. (2013) *Escritos à Margem. A presença de autores de periferia na cena literária brasileira*, Rio de Janeiro: Faperj.

Van Zanten, A. (2001) *L'École de la Périphérie : Scolarité et Segregation en Banlieue*, Paris: Presses Universitaires de France.

Yúdice, G. (2003) *The Expediency of Culture*, Durham: Duke University Press.

11

When Co-Creation meets Art for Social Change: the Street Beats Band

Juliet Carpenter

Introduction

The concept of Co-Creation has been interpreted in this volume from a variety of perspectives: approaches from the Global North and Global South, from the perspective of scholars working with artists and non-governmental organisations (NGOs) on Co-Creative projects, as well as from the angle of non-profit organisations, instigating projects that bring together artists and communities to Co-Create knowledge and new understandings in marginalised neighbourhoods. This present chapter draws on work by the author on the interface between two conceptual frames: the notion of Co-Creation (Carpenter and Horvath, 2018 ; Carpenter et al, 2021 forthcoming) and its intersection with the 'Art for Social Change' movement (Marcuse and Marcuse, 2011), exploring the role that creative arts collaborations can have in knowledge creation to effectuate social change.

The use of the term Co-Creation in this chapter aligns with that set out in the Introduction to this volume (Chapter 1): that is, the collaboration of a constellation of different actors (artists, local residents, researchers, community groups and other stakeholders) in cultural production, to address societal challenges such as marginalisation and stigmatisation (see Pahl et al, 2017 for a discussion of academic–artist collaborations). However, as the chapter will illustrate, the boundaries between these different actors are fluid, given that the notion of Co-Creation challenges the rigid binaries between 'academic' and 'non-academic' participants, and the boundaries between professional and non-professional artists. Wrapped up with this fluidity of roles is the way in which the balance of power plays out and shifts between different participants in a Co-Creation project.

This chapter seeks to demonstrate that, while the methodology of Co-Creation holds critical potential as a tool to challenge stereotypes and marginalisation, it nevertheless operates within the structural constraints of deeply embedded power hierarchies and hegemonic discourses that dominate received narratives. Drawing on the example of a Co-Creative project, the Street Beats Band (SBB), a community-based percussion band in Vancouver, Canada, the chapter argues that such projects have potential to build community, empower participants and effectuate change in daily lives. However, it also cautions against framing Co-Creation as a catch-all panacea for social exclusion and marginalisation, given the differentials of power that thread through urban society, related to class, gender, race and postcolonialism.

Conceptual frames: Co-Creation and Art for Social Change

As other chapters have demonstrated, there are a number of different interpretations of the notion of Co-Creation, as understood in the context of this volume. Chapter 1 draws up a general definition of the concept, which involves the Co-Creation of knowledge and understanding around marginalisation, through the collaboration of residents, artists, researchers and urban stakeholders in creative arts practice. One of the key components is the disruption of existing hierarchies of knowledge production and social power, bringing together alternative perspectives through collaborative creative practice in order to interrupt traditional thinking and challenge stereotypes.

Co-Creation also necessitates a fluidity of functions, blurring the boundaries between traditional knowledge producers (researchers) and creative practitioners (artists), as well as collaborating with others who may have no previous association with either group (Haviland, 2017). This duality of roles is paramount in the process of Co-Creation, involving crossing disciplinary boundaries, exchanging skills and understanding, and collaborating with people from different backgrounds. Co-Creation involves crossing borders, so-called 'fuzzy boundaries' (Gubrium et al, 2014) between professional and non-professional artists, between researchers and residents as knowledge producers, traversing borders which are by implication wrapped up with power hierarchies, both within the project and more broadly at a community or societal level. The hybridity inherent in Co-Creation implies the need to balance interests, a mediation of alternative understandings and ambiguities which need to be negotiated by those involved in creative production.

There are crossovers between the notion of Co-Creation and the field of 'Art for Social Change' (ASC) (Marcuse and Marcuse, 2011). ASC can be defined as: 'Art that is created collectively by groups of people (who may not self-identify as artists) about what matters to them, through arts or dialogic processes that are facilitated by an artist or group of artists' (Yassi et al, 2016). It is more focused on creative production for social change rather than on knowledge production and engagement with researchers. The key focus of ASC is, therefore, the artistic production and the social change that may result from it. Co-Creation, on the other hand, emphasises knowledge production, as well as a strong relationship between researcher and artist in that process, with the creative output acting as a vehicle for knowledge production. However, the two processes have distinct similarities. Both approaches involve professional and non-professional artists in creative collaboration to explore social issues and engage with participants to find new ways of seeing and understanding their worlds. There are also parallels in relation to the power dynamics at play, both visible and hidden, that need to be addressed within a reflective framework of ethical practice.

Projects harnessing ASC can be driven by different agendas. In exploring participation in art projects, Bishop (2006) argues that there are three main motivations for community engagement in the arts: first, the desire to create empowered and active subjects through arts practice, who are then catalysed to determine their own social and political realities; second, the desire to de-hierarchise art, to share or hand over authorship from the artist to the community; and third, to develop stronger social and community bonds, through 'a collective elaboration of meaning'(Bishop, 2006: 12). ASC projects are driven mainly by the first motive, with the overall objective to allow participants to take control of their social and political worlds.

However, with both Co-Creation and ASC, it is important to engage with the critical debates around the use of arts in social change and community-engaged practice. Some argue that creative practice should not be reduced to a tool to achieve social outcomes, but rather should be seen as a legitimate end in itself (Gray, 2007). Others point to the tension between what is defined as 'quality art' in traditional arts practice, versus the more flexible standards that are applied to community-based arts involved in Co-Creation and ASC (Belfiore, 2002). For example, in community-based projects, there can be friction between the emphasis on excellence of the outcome as assessed through the criteria of aesthetics versus the value of the creative process itself, the artistic journey, and the value that this brings to participants as an end in itself. These debates are important to be aware of when considering Co-Creation and ASC projects and will be explored further in the context of the Street Beats Band, a 'found object' percussion band in Vancouver.

In relation to the methodology, the chapter draws on a number of different sources of data, including documentary evidence, the funding application for the Street Beats Band project, other publicly available sources and a total of 15 in-depth interviews with key stakeholders and project participants which were completed in 2018–19. These included community and professional musicians, 'binners', non-profit organisations involved in the project and representatives from the municipal funder. A total of five semi-structured participant feedback surveys were also completed after the final concert performances in November 2017, which were used in the analysis to feed in to an assessment of the project that was completed by the author in July 2019. The next section provides a background to the project and the constellation of collaborators involved. The chapter then explores the 'materialities' of the Street Beats Band project and the issue of power relations and then draws conclusions on the possibilities for Co-Creation projects such as the Street Beats Band to address social inequalities.

Street Beats background

This chapter is based on the author's collaboration with the not-for-profit organisation 'Instruments of Change', which is based in Vancouver, Canada. Instruments of Change was set up in 2008 by professional flautist and academic Dr Laura Barron. The organisation aims to empower people to become 'instruments of transformative change' in their own lives (Instruments of Change, nd). It leads a variety of Co-Creative, socially engaged projects that work with marginalised communities, both in the Global North and Global South, using musical expression as a vehicle for change.

Much of the work of Instruments of Change is situated at the interface of the two conceptual strands of Co-Creation (as defined in this volume) and ASC: that is, broadly speaking an artistic engagement that impacts social change. This broad definition can take a variety of expressions with different combinations of professional and community participation, but in general, Instruments of Change categorises their projects in one of three ways: (1) work that is community-created and community-presented; (2) work that is community-created and professionally presented; or (3) work that is community- and professionally created, and community- and professionally presented. According to Instruments of Change, when work is Co-Created with the community and professional artists (models 2 and 3), this tends to generate greater social change, with a more sophisticated art output, greater levels of expressivity, and potentially wider audiences, than if the work is created and presented solely by the community.

One of the projects led by Instruments of Change from 2015–17 was the 'Street Beats Band' (SBB) project, which aimed to bring together different communities in Vancouver to rehearse and perform a pre-composed percussion work at the New Music Festival. The Festival was organised by the International Society for Contemporary Music (ISCM) in Vancouver in November 2017. The Street Beats Band project falls under the third model, as the work was both community- and professionally created and presented.

The Street Beats Band was a two-year project that aimed to bring together a constellation of different actors, including Vancouver's 'binner' community, professional musicians and other community members, to collaboratively Co-Create and perform a large-scale, specially commissioned percussion piece, within the framework of an international music festival (Community Arts Grant Application Form, submitted by Instruments of Change to Vancouver City Council, 2017, unpublished).

The project developed in two phases and involved multiple communities. The first phase ran from September 2015 to November 2016 (Year 1) and started by engaging members of Vancouver's binner community and paying them to source recyclable materials to be converted into musical instruments. The binners are Vancouver's recycling community, who collect redeemable containers and other materials from garbage bins across the city to generate income through refunds received at recycling depots. Instruments of Change partnered with the Binners' Project, a non-profit advocacy organisation that coordinates the binners' waste collection throughout the city on a weekly basis, to work with a group of binners to source materials, clean them up and repurpose them as the Street Beats Band's percussion instruments. These ranged from simple buckets, cans and pans to 'created' percussion instruments, such as a shaker made from a tennis ball container half-filled with quinoa.

The project then recruited 40 community members in four different locations across Vancouver to rehearse and perform on these instruments as part of the Street Beats Band. Following six weeks of rehearsals, this urban percussion community band gave two performances at the Roundhouse Community Centre in Vancouver in November 2016, as part of the Modulus Festival run by the not-for-profit organisation 'Music on Main'. This first phase of the overall project was exploratory, investigating the different sounds and rhythms that could be achieved by the four community groups using the 'found object' percussion instruments, exploring the levels of rhythm complexity that the community were able to sustain, and possible teaching strategies to help the players learn the work.

The second phase (Year 2) tied in with Vancouver's hosting of the ISCM World New Music Festival in November 2017, which was also led by 'Music on Main'. The Vancouver-based composer, James Maxwell, was commissioned to write a piece for the Festival, and following Year 1 of the project, he subsequently incorporated some of the rhythms and motifs that were created during that first phase into his new composition, 'Eight or nine, six or seven'. He also accompanied the binners on alley walks and collected soundscapes, both of which also informed the compositional process.

Some 20 community participants then worked in three 'pods' or 'mini-bands', each led by a facilitator, to learn the specially commissioned work over six weeks; the piece was then performed in two shows at the ISCM Festival, on the 'found object' percussion instruments before an international audience. The Street Beats Band were also joined by a nine-piece professional brass ensemble from the Music on Main All-Star Band,including six trombones, a tuba and two professional percussionists, with the whole composition being mixed in with recordings of sonic urban soundscapes (for example, traffic sounds, birds, and rain) that the composer had sampled in the city. The key components of the Street Beats Band project are presented in Figure 11.1.

However, although labels are used to categorise the collaborators (musician, composer, facilitator, and so on), in reality and in line with a Co-Creative approach, the boundaries were blurred between roles. The instigator, Laura Barron was also an academic, a musician and facilitator. The community participants performed alongside professional musicians in the International Music Festival, challenging traditional views of the profile of a 'professional' musician. Furthermore, the composition itself was also Co-Created in response to the community participants, as it was rewritten by the composer in light of the community's initial experimentation with the binners' found instruments, thus disrupting the hierarchy between professional composer and community musician, through the incorporation of the community's inputs into the composition. Similarly, during rehearsals, the professional musicians, composer and conductor all needed to play not only a leadership role, but also a facilitating and empowering

Figure 11.1: Key contributors to the Street Beats Band project.

• **Instruments of Change:** The project champion, a not-for-profit organisation that runs community arts programmes and aims to empower people to use the arts, and music in particular, to promote transformative change in their lives. Led by Executive Director, Dr Laura Barron, who is a professional flautist and was a full-time academic for ten years, and who now dedicates her time to Instruments of Change.
• **Music on Main:** A non-profit organisation that programmes music events in the city and was the lead on Vancouver's bid to host the ISCM New World Music Festival in 2017. Led by David Pay.
• **The composer:** Vancouver-based composer, James Maxwell.
• **The Binner Community:** Engaged through the Binners' Project, a number of binners were employed to collect or 'curate' the instruments at the beginning of the SBB project.
• **Participants from the community-at-large:** Recruited through four community centres in different neighbourhoods throughout the city in Year 1, and through further music-related networks in Year 2.
• **Facilitators:** Three professional musicians, employed as facilitators to guide the community participants in their learning and practice and to lead the performances.
• **Conductor:** Professional conductor, Janna Sailor.
• **Music on Main All-Star Band:** Professional musicians who accompanied the community Street Beats Band with brass and additional percussion sections, in the two performances at the ISCM World New Music Festival, November 2017.
• **Audience members:** Those who attended the Modulus Festival in November 2016 and the ISCM Festival in November 2017.
• **City of Vancouver:** The funder of the project, through the Community Arts Grant Programme.

---

role. There are no rigid binaries between the roles of researcher, artist, non-profit organisation and community participant, rather there are a set of complex, layered and shifting experiences that overlap between them. These are fluid categories where individuals can pass from one to another according to their role in a particular situation.

Co-Creation through the Street Beats Band

Co-Creation through the Street Beats Band started with the involvement of the binners in curating the percussion instruments at the beginning of the project. Binners are very much a part of Vancouver's downtown community, a constant presence on the street, collecting redeemable containers from bins to sustain their livelihoods and divert waste from landfill. Yet their status in the city is marginal, often conflated with begging, and stigmatised due to the nature of their work. The SBB instigator, Laura Barron, built up relations with the binner community over more than a year, to create trust and confidence, and to "gain an appreciation for their expertise, and really humanising them, and getting to know them as people, and being privileged to witness their work" (interview, 31 October

2018). A number of binners were paid to collect materials that could be curated as percussion instruments and were accompanied on their alley walks to collect materials by Laura Barron, and the composer James Maxwell, who observed how they listened to the city, and how they sifted, sorted and selected materials (such as buckets, cans and pans) that could be repurposed as instruments. In this way, the binners themselves contributed to the Co-Creation of the composition, not only through providing the instruments but also through giving the composer insights into their perspectives on the city, which also fed into the composition (Figure 11.2).

The very act of paying the binners for their time had a significant impact on their self-esteem, as it demonstrated the value of their work and an appreciation of their knowledge of the city and their skills in sourcing materials. They were proud to present the materials that they had found on the alley walks. It was also an engagement that involved planning beyond the immediate week ahead, which is the normal timescale of the Binners' Project. Many binners find it challenging to think beyond the coming week ahead, due to complex issues of mental health, addiction or inadequate housing. Their involvement in the project was longer term, stretching over a month, so it challenged participants to think beyond the immediate week and to project themselves forward and plan ahead.

Figure 11.2: The binners curating instruments.

Source: Lani Brunn.

In fact, it was anticipated at the beginning of the project that the binners would be involved much more closely throughout the two years, including taking part in the final performance, which was anticipated as being a 'Binners' Symphony'. However, this longer-term engagement proved unworkable, given the difficult lives that many binners lead, working long and exhausting hours, and not being able to commit to a long-term project. One of the binners was more closely involved, in both curating instruments, attending rehearsals and performing in the first year show, but ill health prevented him from continuing into the second year. So, while the binners were an integral part of the SBB, through Co-Creating the instruments, their absence in the final performance meant that the public audience was not fully aware of their involvement and were not fully challenged about their preconceptions of the binner community.

The final performance, however, did involve a wide range of some 20 participants, from a variety of neighbourhoods in the city, and from different backgrounds, cultures and generations (see Figure 11.3). The experience gave participants a strong sense of community related to the project, in a supportive atmosphere – as the conductor noted: "The little boys would be helping the grandmas with their rhythms" (interview, 14 November 2018) – and helped to build confidence among participants. One facilitator appreciated "the different inputs that different walks of life could bring to the group" (interview, 7 February 2019). Another participant noted that: 'Making music together is a one-of-a-kind bonding experience. People I considered strangers just weeks ago have become a part of me' (Campbell, 2017). Respondents commented that the strength of the community created through participating in the project was an important outcome of their involvement.

Figure 11.3: The Street Beats Band performance, November 2017.

Source: Jan Gates.

Although the Street Beats Band was not focused on community participants gaining a voice in a situation where they may have felt marginalised, as with other ASC projects, it did open up other possibilities, such as the opportunity to play alongside professional musicians, with other benefits of confidence building, the discipline of rehearsals, the focus and time management required, and collaborative skills of working in a group.

Additionally for the binners, further opportunities also opened up from the SBB – to be involved in a parallel project run by Instruments of Change in local schools, speaking to school children about repurposing waste as part of their environmental education class. The binners were empowered as experts, paid to share their expertise in recycling in a school setting, normally an environment from which they are excluded. This also contributed to the destigmatisation of the binners in the eyes of the children and school community, where direct contact with individual binners helped to broaden the children's understanding of the binner community, and their value in society.

For the audience, the performance challenged them to question their preconceived ideas about what community engagement can achieve. The 300 or so audience members over two days were made up of Festival participants, composers and performers from around the world, as well as friends and family of the Band, who were all exposed to the fusion of ages, cultures and backgrounds in the Street Beats Band. They witnessed the high standard of musical ability that is possible with community engagement in the classical music world and opened up their minds to the possibilities of such Co-Creative approaches. A number of audience members provided informal feedback on the achievement of working at such a high level artistically, while also promoting a participatory approach. As one audience member expressed: "It was one of the most successful instances I've seen of combining professional artists with community artists in a truly meaningful way ... the two halves were really co-dependent and integrated" (interview, 14 February 2019).

The project also destabilised accepted thinking of what a musical instrument is, both for the audience and the community participants, in relation to the materiality of the 'found object' instruments. As the instigator Laura Barron commented:

"It shifted paradigms a bit, in relation to their imagining what an instrument can be, and how accessible music making can be, how it can be right at their fingertips, that they don't need to go to the Conservatory, they don't need to buy an expensive instrument, that their voices and their found instruments can make music." (Interview, 31 October 2018)

Individuals benefit from participating in art, because of its potential for learning, emancipation and empowerment (Bacqué and Biewener, 2013). The SBB achieved these outcomes for the participants, but the Co-Creation process goes beyond individual outcomes of community participation in art, to Co-Create new knowledge about places or communities, which challenges previously held views. In this case, although the binners were not as fully involved as anticipated, their association with the project contributed to confront audience views about community-based art and what can be achieved through community engagement in creative production. As an audience member noted: "Too often, I find, the community element could be eliminated without necessarily having an impact on the final presentation. But this wasn't the case with that [the SBB] at all" (interview, 14 February 2019).

These border situations unsettle audiences with new ways of seeing and understanding. The SBB drew on the binners' life experiences in border situations, blurring the boundaries between art and social action. By performing the piece with community participants at an international music festival, the process was also destabilising conventional views about who is 'a musician' and who has the right to be labelled as 'a musician'. In many ways, therefore, the SBB project can be seen as Co-Creation, as it crossed borders, disrupted concepts and disciplines, and questioned existing thinking.

Confronting power differentials in Co-Creation

As Matarasso notes (2019: 107), 'inequalities of power are created in the act of co-creation'. This arises for a number of reasons. The first relates to the level of skill, knowledge, experience and confidence of professional artists (musicians in this case), compared to non-professional community artists, which inevitably places the community participants in an unequal position. The second reason is connected to the power attached to the role of the instigator, who is the hub of the Co-Creation project, connected to all components, ranging from the funding body through to the artists, community participants and beyond. This gives them access to knowledge that underpins their authority in the Co-Creation process. While it is important to have a strong instigator and leader in Co-Creation projects, this concentration of knowledge also brings with it potentially significant command over other participants, a situation which should be acknowledged and negotiated from the beginning and throughout the Co-Creation exercise to integrate strategies for power sharing into the process.

In the case of the Street Beats Band, the instigator Laura Barron was conscious of her privileged role, as the leader of the project, as a professional musician, and as a facilitator. Community participants acknowledged her grounded style, approachability and levelling manner, which contributed to breaking down power hierarchies in the project. However, she did need to make difficult decisions about whether to include certain participants from Year 1 in the Year 2 performance year, due to the mismatch between the skills of some participants and the technicalities of the composed piece. It was felt that some participants would struggle to learn the complicated rhythms that were needed to play the work to a performance level, and so they were passed over in Year 2. She expressed her "deep regrets about having had to make the executive decision to exclude some participants from Phase Two of the project. However, my motivations for making such difficult decisions are always in the interest of what is best for the greater good" (personal communication, 18 September 2019).

This raises issues that are frequently debated in relation to socially engaged arts, that is, the relative importance of the product artistically versus the value of the process to the participants, such as the importance of social relations and dialogical interactions. How important is the quality of the final artistic product, in this case the musical outcome, when the process taken to get there has the potential for significant and long-lasting impacts on the community members involved? While in general, Instruments of Change aims to valorise both the process and the final product equally, in this case, due to the connection with the wider ISCM Festival and the newly commissioned percussion piece, the delivery of the final musical product at the ISCM Festival was given priority, although this meant excluding certain Year 1 participants from continuing into the second year. This tension between the process and the product, between relational outcomes and object-based outcomes, is one that many Co-Creative projects grapple with while trying to bypass binary thinking that positions artistic outcomes against social ones. In each case, the aim is to achieve a balance that is most appropriate in the particular context.

Power relations in a Co-Creation project are also complicated by the issue of who gets paid for their participation and why. Payment to professional artists for their involvement is rarely questioned, but payment to non-professional artists is less common, partly due to funding constraints. In the Street Beats Band, the binners were paid for their time to collect materials and curate them as instruments. They were paid as a way of demonstrating the value of their knowledge and know-how of the city, its alleys and waste materials, in the context of a project that aims to destigmatise a marginalised group in Vancouver society. The professional musicians from Music on Main were paid for their involvement in the final performance, as were the instigator of the whole project, the composer, the facilitators and the conductor. The community participants were seen as volunteers and were not paid. However, if the community participants are recognised as musicians, equally implicated in the act of Co-Creation, there are strong arguments from an ethical and power perspective for them to be paid as well. And yet some would argue that financial remuneration is not necessarily the most appropriate means of compensating community participants for their involvement, given the potential for disempowerment and a sense of obligation if payment is made in exchange for participation. Others argue that community members benefit from participation in non-monetary ways through personal development, capacity building and other skills, so payment is neither necessary nor appropriate. In the Street Beats Band, community members were provided with free food at every rehearsal and refreshments in the Green Room at the two performances, in addition to the 'free' skills-building education they received. These complexities around payment are often resolved by default through a lack of available funds to remunerate all community participants, but they nevertheless raise important questions about fairness and equality of treatment in a Co-Creation project, issues of reciprocity, and the perceived value of different participants' contributions.

Co-Creation aims to disrupt traditional thinking and challenge stereotypes, ultimately to bring about societal change. But these are grand objectives, which are not necessarily achievable through small-scale projects. Many Co-Creation projects achieve significant impacts at individual and community scales. In the Street Beats Band, individual impacts at the personal level were identified through participants gaining skills, confidence and knowledge. At the community scale, the rehearsal groups came together as a whole, shared ideas and resources, and developed trust through their communal experience of practising and performing together. However, wider social transformation is harder to identify, not only because it is a long-term process and the project was a small scale intervention, but also because of the difficulty of accomplishing such change, within a framework of structural constraints that limit wider social transformation related to gender, class, race and postcolonialism. The involvement of the binners in the broader project could have contributed to individual and societal change, but the constraints of their difficult lives meant that they could not and/or did not participate more fully. This case therefore illustrates the potential of Co-Creation to build community and to confront barriers and prejudice, but tempered with a realism of the power of structural constraints that limit deep social change.

Conclusion

Co-Creation aims to be a creative and democratic process through which different voices come together in a common artistic endeavour that brings participants into creative contact, and contributes to their discovering, understanding and sharing experiences. The Street Beats Band brought together the notion of Co-Creation with principles of ASC to empower participants and challenge traditional views of community-engaged practice by marrying professional and non-professional musicians in an international professional setting.

Overall, the project adhered to ASC principles, while also drawing on elements of Co-Creation as defined in this volume, by bringing together different stakeholders to address issues of marginalisation, and emphasising community and empowerment. Although researcher engagement and knowledge creation were not explicit aims of the SBB, one of the outcomes was participants' enhanced understanding of different perspectives and world views of those who took part, particularly through the engagement of the binner community. The project reached significant achievements in the final show at the ISCM New Music Festival, with a high-level work performed mainly by community musicians, some with no formal musical training, playing on repurposed object instruments that had been curated by binners. The binners' connection with the project helped to challenge the community participants' views of the binner community, although as the binners themselves did not perform at the final New Music Festival, the impact on the audience's perception of this marginalised community was more limited.

This case study illustrates that a Co-Creative process such as the Street Beats Band project can build community, as well as confront conventional thinking and challenge ideas and expectations. Participants came together to collaborate and create music together, to make sense of and explore their worlds. The Street Beats Band provided an arena for building voices, confidence, trust and space for dialogue between different groups. But, as the chapter has illustrated, within the Co-Creation process there are inevitable inequalities of power that risk creating dominant and subordinate relations, when professional and non-professional artists collaborate, and when the necessary 'instigator' is required to initiate, lead and make decisions for the project. As Laura Barron commented: "I am well aware of the limitations of this work, and recognise it as an incomplete vehicle for social change" (personal communication, 18 September 2019). Tensions and dilemmas embedded in Co-Creation are unavoidable, due to different visions, interests, and inevitable power hierarchies. These issues should be acknowledged, addressed and negotiated by those involved.

What this chapter has argued is that Co-Creative projects offer critical potential to catalyse individual and collective impacts, with community participants benefiting in a myriad of ways from the creative and collective process of artmaking. These benefits include participants' feeling of achievement, a sense of community and communal identity, and building cross-generational and cross-cultural understanding. However, at the wider societal level, changes are necessarily more limited. While impacts can be seen at the individual and community level, the power of Co-Creative or ASC projects to address some of the deep-seated societal challenges is more limited. As 'incomplete vehicles for social change', as Laura Barron remarked, they cannot dismantle the structural forces that underpin inequalities, but they do have the capacity to impact on the people who can trouble those structural forces, to question inequalities related to gender, class, race and postcolonialism, and challenge societal inequities through the process of Co-Creation.

Funding acknowledgement

This chapter was written with support from the European Union's Horizon 2020 research and innovation programme under the Marie Skłodowska-Curie grant agreement no 749154 (SURGE: Social Sustainability and Urban Regeneration Governance: An International Perspective).

References

Bacqué, M.-H. and Biewener, C. (2013) *L'Empowerment: Une Pratique Émancipatrice?*, Paris: Éditions La Découverte.

Belfiore, E. (2002) 'Art as a means of alleviating social exclusion: does it really work? A critique of instrumental cultural policies and social impact studies in the UK', *International Journal of Cultural Policy*, 8(1): 91–106.

Bishop, C. (2006) 'Participation', in I. Blazwich (ed) *Documents of Contemporary Art*, London: Whitechapel Gallery.

Campbell, T. (2017) *Instruments of Change: Community Sounds in Contemporary Classical New Music*, blog post, [online] 11 November 2017, available from https://tenthousanddaysofgratitude.com/index. php/2017/11/04/instruments-of-change-community-sounds-in-contemporary-classical-new-music/ [accessed 19 September 2019].

Carpenter, J. and Horvath, C. (2018) 'Co-Creation: addressing urban stigmatization, building inclusive cities', Paper presented at the *Urban Affairs Association Annual Congress*, Toronto, 6 April 2018.

Carpenter, J., Horvath, C. and Spencer, B. (2021 forthcoming) 'Co-Creation as an agonistic practice in the favela of Santa Marta, Rio de Janeiro', *Urban Studies*.

Gray, C. (2007) 'Commodification and instrumentality in cultural policy', *International Journal of Cultural Policy*, 13(2): 203–15.

Gubrium, A., Hill, H. and Flicker, S. (2014) 'A situated practice of ethics for visual and digital methods in public health research and practice: a focus on digital storytelling', *American Journal of Public Health,* 104(9): 1606–14.

Haviland, M. (2017) *Side by Side? Community Art and the Challenge of Co-Creativity*, Abingdon: Routledge.

Instruments of Change (nd) *About Us*, available at http://www.instrumentsofchange.org/index.html, [accessed 18 September 2019].

Marcuse, J. and Marcuse, R. (2011) 'Art for Social Change: a call for partnership', in C. McLean and R. Kelly (eds) *Creative Arts in Research for Community and Cultural Change*, Calgary: Detselig Enterprises Ltd.

Matarasso, F. (2019) *A Restless Art: How Participation Won, and Why It Matters*, London: Calouste Gulbenkian Foundation, UK Branch.

Pahl, K., Escott, H., Graham, H., Marwood, K., Pool, S. and Ravetz, A. (2017) 'What is the role of the artists in interdisciplinary collaborative projects with universities and communities?' in K. Facer and K. Pahl (eds) *Valuing Interdisciplinary Collaborative Research,* Bristol: Policy Press.

Yassi, A., Spiegel, J.B., Lockhart, K., Fels, L., Boydell, K. and Marcuse, J. (2016) 'Ethics in community-university-artist partnered research: tensions, contradictions and gaps identified in an "Arts for social change" project', *Journal of Academic Ethics*, 14(3): 199–220.

12

Co-Creation and social transformation: a tough issue for research

Jim Segers

Introduction

This chapter discusses the role of research institutions and researchers in social transformation in an urban context. From the perspective of City Mine(d), an initiator of social change processes, it looks at the ambitions of academic research methodologies like Co-Creation to generate knowledge together with communities and stakeholders.

The first section outlines the argument. Section two describes the evolution many citizen and community organisations have made from protest to proposal. The third section focuses on a practical approach to social transformation inspired by the work of Vermaak (2012) and Orlikowski (1996). Section four is dedicated to the specific tactics for social change developed by City Mine(d). The last section deals with the, at times, ambiguous role of research institutions and researchers, as observer-scientist versus agent-activist, or as producers of knowledge versus initiators of change, in social transformation. A conclusion revisits the main ideas of this chapter.

The argument

In September 2019, the department of Political Sciences of UNAM (National Autonomous University of Mexico) organised a Co-Creation seminar in Mexico City. During the session titled 'Citizen participation and socio-political dynamics', it was argued that grassroots organisations and citizen initiatives are increasingly shifting 'from protest to proposal', no longer aiming to block developments, but formulating alternatives, analysing what is at stake and coming up with better ways of meeting needs. The shift from opposing to proposing has brought grassroots organisations closer to more institutional actors like governments, businesses and industry, civil society organisations, and also research institutions. This raises an interesting question: are institutionalised or informal partners better positioned to initiate social transformation?

The *rapprochement* of these actors has blurred the traditional boundaries between social transformation and social research. Campbell and Vanderhoven (2016) refer to the public benefit of co-producing research, and this volume describes Co-Creation as a methodology for generating creative outputs and knowledge that are relevant to the local community. While this is welcomed by all involved, one should be careful not to confuse social research as a scientific practice with social transformation. Social transformation in this chapter refers to the practice of bringing about change in issues that cannot be solved in a traditional manner. Following Vermaak (2012), these are referred to here as 'tough issues'. These issues are multifactor – knowledge we have about them is incomplete or even contradictory and interconnected, multiactor – many stakeholders and agencies are involved, and multiscalar – they often play at local as well as global levels.

City Mine(d) tends to involve five groups of stakeholders. They are: the government; businesses; civil society (NGOs, non-governmental organisations, that have a relationship with the state); citizens and grassroots organisations; and research institutions. None of these stakeholders has the legitimacy to start a process dealing with tough issues, as each one can be considered suspect by all others: government for consolidating power, business for the profit motive, civil society as an extension of the status quo, and citizens for being occupied only by expressing grievances.

Researchers and research institutions are not considered independent either. On the one hand, a research agenda is deeply embedded in an institutional framework that comes with framing and with an agenda different from the (tough) issue in question. More importantly, academia has a status and adhered power that distorts horizontal or egalitarian decision making. In response to this, and referring to the work of Simmel (1950), City Mine(d) defends a position of 'third actor', or in Simmel's words *'tertius gaudens'*. While Simmel limits himself to three-actor relationships, the broker roles he describes can also be identified in larger networks: the 'mediator' is an equal to or stands above the others; 'divide and rule' is someone who creates conflict to gain a dominant position; the *'tertius gaudens'* on the other hand acts as a gateway between different actors and derives resources (or in case of City Mine(d) stakeholder commitment) from occupying this pivotal position. City Mine(d) proposes to produce a creative answer to a small part of the 'tough issue' at hand. In doing so, it is considered insignificant but also not a threat by the stakeholders. The organisation has no resources to contribute, yet can be considered a potential ally by every other stakeholder. Because it is powerless, it is considered harmless. In addition, City Mine(d) often refrains from promoting a brand image and for each tough issue creates a new identity.

In the light of these remarks about power hierarchies within collaborative projects, the following section will illustrate the shift from protest to proposal as it was experienced in the course of a project in Barcelona initiated by City Mine(d). The chapter will then attempt to set out a perspective on social transformation through the lens of tough issues. Next, the approach of prototyping and its tactic of *tertius gaudens* will be described, and finally some thoughts will be expressed about the relationship between initiatives like City Mine(d) and research and academia in general, and with a methodology like Co-Creation in particular.

From protest to proposal

> *City Mine(d) es proposa recuperar aquest espai com una cuina urbana emergent oberta a tot tipus d'iniciatives que retornin l'espai públic als habitants de la ciutat.*

> City Mine(d) intends to recover this space as an urban kitchen emerging open to all kinds of initiatives to return the public space to the inhabitants of the city.
> (Quaderns de arquitectura i urbanisme, 2006; author's translation)

City Mine(d) is a design practice that was set up in Brussels in 1997. Over the years it has assumed many guises, from 'production house for art interventions in public space' via 'economic development agency' to 'neighbourhood activists in some twenty neighbourhoods throughout Europe' (City Mine(d), 2016). Yet, there are two recurrent themes: on the one hand there is 'the making of things': creation of artefacts that serve their own ends, while also serving as an opportunity to bring disparate – at times even adversarial – parties together. On the other hand, a second, connected, theme has to do with the just and cohesive city. While not well placed to directly increase the socioeconomic well-being or political emancipation of citizens, City Mine(d) does aim to improve the lives of people. Inspired by the work of Nussbaum

(1999), among others, City Mine(d) has become convinced of the view expressed by Nussbaum that 'choice matters. You might have the opportunity to eat a nutritious diet, though you might choose to eat a lousy diet. What matters is the opportunity' (quoted in Adams, 2017).

This 'equal worth of persons as choosers' (Nussbaum, 1999: 57) – which asks, 'what are the individuals of the group or country able to do and be' (1999: 34) – seems dialectically opposed to the need for communities to self-organise in order to overcome barriers to development (see Ostrom, 1990). However, it is precisely this tension between individual liberty and 'the collective power needed to reshape the processes of urbanisation' (Harvey 2008: 23) that fuels the work of City Mine(d). And not just City Mine(d). Research methodologies such as Co-Creation, which aim to combine artistic expression (often a very individualistic endeavour) with community interests, will at some point unavoidably have to deal with it.

As with other similar practices that emerged in the late 1990s, City Mine(d) has a background in environmental, peace and movements in support of the Global South, with roots in direct action. Many of these groups were informed by the 1960s civil rights movements and the anti-nuclear movement of the 1980s, with practices that used non-violent strategies like sit-ins, occupations of buildings or mass demonstrations. More interestingly, these practices used governance principles that are still relevant: horizontal decisionmaking, anti-authoritarianism and self-organisation. Even a research methodology like Co-Creation can aspire to these principles. This chapter will deal with the extent to which this is possible from within academia later.

From its inception, City Mine(d) focused on the city as its *locus operandi* as well as subject of its work. The reasons for action were struggles of social justice manifest through a lack of green and public space, loss of affordable housing, gender imbalance, urban transport and mobility. In more general terms it resisted the top-down development of cities in which planning was left to engineers, who organise space and other resources in the most efficient way. According to Healey (1997: 5), the planning system was designed assuming:

> ... that the state could "take charge" and "control" spatial organisation and the location of development. ... Whereas the economic planning tradition has been dominated by economists and political philosophers, the arena of physical development planning was shaped for many years by

engineers and architects, and by utopian images of what cities could be like. (Healey, 1997)

However, the regeneration of post-industrial areas required financial resources no longer available to public authorities. In light of the macroeconomic difficulties of the 1970s and 1980s, governments cut back expenditure programmes and relied more heavily on private initiatives. Moulaert (2005) in Singocom, concluded:

> The current policy shifts occurring, at all government scales, towards narrowly defined economic and efficiency criteria, a reliance on real estate development for urban regeneration, the privatisation or externalisation of service provision, a re-conquest of public spaces by either private businesses or technocratic local governments are increasingly pushing civil society "change agents" out of the social scene. (Moulaert, 2005)

In the introduction to City Mine(d)'s 'Bruxel' Conference, Swyngedouw (2003) warned that the consequences of market-led urban development would be 'mechanisms of exclusion, social polarisation and diminishing citizenship'. A decade later, European cities are still, unsuccessfully, trying to reconcile claims of social justice and redistribution with dependence on market and private investment.

A shift can now be noticed in the relationship between the powers-that-be and those, like City Mine(d), who try to change cities for the better. Here there is a distinction between 'tactic' and 'strategy'. This chapter uses 'tactic' in the sense defined by Michel de Certeau in *L'Invention du Quotidien* (1980), as opposed to 'strategy'. 'Strategy' is the realm of the powerful, who plan cities and are able to impose a vision, while in de Certeau's reading, 'tactic' is an adaptation of the powerless to the context provided by the strategy of the powerful. He refers to it both as '*résistance*' and as '*bricolage*'. It is precisely between these two terms that the shift is taking place: where the urban struggles mentioned previously were initially mainly forms of resistance against development, the author agrees with the participants of the UNAM seminar that practitioners are trying to change developments by proposing alternatives. In this sense *bricolage*, in its meaning of 'do-it-yourself', describes a non-professional, do-it-yourself way of urban planning and policy making. This happens in regeneration schemes, but also in urban governance and even the management of urban natural resources. This chapter will illustrate the shift from *résistance* to *bricolage* with a process City Mine(d) initiated in Barcelona in 2004, and which itself moved from opposing the development plan of the metropolitan government to *bricoler* a veritable alternative for a specific site.

In the year 2000, Barcelona's metropolitan government accepted the 22@ plan, an urban regeneration scheme aimed at transforming the industrial area of Poblenou into *the* technology and innovation neighbourhood of the city, while at the same time increasing space for housing and leisure. French architect Jean Nouvel was asked to transform a five-hectare piece of land into a 'Central Park'. Right after the scheme was adopted, the metropolitan government started expropriating houses on site, with the last ones demolished in 2003.

A year later the site was still vacant. Users of the factory building and local residents took matters into their own hands and started to build their own park. Initially, the factory walls were painted. Then, on 29 May 2004, action 'ParcCentralPark' followed. About 40 local residents – users of the Can Ricart centre and sympathisers, armed with brooms and spades – started cleaning up the site. Its strategic importance manifested itself immediately in a peculiar way: in no time about one hundred members of the Spanish riot police in full gear removed the cleaners from the site. Once cleared, the site was surrounded and secured by the Guardia Civil as a forbidden zone. When the 'active' citizens focused their attention and spades on an adjacent plot barely a thousand square metres large, that also was stopped *manu militari*. The siesta respected by Guardia Civil as well as Spanish citizens brought the stalemate to an end.

The public demonstration meant that local grievances reached the metropolitan government as well as Nouvel's practice. Residents' associations were consulted, a local artist's work was integrated into the design of the park, and a historic chimney on site was kept and restored as a reminder of the neighbourhood's glorious past. The decision-making process about the full five hectares, however, remained off limits for residents.

Meanwhile, the old factory complex still housed about 60 small- and medium-sized enterprises (SMEs), collectives and arts centres, which together employed 240 people. Among them was Can Font, a space shared among others by City Mine(d). When, in September 2004, the metropolitan government informed users of the imminent demolition of the complex, the platform 'Salvem Can Ricart' (Save Can Ricart) was founded, Can Ricart being the name of the site that holds several factory buildings, among them Can Font. It initiated campaigns such as 'Made in Can Ricart' to promote products made on site. By April 2005, the platform developed a dossier in defence of the site: 'Can Ricart – Parc Central Nou Projecte' (Universidad de Barcelona, 2005). In this dossier, the site's heritage value was emphasised – one of the last three remaining 19th century industrial complexes in Barcelona, its urbanistic importance was explained – a publicly accessible site on which industry and experiment co-existed, and a critique of the 22@ scheme was articulated – the plan interpreted innovation too narrowly, leaving only room for technology. More importantly, the dossier contained an alternative proposal made by the citizen platform that combined existing qualities with ambitions from within 22@. In January 2006, the metropolitan government decided to preserve half of the industrial complex and to adjust the plans according to users' needs.

Tough issues

> One learns about tough issues by addressing them, not by thinking about them beforehand. The latter leads to a 'paralysis by analysis,' where people cannot take action until they have more information, but they cannot get good information until someone takes action. Thus, a process of 'small wins' makes more sense: micro-level changes that actors enact as they make sense of and act in the world.(Wanda Orlikowski (1996), as quoted in Vermaak (2012: 226))

The earlier mentioned lack of green and public space, loss of affordable housing, gender imbalance, decolonisation, urban transport and mobility are instances of 'tough issues' (Vermaak, 2012) or 'wicked problems' (Rittel and Webber, 1973). Policy issues grouped under this label are deemed 'tough' because they are complex in their subject matter (multifactor), in order to be addressed they need the collaboration of many stakeholders (multiactor) and they touch upon different levels of policy and decisionmaking (multiscalar). Rittel and Webber (1973) juxtapose 'wicked problems' with 'tame problems', like playing chess or solving a puzzle. The latter have a clear solution and an endpoint, whereas wicked problems lack a clear formulation of the problem, have no right or wrong solution and each one is unique (see also Conklin, 2006). This also means that 'tough issues' escape the prevailing logic that all issues can be solved by algorithms. They show us the edges of today's dominant notion that all problems can be reduced to a mathematical formula which, with the right input of data, then solves itself.

The problem of urban transport and mobility provides an interesting example of a tough issue. In a study on Munich and Birmingham, Hendriks (1994) identified three cultural positions towards the dilemma of more roads versus fewer cars. There are those who value individual freedom most and who put their trust upon the environment recovering; a second group counts on keeping matters orderly with a structured framework, and relies on determining the boundaries of environmental resilience and taking action before chaos erupts; and a third group values equal access, sustainability and liveability, and for them the environment is always on the edge of collapse. Within a single city, these three visions compete for power to shape the built environment and to decide and implement regulation. Often, this takes place within a system of governance in which the municipal vies for the final word with regional, national and even transnational institutions, in addition to government and private sector interests. As such, urban transport and mobility is a clear example of a 'tough issue'. There is only one physical space, and the visions are incompatible.

In City Mine(d)'s approach to social transformation, 'tough issues' form the subject and cause of collaboration. Urban populations and their governments are confronted with a plethora of 'tough issues' and deal with them with a limited degree of success. Rittel and Webber's (1973: 156) remark, 'Now that the relatively easy problems have been dealt with, we have been turning our attention to others that are much more stubborn', is true when it comes to stubbornness. Solutions to 'tough issues' are still outsourced away from democracy to experts, taskforces or think tanks, excluding citizens from the thought process and making citizens reluctant to accept, let alone adopt, the remedy (Vermaak 2012). 'Tough issues' demand an approach in which all who have a stake – for once, the jargon is spot on in calling them 'stakeholders' – take part in understanding the problem and designing a solution. As Orlikowski (1996) suggests, it takes an agent to take a first step in order to gain information to move on to the next step. This practical way of working is what inspired City Mine(d) in an approach it now refers to as 'prototyping'.

The prototyping third

> Often the relation between the parties and the non-partisan emerges as a new relationship: elements that have never before formed an interactional unit may come into conflict; a third non-partisan element, which before was

equally unconnected with either, may spontaneously seize upon the chances that this quarrel gives him; and thus an entirely unstable interaction may result which can have an animation and wealth of forms, for each of the elements engaged in it, which are out of all proportion to its brief life. (Simmel, 1950: 154)

The prototyping approach was inspired by Suchmann et al (2002): '... the prototype, an exploratory technology designed to effect alignment between the multiple interests and working practices of technology research and development, and sites of technology-in-use'.

The exploratory character of prototyping is important, as it goes beyond the comfort zone of engineers and specialists. It goes into uncharted territory, where it touches upon different interests. Yet, it is more ambitious than community arts projects, as it aspires to be relevant within its tough issue, and function at the same time. It is a working model, rather than an expression of (community or individual) sentiments or grievances. In addition, it avoids the issue of 'instrumentalisation of art' which, according to some critics, leads to a lower form of artistic expression.

In their article 'The role of the Tertius as initiator of urban collective action', exploring the role of City Mine(d), Moyersoen and Swyngedouw (2005: 309) write:

Initially, the initiators, ... had no reputation, no financial means and very limited power to start, let alone impose, an urban renewal process. ... [They] adopt the role of Tertius (Simmel, 1955). The 'tertius' role is the intermediary role between groups in situations of friction resulting from open competition and/or from a state of non-communication between rival groups. From this perspective, the core-group exploited the 'vacant' institutional and socio-political space between the diverse and non-communicating local community. (Moyersoen and Swngedouw, 2005; see also the previous quote by Simmel, 1955.)

The question for research methods like Co-Creation becomes: to what extent is a research institution a third, non-partisan element? Is scientific research an end in itself, and would, therefore, a community feel instrumentalised by contributing to research; or can the research truly coincide with the needs and aspirations of a community, even if it has to abide by the laws of academia?

While the development of a prototype serves a purpose in itself, namely that of technological exploration and innovation, it also serves a secondary purpose, namely that of providing the different stakeholders in a tough issue with the opportunity to come together in a non-rival context. Suchmann et al (2002) refer to it as 'alignment', City Mine(d) calls it the 'creation of a coalition'. The coalition's main reason for being is to build the best possible prototype, but, while working on it, different stakeholders meet in an informal context and have the opportunity to get to know each other's perspective on the tough issue. As already mentioned, the knowledge about tough issues is always incomplete, contradictory and interconnected, so it makes a lot of sense hearing other stakeholders' perspectives.

City Mine(d) tends to look for five groups of stakeholders. The starting point is citizens and communities, often at the scale of a small neighbourhood. It distinguishes citizens from civil society in a Gramscian way, in the sense that civil society (in its meaning of non-governmental organisations and institutions that manifest interests and will of citizens) has an intimate relationship with the state. As Gramsci notes (1971: 263): 'The general notion of State includes elements ... of civil society (in the sense that one might say that State = political society + civil society, in other words hegemony protected by the armour of coercion).' The government in itself, at the different levels on which the tough issue is at play, is obviously also a stakeholder. The shift from government to governance, aptly described by Swyngedouw (2004), makes the relevant business actors indispensable in a coalition. The fifth actor is research institutions. They are invited for their contribution of basic as well as applied research, but also from the notion that research influences policy. In that sense it is an indirect way to shape society. Yet, their role is not entirely unproblematic. Whereas government and industry are aware of being 'hegemonic actors', research and civil society institutions are often less so. The next example will explore this further.

A coalition on electricity that is developing at the time of writing can provide an insight into the first stages of this process. An article published in *The Guardian* in December 2016 (Magnin, 2016) quotes a study showing that by 2050 half of the European population could be producing their own electricity, 'either at home, as part of a cooperative, or in their small business.' The electricity sector is on the verge of a major shift. Factors such as increasing electrification, growing awareness of the environmental impact of energy consumption and a retreat of the state that makes the sector predominantly profit-driven are bringing about a transformation comparable only to the creation of the national grid a century ago. In this shift, City Mine(d) sees an opportunity to approach the mountain of climate change from a less steep flank. In other words, climate change increasingly pitches believers against non-believers, to the point where the subject becomes so vast that it ends up being incapacitating. Yet, within this broad field of a sustainable environment, City Mine(d) is looking for opportunities, rather than engaging with the threats, the opportunity here being the shifting electricity landscape that provides a chance to tilt the playing field in favour of citizens and cooperatives. The location is Brussels' Quartier Midi, one of Europe's most densely populated areas and with a notoriously stubborn deprivation index (including energy poverty).

From May 2018, experts from industry, research, media, government and civil society were interviewed about their perspective on the changing sector. After the interviews, the interviewees were brought together in a meeting in the Quartier Midi. To take out the differences in status or posture, participants agreed to a first-name basis meeting. Meanwhile, a local group had been formed, and a name had been chosen for the project: 'La Pile' (The Battery). Thirty-five stories of local residents of the Quartier Midi and their relationship with electricity were collected and contributed to an overall perspective on the sector. Next, the vast amount of information gathered from interviews, meetings and collected stories was made digestible in three ways. One was a roadmap, entitled 'How to face up to the cost of electricity', with tips and tricks and useful contacts. The second way was an exhibition that aimed to inspire the general public, but particularly those involved in the prototyping stage in Brussels' Quartier Midi. The La Pile Expo was launched in Brussels' prestigious arts centre Bozar before it moved to the Quartier Midi and then travelled across Belgium and abroad. The third way of sharing information was a board game called 'Exploration Game'. Playing the game gives players an opportunity to familiarise themselves with what local electricity production involves (and its limits), yet at the same time through roleplaying to gain a better understanding of the interests different stakeholders have to take on board.

The truth is out there

¿Qué es la razón? La razón es aquello en que estamos todos de acuerdo, todos o por lo menos la mayoría. La verdad es otra cosa, la razón es social; la verdad, de ordinario, es completamente individual, personal e incomunicable. La razón nos une y las verdades nos separan.

> What is Reason? Reason is what we all agree upon, all or at least the majority. Truth is something else, Reason is social; Truth, ordinarily, is completely individual, personal and incommunicable. Reason unites us and Truths separate us.
> (Miguel de Unamuno, 1927: 9; author's translation)

One of those interviewed as part of La Pile was Ilse Tant, chief officer of community operations at Elia, Belgium's electricity transmission operator. Her role is to mediate between the company responsible for installing high voltage cables across the country, and communities that have to live with the cables. In her view, the difficulty is to convince engineers from her company that they have only part of the picture, and that local communities also hold an important part of the truth. Her experience sounds true for many experts. The curse of knowledge, a term coined by Camerer, Loewenstein and Weber (1989), is easily described as the inability to unknow what we know. This is problematic in a coalition, as the asymmetry of information puts members of the research community always at an advantage. They have access to the latest information and it takes a very conscious researcher to overcome this bias. Gladwin (1989: 13) provides us with an interesting thought on social sciences in particular:

> [Like other] models in the social sciences, [decision tree models] are simplified pictures of a part of the real world, like model trains. They are simpler than the phenomena they are supposed to explain or represent, just as a model train has some characteristics of a real train but not all (e.g., its size). (Gladwin, 1989: 13)

The main concern is, however, a political one. As mentioned before, research institutions are hegemonic actors, which excludes them from roles like community actors or grassroots activists. Illich (1971: 26) warns us that universities 'have a monopoly of both the resources for learning and the investiture of social roles. [They] co-opt the discoverer and the potential dissenter'. This is important not only for the stakeholders City Mine(d) brings together in a coalition, but also for research methodologies like Co-Creation. Research institutions can be key actors and stakeholders in a social transformation process, but it is very hard for them to be the initiator. The question of whether researchers can dissociate themselves from the research institution, to what extent, and what new role in addition to citizen that would confer on them, remains to be dealt with, preferably by researchers themselves.

Yet, Co-Creation can become a valuable tool for studying social change in a more inclusive way. In an interview on the topic of Co-Creation in science, Xavier Hulhoven, scientific adviser to the Brussels Regional Institute for Scientific Innovation Innoviris, talked about two participatory schools within scientific research: there is, on the one hand, participatory action research, which is very much toolkit- and methodology-oriented; and on the other hand there is a school of Co-Creation:

> "… more based on principles, which tell a story of a community, of how people are taken into account, and how the freedom to experiment and to take risks is guaranteed. And to make sure the values of scientific research are respected, be they a slow pace ('*la lenteur*'), reflection, nuance, possibility to experiment and consequently to fail, contradiction." (Hulhoven and Vangeebergen, 2019)

He admits that these values are meaningful beyond the realm of scientific research. His colleague, Thomas Vangeebergen, adds values such as questioning ('*remise en question*'), doubt, even creating some discomfort or confusion which conjures up a series of questions.

> "This is politically important. For everyone's comfort, we are forced to eliminate all forms of risk, we need to eliminate all uncertainties, we need to eliminate questioning. [Co-creation] is not about win-win alliances, in which each can find his or her thing; it is rather about embarking on a journey of shared exploration with all the risk-taking that entails." (Hulhoven and Vangeebergen, 2019)

Clearly, these are the values that inspire both the Co-Creation methodology described in this volume, as well as City Mine(d). Loftus (2003: 39), describing the work of City Mine(d), wrote:

> … to use the now hackneyed aphorism of Antonio Gramsci, the projects show a true optimism of the will in the face of a pessimism of the intellect. As several authors have suggested however, it is conceptually lazy to fall back on Gramsci's maxim without also changing our own praxis (see Harvey 2000). What is needed is a renewed optimism of the intellect, or better still a renewed synergy between theory and practice. (Loftus, 2003: 39)

Conclusion

This chapter builds on the observation that many grassroots and citizen initiatives are shifting away from blocking developments towards proposing alternatives. It borrows from the vocabulary of Michel de Certeau (1980) to describe a shift from '*résistance*' to '*bricolage*'. The Barcelona case study illustrates how this shift can occur within a project of merely five years. The chapter also considers an important tension between the individualistic capabilities approach as described by Nussbaum (1999) and the need for collective action which emerges from the work of Ostrom (1990). This seeming contradiction can often be found at the core of social transformation. In issues of climate change, urban transport and mobility or economic redistribution, the individual needs and entitlements often collide with a collective and long-term view.

This chapter has drawn on a reading of social transformation that is based on the notion of 'tough issues'. Defined by Vermaak (2012) as multifactor, multiactor and multiscalar, 'tough issues' are a performative way of stating the challenges society is faced with. The issue can be unpacked in smaller, more practical challenges, and small wins allow for progress even in over-complex matters such as climate change. Informed by the notion of 'tough issues', City Mine(d) has developed a tactic for social transformation it refers to as 'prototyping'. 'Prototyping' is what gives City Mine(d) its role of third actor (Simmel, 1950). Prototyping brings together a group of five stakeholders, which are (in addition to citizens) civil society organisations, business actors, governments and research institutions. The latter, particularly, have an ambiguous relationship with social transformation. The chapter identifies two reasons: on the one hand they suffer from the curse of knowledge, yet on the other, they are also, willingly or not, imbued with power. This makes it harder for them to initiate processes of social transformation. Yet the chapter concludes by noticing that initiatives like City Mine(d) and research methodologies like Co-Creation have many values in common: a slow pace, reflection, nuance, the possibility to experiment and consequently to fail, contradiction. To name but a few.

City Mine(d) emphasises its role as '*tertius gaudens*' because this is a position none of the five other stakeholders can achieve. Urban lives are very much shaped by structures that impose power and a form of coercion upon citizens. These are not solely the state or market-related actors. As a matter of fact, the distinction between the five stakeholders comes from the fact that each of them has a different degree of power, while at the same time has to live with a different set of constraints. The five are chosen because they cover a very wide spectrum of power that shape cities. Compared to these five actors, City Mine(d) – in that sense also any arts organisations – wields no power, but at the same time suffers little constraints.

The perspective of 'tough issues' can prove valuable to all sorts of actors aspiring for social transformation. As mentioned before, it makes the challenges communities and even societies are faced with more practical and allows for progress in the right direction without actually solving the issue immediately. In research methodologies like Co-Creation, 'tough issues' can prove a meaningful way to identify the overlap between the research agenda and community concerns. The prototyping approach City Mine(d) proposes is but one way of making small wins and progressing towards dealing with the true issue. Others, including research or arts-related approaches, could prove at least as valuable.

References

Adams, W. (2017) 'Martha C. Nussbaum talks about the humanities, mythmaking, and international development', *Humanities*, 38(2) [online] available from https://www.neh.gov/humanities/2017/spring/conversation/martha-c-nussbaum-talks-about-the-humanities-mythmaking-and-international-development [accessed 30 July 2019].

Camerer, C., Loewenstein G. and Weber, M. (1989) 'The curse of knowledge in economic settings: an experimental analysis', *Journal of Political Economy*, 97(5): 1232–53.

Campbell, H. and Vanderhoven, D. (2016) *Knowledge That Matters: Realising the Potential of Co-Production*, Manchester: N8 Research Partnership.

City Mine(d) (2016) 'City Mine(d) en Friche', August 2016, Brussels.

Conklin, J. (2006) *Dialogue Mapping: Building Shared Understanding of Wicked Problems*, Chichester: Wiley Publishing.

de Certeau, M. (1980) *L'Invention du Quotidien*, Paris: Union Générale d'Editions.

de Unamuno, M. (1927) *Como se Hace una Novela*, Buenos Aires: Alba.

Gladwin, C. (1989) *Ethnographic Decision Tree Modeling: Sage University Paper Series on Qualitative Research methods Vol. 19*, Beverly Hills, CA: Sage.

Gramsci, A. (1971) *Selections from the Prison Notebooks*, New York, NY: International Publishers.

Harvey, D. (2000) *Spaces of Hope*, Edinburgh: Edinburgh University Press.

Harvey, D. (2008) 'The right to the city', *New Left Review*, II (53): 23–40.

Healey, P. (1997) *Collaborative Planning: Shaping places in Fragmented Societies*, London: Macmillan Press.

Hendriks, F. (1994) 'Cars and culture in Munich and Birmingham: the case for cultural pluralism' in D.J. Coyle and R.J. Ellis (eds) *Politics, Policy and Culture*, Boulder, CO: Westview.

Hulhoven, X. and Vangeebergen, T. (2019) Interview with the author, 18 July 2019.

Illich, I. (1971) *Deschooling Society*, New York: Harper & Row.

Loftus A. (2003) 'Democratic interventions in the urbanisation of nature' in J. Moyersoen and J. Segers (eds) *Generalised Empowerment: Uneven Development and Urban Interventions*, Brussels: City Mine(d), pp 28–39.

Magnin, G. (2016) 'Let the people lighten energy load with citizen-owned schemes', *The Guardian*, 29 November 2016, available from https://www.theguardian.com/environment/2016/nov/29/let-people-lighten-load-citizen-owned-energy-schemes?CMP=share_btn_tw [accessed 30 July 2019].

Moulaert, F. (ed) (2005) *Social Innovation, Governance and Community Building (SINGOCOM)*, Brussels: European Commission.

Moyersoen, J. and Swyngedouw, E. (2005) 'The role of the Tertius as initiator of urban collective action: the case of LimiteLimite in the Brabantwijk (Brussels) as a socially innovative urban redevelopment process' in F. Moulaert (ed) *Social Innovation, Governance and Community Building (SINGOCOM)*, Brussels: European Commission.

Nussbaum, M. (1999) *Sex and Social Justice*, Oxford: Oxford University Press.

Orlikowski, W.J. (1996) 'Improvising organisational transformation over time: a situated change perspective', *Information Systems research*, 7(1): 63–92.

Ostrom, E. (1990) *Governing the Commons*, Cambridge: Cambridge University Press.

Quaderns d'arquitectura i urbanisme (2006) *Cityborg, ParcCentralPark, Straddle3*, Febrero 2006, Barcelona: COAC.

Rittel, H. and Webber, M. (1973) 'Dilemmas in a general theory of planning', *Policy Sciences*, 4(2): 155–69.

Simmel, G. (1955) *Conflict*, Glencoe, IL: Free Press.

Simmel, G. and Wolff, K.H. (1950) *The Sociology of Georg Simmel*, Glencoe, IL: Free Press.

Suchmann, L., Trigg, R. and Blomberg, J. (2002) 'Working artefacts: ethnomethods of the prototype', *British Journal of Sociology*, 53(2): 163–79.

Swyngedouw, E. (2003) *Cities, Urbanity and Urban Interventions, Background to the Bruxel-conference*, Brussels: City Mine(d).

Swyngedouw, E. (2004) 'Governance innovation and the citizen: the Janus face of governance-beyond-the-state', *Urban Studies*, 2004(42): 1–16.

Universidad de Barcelona (2005) *Can Ricart – Parc Central Nou Projecte*, available from http://www.ub.edu/geocrit/b3w-580.pdf [accessed 30 July 2019].

Vermaak, H. (2012) 'Facilitating local ownership through paradoxical interventions', *The Journal of Applied Behavioral Science*, 48(1): 225–47.

13

We Can Make: Co-Creating knowledge and products with local communities

Martha King, Melissa Mean and Roz Stewart-Hall

Introduction

This chapter explores the role that Co-Creation plays in the work happening at Knowle West Media Centre (KWMC), Bristol, UK, through the lens of two case study projects: The Bristol Approach, which is about addressing digital exclusion and tackling inequalities, and We Can Make, which is about Co-Creating new approaches to housing. Both projects help to demonstrate how KWMC has been working, since 1996, in ways that start with people and bring together arts, artists, other expertise, digital tools and data to explore and address people's concerns and priorities through Co-Created creative interventions.

For KWMC, Co-Creation is understood to be: '... a cooperative process whereby people with common interests, often with diverse skills and experiences, work together non-hierarchically towards a change they want to bring about' (KWMC, nd). A key aspect that allows this 'non-hierarchical' practice to function is the collaborative definition of an overarching common goal around which people from different backgrounds (both in terms of socioeconomics, cultures and disciplinary specialisms) can cluster and focus energy. At the start of every project, it is essential to give time to defining and Co-Creating a shared mission of change. With a clear headline intent, participants can then voluntarily contribute as little or as much as is appropriate and could be involved in only one small aspect, knowing that their participation is still moving towards the overall mission. To enable this process to work everyone has to have a willingness to contribute to the overall shared goal as well as the agency to participate and contribute in different ways. Facilitators of Co-Creation play a key role in ensuring a process of 'non-hierarchical' Co-Creation is possible. Rather than denying different knowledge and expertise, KWMC facilitators apply processes where all skills are valued and acknowledged, ground rules are established early on, and in turn safe spaces that flatten hierarchical power dynamics are created. Artists are often employed as facilitators using tactics such as 'play' to cross boundaries, remove fear and create spaces where change on both a community and individual level can happen.

It can be argued that the transformative potential of engagement in the arts has sometimes led to an unhelpful set of assumptions about who or what it is that is in need of transformation. François Matarasso has written about this, clearly articulating some of the issues there are with pervasive notions of 'impact':

> In this thinking, the social art project is conceived as an experience whose 'impact' changes those who take part. And in this context, 'change' means 'improve', in terms of the problem-solving mission identified, more or less cooperatively, by the artist and the commissioner. (Matarasso, 2015: 5)

Matarasso uncovers a set of problematic assumptions, which underpin this way of thinking, that some people are 'in need of improvement'. At KWMC, there is no such assumption about who or what is in need of improvement. Instead, a process of Co-Creation is used to identify the broad and diverse changes that need to take place in order to make radical, long-term positive differences.

Co-Creation, in practice, demands a recognition that change may need to happen in many places, spaces and people, including within the organisations or for the individuals involved in a process (such as at a gallery or for a researcher), or at organisations and with individuals that are not directly involved (such as councils or policy makers). The sites for change are only identifiable through the Co-Creation process and reflection on the exchange and learning that takes place through such a process. In such a context, the notion of 'impact' is usefully unsettled in terms of who has impact upon whom, and it is less predictable than the everyday use of the term often implies.

This chapter will explore some of the challenges, possibilities and limitations of Co-Creation, suggesting that positive social change can be enabled by Co-Creation processes that:

• start with people and their interests;
• work towards a shared goal;

- use creative approaches and arts practice to work across disciplines and power structures;
- create space for reimagining;
- democratise and demystify the tools and means of production.

The authors will discuss some of the challenges around incentivising and enabling people from different socioeconomic backgrounds and positions of power to participate in Co-Creation projects. They will also demonstrate how artists and arts-led creative approaches can allow diverse contributions towards common Co-Creation goals. Before doing so through two case study examples the next section provides some context about Knowle West and KWMC.

Knowle West Media Centre

KWMC is an arts organisation and charity based in Knowle West, south Bristol, an area of approximately 5,500 households that roughly corresponds to the electoral ward of Filwood. It ranks highly in government indices of deprivation, with 35 per cent of people experiencing income deprivation in some parts of the area, which is ranked in the most deprived 1 per cent of areas in England (Bristol City Council, 2019).

KWMC offers a wide range of activities for people of all ages, including skills training and employment opportunities for young people, a programme of regular talks and exhibitions, and creative projects working with local residents to explore issues ranging from health to housing. As the Bristol Living Lab (part of the European Network of Living Labs), KWMC brings together people from different backgrounds to explore and test creative solutions to the challenges that affect them in a 'real world' setting.

KWMC also runs The Factory, an award-winning making and training space, based at Filwood Green Business Park. The Factory, established in 2015, provides access to new digital manufacturing technologies (such as CNC routers and 3D printers), offers product design and prototyping services for clients, and delivers a range of free training courses.

From its beginnings in a 1996 photography project run by KWMC Director Carolyn Hassan, the organisation and its ethos were forged at a 'grassroots' level, with Knowle West residents and young people involved from the outset. KWMC was formally constituted as a charity in 2002 and, in 2007, a group of young people helped to develop designs for an innovative environmental building to house KWMC's expanding staff team and portfolio of projects.

When it opened in 2008, KWMC's new building was the largest straw-bale construction in the South West. In 2014, on the ten-year anniversary of her involvement with KWMC, one young woman involved in the building project tweeted: 'It's a big part of my life and helped carve my future'.

KWMC now works across generations and communities in Bristol, as well as with enterprises, universities, local governments and networks across the UK and the world. Knowle West remains at the heart of KWMC's work and it is committed to being a nationally relevant organisation with a local focus.

Through its creative and accessible activities, KWMC hopes to inspire people to make a difference to their lives, communities and environment. A former volunteer described the impact that KWMC has had for her, saying: "It's a great place to regain your confidence and make you feel like you've made a difference".

KWMC was recently cited by the Joseph Rowntree Foundation as an example of innovative SEO (Social Economy Organisation) activity and an exemplar for innovation and knowledge sharing. (Vickers et al, 2017). Sharing learning from 23 years of Co-Creation, and continuing to evolve and explore what Co-Creation means, is key to KWMC's practice. For example, the organisation is currently a core member of the national Co-Creating Change network, which is coordinated by Battersea Arts Centre and is working as a partner on a community-led Creative Civic Change arts project led by Filwood Community Centre in Knowle West and funded by Local Trust, National Lottery Community Fund, the Calouste Gulbenkian Foundation, and the Esmée Fairbairn Foundation.

The Bristol Approach

The Bristol Approach is a project that highlights a strand of KWMC's work that is about addressing digital exclusion and tackling inequalities by Co-Creating relevant tools to address contemporary issues. Between 2015 and 2018, KWMC worked with Bristol City Council (BCC) and Ideas for Change (a Barcelona-based innovation company) to develop The Bristol Approach to Citizen Sensing, which sought to address the extent to which 'smart city' programmes are often developed and driven by the few and do not always take into account the majority of people who live in, work in and collaboratively make the city. Citizen sensing is a democratic approach to the collection, analysis and use of sensor data (including and often combining digital and human sensing) that actively involves and engages citizens in all aspects of data sense making.

A report by Nesta, a UK innovation foundation, identified things that have held 'smart cities' back from delivering real value:

- not addressing the issues people really care about;
- not taking human behaviour as seriously as technology;
- a lack of focus on the skills people need to use smart technologies;
- a lack of integration with other things going on in cities;
- not providing clear roles for people;
- not focusing on shared, open resources. (Nesta, 2015)

These barriers intensify existing challenges of urban disadvantage and social injustice that confront those cities struggling to be socially cohesive in this era of economic uncertainty. To counter this dominant trajectory – and with the belief that all people, whatever their background, should be able to imagine, design and build the future they want to see, for themselves and their city – The Bristol Approach to Citizen Sensing was developed as a framework to enable 'smart cities' to be Co-Created.

The framework included six steps and was underpinned by a philosophy of the 'commons'. This is a potentially powerful conceptual and methodological framework to collectively manage, or govern, shared resources, and offers an alternative to privatisation or monopolistic public regulatory control. While there is no single definition or uniform application of the commons, the aim of enabling collective change making, through gathering a wide range of contributions from citizens and different stakeholders, forms a critical part of the approach. The approach is gaining momentum with a growing number of places, from Bologna to Bolivia, adopting it as a practical tool and mind-set to help guide collaborative decision making and structuring participation in how commons resources (everything from natural assets to data) are contributed to and shared among diverse populations.

The steps of The Bristol Approach commons inspired framework are:

- **Identification:** identifying issues people care about, mapping communities, organisations, businesses and others affected by the issues who might be interested in working towards a solution.
- **Framing**: exploring issues and framing them as shared goals. Identifying if and how technology and data could be utilised,

uncovering resources that are available and identifying gaps in resources or knowledge.

- **Design:** working with people to Co-Create tools, governance and data infrastructure to tackle issues.
- **Deployment:** taking the tools created into communities to test.
- **Orchestration:** drawing attention to what has been made, encouraging others to use tools created and data collected, and to celebrate what has been Co-Created.
- **Outcome:** assessing if and how goals have been achieved, finding out what has been learned, sharing insights, creating solutions to issues, identifying opportunities and making changes to available infrastructure. (Bristol Approach, 2018)

The framework aimed to enable relevant citizen-generated data to be collected and used for the common good and for the service of citizens. It was structured to ensure that smart city programmes are driven by issues that are relevant to local needs and take place at a community level, with local people actively involved in designing, testing and evaluating. As with all KWMC's work, it starts with people who have expertise and/or lived experience regarding the issues facing their communities.

Pilot projects, led by KWMC, took place in 2016 to test how the Bristol Approach framework works in real communities, with real issues. The purpose was to learn from this process, to improve the framework as a guide for citizens and cities, and to help inform the design and development of smart city programmes. One of the pilot projects focused on damp in homes. The issue of damp homes was identified as a key area of concern after conducting a broad city-wide analysis of key issues through visiting community activist groups, having conversations with city leaders and subject specialists and employing artists to engage residents in conversations through more creative means. Once damp homes had been identified as an issue that was impacting negatively on many people's lives, and which citizen sensing could help to tackle, then a broad range of people were invited (via various on- and offline channels) to participate in a series of Co-Creation workshops.

Workshops were facilitated by artists and first focused on framing shared goals, moving towards Co-Creating solutions and then on to hands-on making. Artists used creative approaches to enable conversations, which helped dissolve hierarchies and persistently underlined the human aspect of technology. This process opened up new ways of looking at things and brought people together through play and making. The starting point for The Bristol Approach is the belief that citizens should have a leading role in imagining, designing and building their future.

The initial framing workshops were attended by residents who had damp in their homes, energy experts, housing charities, designers, hackers, artists and community activists. The group decided to call the project 'Dampbusters'. Once an overarching goal had been agreed, smaller working groups were formed with different leaders. Through creative Co-Creation workshops, people decided to make frog-shaped cases to house damp sensors for measuring temperature and humidity. They also designed an online damp-reporting tool and a community 'dampbusting' team of people trained to support their neighbours. These tools were prototyped and tested with residents in east Bristol. Prototype testing was followed up with evaluation and collaborative interpretation sessions with residents. Ensuring that the people collecting the data were also the ones making sense of that data and involved in the decision making around what to do with the data was important.

The project nurtured a greater sense of people's own individual potential to bring about change and supported people to have greater autonomy in understanding and using data as a useful asset for bringing about positive social change:

> "I've realised how much power I have to affect change and how much power we have working within a team." (Workshop participant, The Bristol Approach)

> "It's a big step to make local people feel like they've got the power, explaining data, taking the fear out of that space, and then getting them in an empowered space where they can actually be involved." (Workshop participant, The Bristol Approach)

The Bristol Approach enables the creative generation of solutions to issues that are apparent but also, because of its integrated and holistic approach, it ensures that people become familiar with data and how it can be used to tackle issues. People are therefore better equipped to tackle unforeseen issues that they may encounter beyond the project remit. Furthermore, through the collaboration between the human and digital sensing that is necessary in citizen sensing, or environmental data gathering, people often become more attuned to their environments and start using their own bodily senses more to notice changes in their environment.

Beyond individual agency the project, due to the Co-Creation processes applied, also increased a sense of community and shifted notions of data collection, that are often focused on self-improvement and self-quantification, to be oriented towards a shared goal for the common good. For example, participants commented on how they would happily contribute information about the interior of their homes to collective data sets if it would help their neighbours or others suffering with damp homes.

Data sense making was a phase where the range of participants needed to expand once again, to ensure that government officials, charities, policy makers, industry professionals and so on were present alongside residents and community activists to Co-Create solutions around the collected data. Sense making or 'solutions workshops' demonstrated the potential of Co-Creation projects to inform the development of city services, infrastructure and new models of community action and business development. Partners and experts highlighted the contemporary significance of Co-Creation approaches in a society where the sands are shifting considerably in terms of the resources available. For example, a member of Bristol City Council's environmental health team explained that they have to use a severity index regarding damp, whereby they have to be sure of the severity of a situation before being able to investigate it:

> "I'm a senior environmental health officer … and am really interested in this project. We can investigate problems with damp and mould growth in privately rented houses and flats, and if it's severe enough we do have legal powers … In the past, we'd try to help by giving advice and guidance to tenants and landlords but recent cutbacks mean we just don't have the resources to do this anymore. Therefore your project might go a long way to help plug this gap." (Senior environmental health officer at Bristol City Council)

The pilot showed that Co-Creation projects such as this require a wide range of expertise and skills, including: knowledge about neighbourhoods and networks, people and communications skills, data infrastructure and governance, coding, interface and user experience design, product design, behaviour, economics, anthropology, visualisation, sensor hardware, workshop facilitation, documentation and sharing. It was clear that technology was only a small part of citizen sensing work and that a much wider combination of tools and resources are needed to make change. 'Dampbusters' illustrated how key issues can be identified and then tackled through Co-Creating and working together across disciplines and power structures. Sharing and collaboration are key in this era of increased funding cuts. It is not for councils or others in positions of power to absolve responsibility, but to establish an equality of input through participation as one of the many players needed in the process of Co-Creation.

However, the willingness of those in decision-making positions to engage in processes of collaboration and Co-Creation can be a challenging sticking point; often the pressures to make fast decisions and reach large numbers of people on a surface level wins over deeper more sustained localised processes of Co-Creation, which require much more advocacy. Lengthy advocacy work for the value of Co-Creation and the participation in such approaches can end up distracting facilitators from the actual work of Co-Creation. However, finding ways to articulate and demonstrate the value of Co-Creation processes and approaches to working across disciplines and hierarchies is essential in order to achieve the necessary diversity in such processes, as well as ensuring Co-Creation happens beyond silos and can gain the necessary support to sustain projects.

KWMC has sought a range of ways to tell the story of successful Co-Creation over 23 years, such as through seizing the value in co-publishing articles, papers and chapters with academics, but also importantly in supporting Co-Creation participants to tell their own story through a range of digital media, often working with artists as well as professional industry mentors to enable this. Balancing the need to articulate the value of Co-Creation practices in order to continue working sustainably, while also needing to be immersed in the practice, can be a challenge.

We Can Make

We Can Make is another example of KWMC's work that successfully engages decision makers, alongside local community members and specialists from other disciplines in processes of Co-Creation, and has done so from its inception.

Home is shelter, safety, and stability. Yet, 100 years on from David Lloyd George's promise of 'homes fit for heroes' and the 1919 Addison Act, which ushered in Britain's first mass wave of council homes, people's ability to access a secure, affordable home is more challenging than ever before. Housing needs spill over into every part of a person's life, affecting relationships, work, education, physical and mental health; this makes stark the inadequacy of our collective response. Conventional strategies to access housing can be understood as reductively competitive, as they either require people to divert more of their wages and savings to get on a property ladder devoid of bottom rungs, or compel people to prove how 'weak' and 'incapable' they are in order to win eligibility for austerity-rationed social housing. Instead of relying on speculative developers or last resort state provision, we need new ways in which people and communities can meet their own housing needs.

We Can Make was born of the frustration expressed by local residents that the housing market and system was not working for them. KWMC set up a Co-Creation 'test space', as part of a broader strand of We Can Make activities, to explore whether and how housing could be done differently if the starting point was the needs and knowhow of people and communities. The subsequent process of We Can Make illustrates some of the key elements of Co-Creation practice.

Co-Creation requires working across different boundaries and disciplines, the mixing together of ideas and experiences, and using different tools and approaches to explore them. Housing is often treated in a silo, as if it is disconnected from other issues such as health, employment, environment, governance and adult social care. Early on, at one of its first Co-Creation workshops, We Can Make worked to break these silos by hosting an 'open data jam', where people from different disciplines, and experiences – from local residents to computer programmers and from artists to engineers – came together to explore a wide range of open data sets that could be shaping people's experience of housing in Knowle West. Working in small mixed teams meant that people could pool their expertise and identify emergent issues, into which they could 'deep dive' together. One team used open data tools to analyse all the planning applications made in Knowle West over a six-year period. They compared the data with Clifton (a wealthy neighbourhood in Bristol) and found that planning applications were twice as likely to be rejected in Knowle West compared with Clifton. By highlighting this issue, the analysis indicated that, if housing prospects in Knowle West were to change, then wider transformations in culture, regulation, and access to resources would need to be Co-Created.

KWMC works with the concept of 'low floor, high ceiling', whereby people can step into a space or place and contribute quickly, easily and simply, but at the same time there is no limit on how lengthy, complex or sophisticated their contribution might become. KWMC often works with artists as facilitators of Co-Creation processes, as they are often excellent mediators and use tactics of play and hands-on making that effectively release inhibitions and allow people to feel safe and treated

Figure 13.1: Charlotte Biszewski and her Mobile Wallpaper Making Machine.

Source: Ibi Feher.

as a 'whole person'. Artists can also help incentivise participation in Co-Creation processes through more subtle, tangential and dialogic engagement approaches, which are often more effective than traditional invitations to participate in workshops or events.

We Can Make deployed this arts-led 'low floor, high ceiling' approach from its inception with a six-month residency with artist Charlotte Biszewski (see Figures 13.1 and 13.2). The residency focused on surfacing the experience of housing in Knowle West through a process of door-to-door conversations with people, through which the day-to-day struggle for adequate housing of many individuals and families in Knowle West was manifest. As is articulated in Charlotte's artist blog on the KWMC website, this involved in-depth and often highly emotive exchanges on people's doorsteps:

> I wanted to open up questions of home and what makes a home. I wanted to look at objects, what we surround ourselves with, how we adorn the place we live and why we do this. How the physical space inside our homes makes us feel 'at home' ... .
>
> I couldn't imagine that asking up-front would work. So I built a mobile cyanotype unit using a bike trailer; it was something I could take door to door, asking people to

Figure 13.2: Charlotte Biszewski with wallpaper cyanotypes.

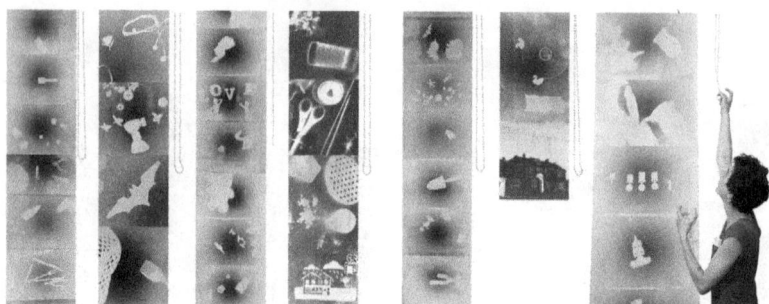

Source: Ibi Feher.

bring me an object and take part in making long wallpaper hangings (using a mobile wallpaper making machine). This is how a typical encounter looked:

Knock, knock.
Resident: Yes?
Charlotte: Hello, my name is Charlotte, I work at the Media Centre.
The door remains ajar, the owner unwilling to open it fully to this stranger, who has just turned up at their house uninvited. There is a silence.
Charlotte: Do you know it? Yes? Well I work there, I am an artist. I am creating a large wallpaper hanging. In my trailer here I have wallpaper covered in this photographic formula.
I bring out my scraggly piece of tattered blue demonstration wallpaper – it shows the silhouettes of coat hangers and lace curtains, captured in the deep blue of cyanotype. They look at me curiously – untrusting but interested.
Resident: I'm sorry we already have wallpaper and we don't want to buy any more.
Charlotte: No, I'm not selling it, I am making it. I am asking residents of Knowle West to bring me an object. I put it in the trailer, and I expose the silhouette onto the wallpaper, it will be a long hanging artwork out of everyone's objects from the area ...
They pause, their face continues to be unimpressed, deadpan.
We wait like that for a few seconds, me expecting them to slam the door on my face, or tell me to politely jog-on.

Hang on a minute! They turn back for a minute and return, triumphant-looking, with a child's toy/glass ornament/frog statue/ brass ring/some strange cooking implement.
Resident: Will this do?

And then we put it in the trailer and wait for ten minutes [for the cyanotype to develop]. In these ten minutes, we are locked into a conversation. In this time they tell me their stories. Their lives in Knowle West, how they came to acquire the object, the way their neighbourhood has changed, their successes in Weight Watchers, the pain of losing a partner, mother, son, the difficulties in finding a job, a place to live, a recent pregnancy. They show me war medals, Crufts awards, trinkets, gifts, tools and cups of tea. I am sniffed by a hundred different pugs, poodles, Dobermans and a Jack Russell who licks my leg for about ten minutes.

The people of Knowle West are as generous with their personal life stories as they are with their offers of tea and biscuits. It has been eye-opening – not just to the objects and stories but the people behind each door who surprised me every time. (KWMC, 2017)

These intimate exchanges and relationships of trust, developed on doorsteps, created the conditions for a first act of collective making among local residents and neighbours and formed the foundations and possibilities for deeper participation. For example, some of the people who worked with Charlotte came to KWMC to see their artwork and participated in Co-Creation workshops to develop new ideas and practical tools to address housing needs. These are people who may never have engaged in a process of Co-Creation if they had been asked to in a more conventional way.

Another critical part of Co-Creation is making visible and valuing the assets and resources available to Co-Create with. Through processes such as Charlotte's Mobile Wallpaper Making Machine, which invited people to have a different kind of conversation about 'housing need', We Can Make was able to surface and map the rich resources with which to Co-Create a different kind of approach to housing in Knowle West. These resources included a high level of knowhow and skill in construction trades among local people, and a high level of everyday resilience, with networks of families and friends helping to meet people's housing needs through mutual support and mixing and matching of rooms available.

The resources also included identifying a new supply of land already in the hands of people; micro-sites distributed in large back gardens, between buildings and leftover patches of land. Knowle West is a typical 1930s neighbourhood, made up of mainly redbrick semi-detached homes, all built at very low density. The research identified that over 2,000 potential micro-sites exist in Knowle West, in each of which a new one- to two-bedroom home could fit. The approach thereby opens up the possibility of housing provision as 'urban acupuncture', allowing families to grow, ageing residents to downsize, and those with changing mobility needs to adapt, without having to leave their community. This, importantly, creates a citizen-led alternative approach to the more conventional developer- and council-led 'demolish and densify' top-down regeneration tactics.

A vital part of Co-Creation, which perhaps surprisingly often gets forgotten, is the importance of actually creating something. Co-Creation is an imaginative process, but it is not just a thought experiment. We Can Make has sought to manifest tangible change in a number of ways. These include building a prototype We Can Make home on a micro-site next to a community centre. The build used innovative flat-pack construction methods, employed local people in the construction crew, worked with artists and local people to make the fittings and furnishings, and is now available for local people to visit and stay in, as a way of testing out different ways of living. Local people have Co-Created a community design code which is a live document that helps set the rules for what any new home on a micro-site should look like, what materials it should use, and sets standards for energy efficiency and biodiversity, which are all priority issues for local people. We Can Make has just secured funding to support its next phase which is working with local families and the community to develop the pilot batch of 16 homes on micro-sites.

The importance of who tells the story about Co-Creation runs through the We Can Make project. As part of the process to support local people shaping and telling the story, KWMC commissioned artist Lily Green of No Bindings (No Bindings, nd) to help produce a resident-led chat show. Knowle Westers are the hosts and guests on this bi-monthly show that is recorded and being collated into a series of broadcast podcasts. The hot topics for discussion come from local people and the process of the wider We Can Make project. Each episode also features a guest artist, such as Bristol City Poet, Vanessa Kisuule and artist Rediat Abayneh, who create new writing and artwork inspired by the conversations. The artist's response to each chat show conversation helps to manifest the character and value of the conversations, so again they can be shared and invite ever more diverse participants and audiences into the Co-Creation process.

The creative contributions to the We Can Make project are wide ranging, from someone contributing an object that becomes part of a cyanotype printed wallpaper, to a resident standing up in a council meeting and suggesting that things could be done differently, to someone helping to build a new prototype house. They are all feeding into the overall goal of social change, all contributing to the story, all helping to shift both perceptions and the actual practical way housing is developed. To Co-Create does not have to mean all sitting in a room together participating in every aspect. Co-Creation can be a collection of diverse acts all curated in a shared direction. The innovative quality and potential for impact of We Can Make was recognised when it was named as one of *The Observer* and Nesta's 2018 'New Radicals' (Nesta, 2018), a bi-annual showcase of the most innovative ideas changing the UK for the better.

Conclusion

Through these case studies we have begun to understand how, as was shown at the beginning of this chapter, KWMC's practice of Co-Creation achieves its goal to always:

- start with people and their interests;
- work towards a shared goal;
- use creative approaches and arts practice to work across disciplines and power structures;
- create space for radical reimagining;
- democratise and demystify the tools and means of production.

This chapter has illustrated how creative processes and skilled artist facilitators can nurture intimate exchanges and develop relationships of trust, dissolving hierarchical assumptions and opening up new possibilities in terms of what can be imagined and what can be made through Co-Creation. It has discussed how pivotal it is for those involved in Co-Creation to articulate their own stories, and how this can help extend understanding, in terms of both depth and reach, about the value of Co-Creation.

This chapter has also discussed some of the challenges around the advocacy work needed to engage policy makers and decision makers in participatory processes. Indeed, the challenge remains to galvanise and secure this wider recognition and shift in resources and power relations to ensure that more people can work together effectively and non-hierarchically towards the change they want to bring about in their communities.

More research is now needed to better understand the role of policy makers and decision makers, and how they can better engage with communities on non-hierarchical terms, and how a step up in terms of commitment, scale, and ambition to champion Co-Creation processes and practices can best be achieved. As ever, the success and impact of Co-Creation processes depend upon remaining open and mindful about what and who is in need of transformation.

References

Bristol City Council (2019) *State of Bristol, Key Facts 2019*, October 2019 Update, available at www.bristol.gov.uk/documents/ 20182/32947/State+of+Bristol+-+Key+Facts+2018-19.PDF.

Bristol Approach (2018) Bristol Approach website, available at www. bristolapproach.org/.

KWMC (nd) Knowle West Media Centre website, available at https:// kwmc.org.uk/projects/co-design/.

KWMC (2017) 'We Can Make: Artist Reflections Part Three', available at https://kwmc.org.uk/communityhousingblogpartthree/.

Matarasso, F. (2015) 'Music and social change: intentions and outcomes', *A Restless Art* [online], available from https://arestlessart. files.wordpress.com/2015/10/2015-music-and-social-change.pdf.

Nesta (2015) *Rethinking Smart Cities from the Ground Up*, Nesta [online] available from https://www.nesta.org.uk/report/rethinking-smart-cities-from-the-ground-up/.

Nesta (2018) *New radicals, 2018*, Nesta, available from www.nesta.org. uk/feature/new-radicals-2018/.

No Bindings (nd) No Bindings website, available from www. nobindings.co.uk.

Vickers, I., Westall, A., Spear, R., Brennan, G. and Syrett, S. (2017) *Cities, The Social Economy and Inclusive Growth: A Practice Review*, York: Joseph Rowntree Foundation.

14

Innovative collaborative policy development: Casa Fluminense and Rio's public agenda challenges

Inés Álvarez-Gortari, Vitor Mihessen and Ben Spencer

Introduction

This chapter explores some of the innovative ways in which collaborative approaches to developing urban policy have been undertaken by the Casa Fluminense organisation (Casa Fluminense, 2019a) in Rio de Janeiro, Brazil. It introduces the work and values of Casa Fluminense, which has built on a recent history of participatory planning and policy making in Brazil to develop and test public policy proposals in the Rio de Janeiro Metropolitan Region (RJMR). After introducing the current Rio de Janeiro context and the extreme inequalities experienced across the RJMR, the chapter then tackles the question of how these urban challenges could be addressed through the collaborative work of Casa Fluminense and to what extent their work can be understood as including Co-Creation approaches.

The authors conclude that Casa Fluminense's work includes many successful elements of Co-Creation, especially when working at the neighbourhood level. These feed into the effectiveness of the organisation in developing policy at the metropolitan level where many, but not all, of the Co-Creation principles are utilised, particularly in terms of mapping, networking and collaborative actions. The authors argue that this constitutes a hybrid model of Co-Creation particularly suited to the challenging context of Rio de Janeiro and having an impact at the neighbourhood and metropolitan scale.

Inequality in Rio de Janeiro

The RJMR is an area facing chronic issues of governability, insecurity and inequality and includes 21 municipalities with extremes of marginalisation, exclusion and stigma and with urban issues that are growing ever more socially, politically and physically complex (Ribeiro, 2017). The 21 municipalities are subdivided into three regions: the municipality of Rio de Janeiro itself, which has six million inhabitants; the Baixada Fluminense, made up of 13 municipalities with a population of three million; and the Leste Fluminense which has seven municipalities and also has around three million inhabitants (See Figure 14.1).

To provide an overview of the multiple challenges facing the residents of RJMR, some key facts collated by Casa Fluminense in the form of inequality maps (Casa Fluminense, 2019b) are presented here. In terms of transport, every day around two million people commute from the municipalities where they live to work in the city of Rio de Janeiro, where 74 per cent of jobs in the RJMR are concentrated. Just over a quarter (26 per cent) of workers spend over an hour in their commute to work. A person on a minimum salary who commutes daily by bus will spend 20 per cent of their salary on their bus fare. Only 31 per cent of the population in the RJMR is close to a train station, metro station, Bus Rapid Transit or tram stop. Currently, after decades of underinvestment and infrastructure degradation, Rio's intermunicipal trains transport an average of just 800,000 people per day, compared with 1.5 million in the 1980s.

The situation regarding citizen safety is also unbalanced, with homicide rates (per 100,000 population) as high as 134.9 in Queimados,

Figure 14.1: Map of the Rio de Janeiro Metropolitan Region (RJMR) showing the three regions and the central area where commercial activity is concentrated.

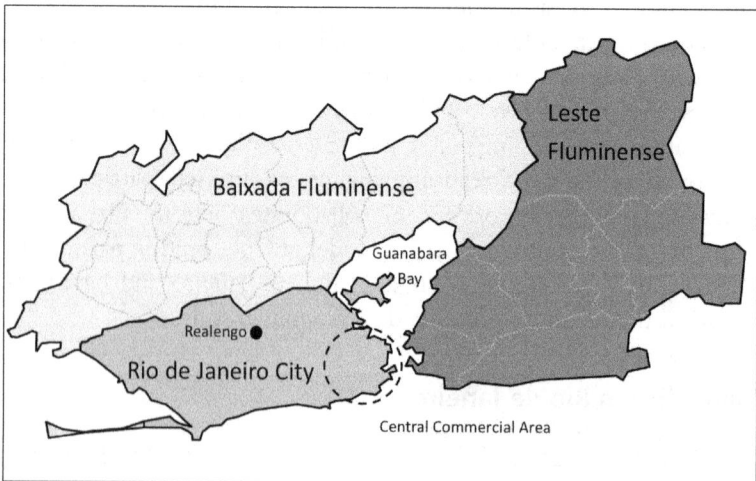

Source: Ben Spencer.

in the Baixada Fluminense, in contrast to 29.3 in the city of Rio de Janeiro. Similarly, in terms of sanitation, provision of sewers in RJMR varies from 83 per cent in the city of Rio de Janeiro to 33–46 per cent in much of the Baixada Fluminense, falling to just 12 per cent in Maricá, situated in the Leste Fluminense. Fresh tap water availability varies from 98 per cent in the city to 58 per cent in Maricá.

Unemployment in the city of Rio de Janeiro stands at 8 per cent, rising to 13 per cent in parts of the Baixada Fluminense, while average income varies from 2,155 Brazilian *reals* (BRL) (£430/US$540) per month in the city, to as low as 607 BRL (£120/US$150) in the municipality of Japeri. Partly as a result of these challenges, there is a widely held association between the Baixada and Leste Fluminense regions and violence, which ignores other aspects of residents' everyday lives, something that Casa Fluminense seeks to challenge.

Participatory planning in Brazil

Following a growing interest in a rights-based approach to urban development and management in Brazil in the 1980s, the 1988 Constitution included articles affirming direct participation in urban policy making (Friendly and Stiphany, 2019). In the late 1980s and 1990s, experiments with participatory budgeting were developed, notably in Porto Alegre, and in 2001 Brazil's City Statute finally included the legal requirement for participation in the planning process. In the following years, participation took place through processes that were genuinely inclusive in some cases, using participatory budgeting, municipal councils, the development of masterplans and town hall housing meetings. However, it has been argued that this happened within the broader context of a continuing political-electoral game that maintained City Council control over urban development, reduced the potential of participatory approaches to guarantee rights to the city (Rolnik, 2013) and privileged wealthier citizens who could engage more easily with the system (Caldeira and Holston, 2015).

Casa Fluminense

With the imminent hosting of the 2014 FIFA World Cup Finals and the 2016 Summer Olympic Games in Rio, Casa Fluminense was founded in 2013 by activists, researchers and citizens who shared a vision of a socially just, democratic and sustainable Rio de Janeiro. The founding of Casa Fluminense was the result of conversations held among a group of people working, in their respective institutions, towards Rio's democratic development. Among Casa's founding members were human rights advocates and community leaders from Rio's favelas, academics (including anthropologists, political scientists and economists) from Rio's Federal University (UFRJ) and State University (UERJ) as well as people from arts-based organisations working with educational and cultural projects with young people.

Therefore, from the outset Casa Fluminense can be seen as a collaboration between those in academia, those in public and private sectors and those in civil society. All the organisations involved worked at the neighbourhood or municipal level, not at the metropolitan level; Casa was created to bring these organisations together to have influence at the metropolitan level . The organisation's mission was developed by this group, so as 'to expand the public sphere and foster the construction of public policies targeting the promotion of equality, democracy and sustainable development in the entire metropolis and state of Rio de Janeiro'. The creation of this vision rested on the recognition that the challenges facing the city, such as the high levels of pollution in the Guanabara Bay (the large bay in the centre of RJMR) and very long commuting times from the periphery to the centre, were the result of factors at the metropolitan and state scale which required action beyond the neighbourhood or municipal level. Casa also wanted to change the way in which the periphery of the city was seen and imagined, with the Baixada and Leste areas being predominately associated with the stigma of violence.

Casa Fluminense is structured as a non-profit civil society organisation that is independent and non-partisan. Casa Fluminense's wider network of over 70 organisations (Casa Fluminense, 2019a) is regarded by Casa as its key strength. The organisation's strategic planning cycles are open for all its members to participate in and it encourages transparency through publishing its work plans. The management and governance of the organisation are structured through three components. The Board of Directors has overall responsibility for the direction of the organisation, with the Consulting Council in turn responsible for supporting the activities of the Casa network through the Executive Nucleus. The Executive Nucleus is made up of a team of ten full-time staff members who carry out Casa's day-to-day activities. The organisation is funded by donations and grants from private foundations such as the Open Society Foundation and Ford Foundation. The overall budget is around 2 million BRL (£400,000/US$500,000) per annum.

Casa Fluminense implements a three-pronged strategy of advocacy and the strengthening of civil society. This is achieved through:

- **Monitoring public policy**, with a focus on public investments and specific programmes, keeping in mind the goals of equity, respect for human rights and government transparency.
- **Organising capacity building and information dissemination activities and debates** in the form of courses, seminars and working groups that involve leaders and social actors from across RJMR.
- **Developing proposals targeted at overcoming the main challenges in Rio's public agenda** and guiding innovative ways of collectively conceiving policies.

Casa Fluminense works through collaborative initiatives, including the monitoring of public expenditure and policy and through collating and publishing information in a form that is easy to digest and use. An important example is the mapping of inequalities across metropolitan Rio, including aspects of mobility, work, income, education, safety, health and sanitation as previously referenced. Another key strand of work is the appraisal of the existence and implementation of municipal policies, such as masterplanning, through an online monitoring panel (Casa Fluminense, 2019c). After the founding of Casa Fluminense and an initial information–gathering and mapping exercise, the priority policy themes of urban mobility, public safety and sanitation were chosen by the Casa team for the development of policy solutions.

Capacity building in the 21 metropolitan areas has been enabled through an annual short course on public policies. The aim is to provide a diverse range of civic and community leaders, activists, journalists, young academics and other actors from across the metropolitan region of Rio de Janeiro with the skills and confidence to engage with public policy debate and formation. Since it first ran in 2016, over 200 people have completed the course. Each year the course is run in a different municipality and, in a typical year, course participants will come from at least 15 different municipalities across the metropolis. Some alumni have gone on to found their own organisations, some have run in municipal elections, while others have been involved in planning and delivering later versions of the course and its expansion to be run in São Paulo and Brasilia. The course has been evaluated by participants at the mid-point and on completion of the series of weekly classes over the three to four months it runs. Recognising how hard it can be to measure the impact of this and other programmes, Casa staff are participating in training to learn more about approaches to the evaluation of programmes run by third sector organisations.

In 2016, the Casa Fluminense Fund was established to support grassroots social movements, local institutions and activists who propose to organise monitoring and/or advocacy initiatives on public policy issues aligned with Casa's themes. That year, grants of up to 200 BRL (£40/US$50) were allocated to initiatives promoted by the members of Casa's network. These mostly included workshops, campaigns and other events, all with general support and advice from Casa. The following year, grants of 300 BRL (£60/US$80) were made available and activities expanded to include more campaigns and events as well as the legal formalisation of organisations.

Over the following years, the sums available increased further. In 2018, the funding was separated into a small grant scheme, with minimal bureaucracy, for sums up to 300 BRL (£60/US$80) and larger grants of 4,000 BRL(£800/US$1,000) which were available to the public, whether organisations or individuals, through an application process. The larger sums available led to an increase in creative approaches to raising and understanding issues. For example, a series of four videos was made by different collectives from across the metropolitan region about urban mobility issues. They were screened at an event in the Complexo do Alemão favela organised by one of Casa's partners, Institute Raízes em Movimento (Roots in Motion Institute). The event included artistic performances such as a poetry slam ('Slam na Laje') and debates.

In dispersing its grants, Casa is effectively operating as a 'regranter' channelling funding from international sources to the local level. This means that barriers to accessing international funding, such as high levels of literacy in English, appropriate contacts and the ability to navigate complex application and monitoring systems, are removed. This results in Casa being able to act as a catalyst, irrigating grassroots activity by taking on advisory, administrative and accountability roles. In addition, the legal formalisation of local organisations means that they are able to access other sources of funding directly themselves, thus the Casa Grant Funds can have a multiplier effect.

This mapping, monitoring and capacity development leads directly into Casa's own collaborative policy development process which culminates in the publication of its 'Agenda Rio' document, produced every two years to coincide with state and municipal elections. Each updated version is organised differently, according to the main themes of the moment, but always prioritising urban mobility, public security and sanitation. The latest edition in 2018 aligns itself with the United Nations 2030 Sustainable Development Goals (United Nations, 2019) and hence is called 'Agenda Rio 2030'. This identifies policy solutions for each of the eight current key Casa themes. These are Metropolitan Politics; Employment and Income; Urban Mobility; Public Safety and the Right to Life; Basic Sanitation and Guanabara Bay; Access to Health, Education and Culture; The Liveable City; and finally, Public Administration, Transparency and Participation.

During the process of developing Agenda Rio, the Fórum Rio is a key event for Casa's network members to make contributions to the document. The Fórum Rio originally took place three times a year, each time in a different location in the greater Rio area. The process of policy development used by Casa Fluminense was initially conceived using the 'design thinking' approach (Interaction Design Foundation, 2019). In practice, it brought together Casa's network of partners for a whole day to discuss the most pressing issues in the metropolis. Through reviewing the success of the approach, the process has now been refined to one meeting per year and employs a strategy whereby its website is used in advance of the face-to-face meeting to invite participants to make suggestions on proposals addressing the key Casa themes. These are then voted on online and combined using a collaborative process, first on the website and then at the meeting. The 12 Fórum Rios that have already taken place have mobilised around 2,000 people and over 60 civil society organisations from across Rio's metropolitan region. The Fórum Rio process opens up space for Casa to create new partnerships with institutions that appear on its radar, enabling Casa to have a more direct link to institutions from the full range of municipalities and also specific policy interests, such as active mobility (walking and cycling) or water quality.

The current Agenda Rio 2030 document captures the 40 resulting policy proposals, with five for each of the Casa themes. The printed Agenda Rio 2030 document is widely distributed among politicians, especially municipal mayors and city councillors in order to influence decision-making processes and to promote the principles of democracy, accountability, and sustainable development. At the last municipal election, the document was given to 96 candidates, of whom 19 were elected. The document is also available in an online format (Casa Fluminense, 2019d).

Casa Fluminense also works closely with partners from outside Rio. In 2017, it worked on the Virada Sustentável (Going Sustainable) event. This has become the largest sustainability initiative in Brazil. Starting in São Paulo, it expanded to other cities including Manaus, Porto Alegre and then Rio de Janeiro. Planning the debates, playful activities and public events involved the participation of civil society organisations, cultural and social movements, museums, businesses, schools and universities, among others, with the common goal of presenting a positive and inspiring understanding of sustainability. The event is also based on the 17 United Nations Sustainable Development Goals, which guide the projects implemented by the groups involved and so is a good strategic fit with Casa Fluminense. Casa was one of the curators of Virada Sustentável events in Rio and held its largest network meeting in São João de Meriti, a municipality in the Baixada Fluminense in the north of the metropolitan area.

Example of a Casa Fluminense neighbourhood project: Parque de Realengo Verde

Realengo is a neighbourhood in the West Zone of Rio de Janeiro (see Figure 14.1), an area with few leisure spaces in comparison with those in the South and Central parts of the city. The neighbourhood contains an abandoned space next to a former munitions factory. Since the closure of the factory in the 1970s, residents have been campaigning to transform the space into a green public park, to be known as 'Parque Realengo Verde'. In addition to the recreational value of the park, residents have argued that it would improve security, create new pedestrian routes and counteract very high summer temperatures and local flooding.

Following approval through the process of developing Casa Fluminense's Agenda Rio 2030, the project 'Lata Ocupa' was devised as a starting point for the permanent artistic and environmental occupation of the space. This was led by the local Lata Doida Cultural Association and its partners, who Casa awarded a grant of 4,000 BRL (£800/$1000).

The recent history of plans for the open space had been controversial. In a neighbourhood consultation meeting in March 2017, which was attended by the City Mayor, residents voted to create the park in place of the construction of a condominium. This resulted in the Realengo Park being included in both the city's Strategic Plan and a city government decree. However, the park was not created as planned and the Mayor then proposed to split the park in two, constructing a condominium on one half and creating a park in the remainder. This proposition was again rejected by the community, who continued to campaign for the whole area to be turned into their vision for Parque Realengo Verde.

In the existing space there were some limited uses, with two football pitches and a junkyard, but much of the area was consumed with dumped rubbish and rubble. Before the start of the Lata Ocupa event, volunteers were mobilised to clear the area, supported by COMLURB (the Council company responsible for cleaning of public spaces). The removal of rubbish and rubble freed up considerable space that had previously not been accessible.

The Lata Ocupa event was held over a weekend in early August 2019. Saturday morning included breakfast and more clearing of spaces along with tree planting, building a structure with a green roof, creating a musical installation for children to play, building artistic installations, making graffiti and high school students constructing a medicinal garden. Following lunch, a series of workshops were held, followed by a party and musical performances that went on into the evening. The Sunday followed a similar pattern but with an evening meeting with local leaders and community groups focusing on local sustainability issues and occupations of public spaces. Finally, there was a large party to close the event.

Media coverage of the event, including by the television station Globo Rio de Janeiro (Globo, 2019), was positive, helping to counteract a horrific school shooting in 2011 which many associate with Realengo. Following the event, a petition 'Parque Realengo 100 per cent Verde', coorganised with another non-governmental organisation (NGO), Meu Rio, gained over 10,000 signatures.

Comparing Casa Fluminense and Co-Creation approaches

The following section explores the similarities and differences to Co-Creation approaches to better understand the potential of Casa Fluminense methods to inform approaches to addressing issues of marginalisation, exclusion and stigma in other cities.

The strategies used by Casa Fluminense include many of the principles of Co-Creation (see Chapter 1, Figure 1.1). Collaborative actions are developed with network members and the wider civil society in a respectful and ethical manner that builds trust. Power relations are affected by the nature of the Casa staff team who are diverse, coming from across the metropolitan region and not being 'BBB', a term in Brazil from the Portuguese 'Branco, Burguês, Bem-intencionado' which means white, bourgeois and well-intentioned.

Power relations within Casa were examined in an action research study (Amann, 2016) which identified issues with the opportunities for making proposals and decisions in the Network, Executive Nucleus, Consulting Council and Board, and also noted the complex and overlapping relations between them. However, Amann recognised that this was a dynamic organisation, seeking to adjust so as to address these issues and that, overall, there was the 'astonishing ability of Casa to unite actors coming from different backgrounds and topic areas, throughout the whole metropolitan region of Rio' (Amann, 2016: 28).

Casa's activities are grounded in very detailed mapping of the wider context, monitoring of policy and targeted capacity building through the public policies course and the Casa Fluminense Fund programme of grants. Through moving their meetings to different locations across the metropolis, with an emphasis on the peripheral communities of the Baixada and Leste Fluminense, and developing the skills and knowledge of local representatives through the public policies course, both the events and the participants are embedded in their locality while also benefiting from the wider perspectives of network partners. The development of all policy recommendations is clearly attributed to the whole family of the Casa Network in the Agenda Rio documents. The workshop and short course outcomes include intangible products such as networks, skills, knowledge and shared understanding along with more tangible policy recommendations which are captured, communicated and evaluated. Amann gives examples of the strength of Casa's approaches to opening up spaces for social change:

> Giving a young black girl from the outskirts the opportunity to speak to public power holders at the launch of the Agenda Rio 2017. Providing legitimate and valuable information in the form of art. Connecting actors and problems in the broader level of the metropolitan region. These all are achievements in which Casa shifts what can be done and whose knowledge counts. (Amann, 2016: 28)

During their work with Virada Sustentável, Casa Fluminense was introduced to the concept of Co-Creation as used by that organisation. However, having considered using the term Co-Creation for their own Fórum Rio events, they decided it was not appropriate. This was after reflecting on the fact that Casa had already developed a starting point of identifying its eight key policy themes and that they had developed a tried-and-tested methodology for organising and running meetings that they wished to use – rather than actively Co-Creating them. These two factors resulted in the feeling that this aspect of the Casa approach was not truly Co-Creation and that they would be misrepresenting themselves and the principles of Co-Creation if they used that label for the overall process. Following criticism of the extent of truly Co-Creative opportunities within the Virada Sustentável approach, that organisation has also stopped using the term. This reveals an informed questioning of the use of the Co-Creation terminology and a need for its careful use.

The development and expansion of the Casa Grant Fund over the last four years has provided increasing resources for local communities and actors to create their own forms of advocacy within the framework of the Agenda Rio 2030. It can be argued that this is much closer to the spirit of the Co-Creation principles and it is notable that, given this flexibility in the Casa grant funded projects, they have become increasingly creative in their work with artists and use of artistic practices to explore issues and engage with communities.

By using this range of approaches, it can be seen that Casa's goal of improving social engagement in public policy debate across the whole metropolis is achieved at a range of connected scales. At the metropolitan level, information and policy are mapped and made available for campaign use municipality by municipality. Across RJMR the key themes are agreed collaboratively with partners through Fórum Rio using a pre-determined methodology. Following participatory action research framing, this can be seen as an 'invited space' for participation where the rules are already set (Gaventa, 2006). By virtue of the fact that Casa Fluminense is working at the metropolitan scale, there is also a mismatch with Co-Creation's focus on the neighbourhood, and artists or artistic practices are not employed in their work at this scale.

However, at the neighbourhood level, participation in the public policies short courses and, especially, the Casa Grant Funds can be seen as enabling something closer to 'claimed spaces' (Gaventa, 2006), that are created more autonomously by less powerful people and provide empowerment and resources for action by communities and local leaders. As emphasised by Amann: 'This communication – not the one Casa is doing, but the one it is allowing – is very important. … These exchanges between people amplify the vision of people: they manage to see what is happening on the other side' ('Danilo', quoted by Amann, 2016: 29)

These actions, along with Fórum Rio, which holds its face-to-face meetings in peripheral neighbourhoods, in turn contribute to Agenda Rio 2030, which is oriented to the metropolitan level. This means that a hybrid approach to Co-Creation is being used in the context of RJMR. A more recognisable and complete form of Co-Creation is enabled at the neighbourhood level, which is in turn contributing to policy development and actions at the metropolitan level. This is an important way for Casa to inform and legitimise their policy proposals. As noted here, many of the most challenging issues facing the residents and workers of Rio cannot be effectively tackled solely at the neighbourhood level. For example, tackling pollution in Guanabara Bay requires combined action across the many municipalities in its watershed.

Conclusion

The Casa Fluminense collaborative approach shares many similarities and strengths with Co-Creation, in that it is based on detailed mapping of the context, building networks and trust, increasing local capacity for action, and monitoring the impact of policy interventions. Divergence comes in terms of scale and related practices. At the top level, Casa Fluminense provides a carefully developed overall framework of policy themes (linked to the UN Sustainable Development Goals) within which it works with its network of organisations to produce policy outcomes. This process does not involve artistic practices or a neighbourhood scale and it is notable that Casa has been uncomfortable about adopting the term Co-Creation for their work. In the Brazilian context another organisation, Virada Sustentável, has also retreated from using the terminology following criticism that they were not fulfilling the ideals of Co-Creation. This demonstrates a positive critical engagement with the use of both language and methods and the challenge of following the principles of Co-Creation.

However, at the neighbourhood scale, nested within Casa's framework of themes, this chapter has described how there are opportunities for more truly Co-Creative approaches to flourish. This is through using the Casa Grant Funds programme to enable residents, artists and stakeholders to use arts-based methods, if they wish, to understand and communicate about urban challenges at the local level and then to contribute this knowledge to wider policy recommendations at the metropolitan level. The strength of this approach is in fusing the benefits of Co-Creative activities at the neighbourhood level with mapping, networking and policy development at the metropolitan scale to provide a hybrid approach to Co-Creation suited to the context and challenges of Rio. This has the potential to improve the living conditions of marginalised and stigmatised people across the wider city. It also suggests an approach that could be adopted more widely to create greater impact from neighbourhood Co-Creation initiatives in other cities at the metropolitan scale.

References

Amann, D. (2016) 'Inside the network hub: learnings and reflections from a network of NGOs, activists & researchers in Rio de Janeiro', unpublished MA dissertation, Institute of Development Studies, Sussex University.

Caldeira, T. and Holsten, J. (2015) 'Participatory urban planning in Brazil', *Urban Studies* 52(11): 2001–17, available from https://doi.org/10.1177/0042098014524461.

Casa Fluminense (2013) 'Projeto Geral e Plano Estratégico', *Casa Fluminense* [online], available from https://casafluminense.org.br/wp-content/uploads/2016/05/Projeto-Geral-Agosto-2013.pdf [accessed 22 May 2020].

Casa Fluminense (2019a) 'About Casa Fluminense', *Casa Fluminense* [online], available from http://casafluminense.org.br/a-casa-en/ [accessed 4 July 2019].

Casa Fluminense (2019b) 'Inequality map', *Casa Fluminense* [online], available from http://casafluminense.org.br/inequality-map/ [accessed 20 August 2019].

Casa Fluminense (2019c) 'Monitoring panel of the municipal management', *Casa Fluminense* [online], available from http://casafluminense.org.br/projetos/monitoring-panel-of-the-municipal-management/ [accessed 20 August 2019].

Casa Fluminense (2019d) 'Agenda Rio', *Casa Fluminense* [online], available from http://casafluminense.org.br/agenda-rio-2/ [accessed 20 August 2019].

Friendly, A. and Stiphany, K. (2019) 'Paradigm or paradox? The "cumbersome impasse" of the participatory turn in Brazilian urban planning', *Urban Studies*, 56(2): 271–87, available from https://doi.org/10.1177/0042098018768748.

Gaventa, J. (2006) 'Finding the spaces for change: a power analysis', *IDS Bulletins*, 37(6): 23–33.

Globo (2019) *Moradores de Realengo fazem mutirão de limpeza* [online], https://globoplay.globo.com/v/7852967/ [accessed 11 October 2019].

Interaction Design Foundation (2019) '5 Stages in the design thinking process' *Interaction Design Foundation* [online], available from https://www.interaction-design.org/literature/article/5-stages-in-the-design-thinking-process [accessed 5 July 2019].

Ribeiro, L.C. de Q. (ed) (2017) *Urban Transformations in Rio de Janeiro: Development, Segregation, and Governance*, New York: Springer.

Rolnik, R. (2013) 'Ten years of the City Statute in Brazil: from the struggle for urban reform to the World Cup cities', *International Journal of Urban Sustainable Development*, 5(1): 54–64, available from DOI: 10.1080/19463138.2013.782706.

United Nations (2019) 'Sustainable Development Goals: 17 goals to transform our world' *United Nations* [online], available from https://www.un.org/sustainabledevelopment/ [accessed 5 July 2019].

15

Working the hyphens of artist-academic-stakeholder in Co-Creation: a hopeful rendering of a community organisation and an organic intellectual

Bryan C. Clift, Maria Sarah da Silva Telles and Itamar Silva

Introduction

Perhaps it is easy to look at a city like Rio de Janeiro and despair. The urban inequalities are nowhere more noticeable than in the city's favelas, where approximately one fifth of the local population lives. Brazil's favelas, like other areas of apparent temporariness and marginality around the world, are fast becoming dominant modes of current urbanity (Davis, 2006). Frenzel (2016) proposed that two discourses commonly shape popular understandings of the favela. The first is a narrative of despair. This narrative recognises that those who live in favelas (the *favelados*) are situated at the intersection of multiple power formations and inequalities. They experience the stigmatising effects of mainstream media and policy through drug and gang activity, low income levels, unsanitary conditions, lack of education, police brutality, spatial stigmatisation, gender- and sex-based violence, employment and education discrimination, and racism.

The second narrative – which is less prominent – is a narrative of hope. In this narrative, the favela is more of a natural constituent of urbanisation; its spaces are neighbourhoods, sites of the vibrancy of urban life, collective agency, self-reliance, creativity, and entrepreneurialism. The winning of rights and legal positions or increased access to public services are examples of the progress of this narrative. Rio de Janeiro is replete with narratives of both despair and hope (Perlman, 2009). It is on a narrative of hope, and in particular the creative activism in one favela, Santa Marta, that this chapter focuses. Co-Creation is capable of responding to urban stigma through creativity, collectivity, and activism, and thus also capable of generating the narratives of hope, which this chapter develops.

From 2016 to 2019, a team of more than 30 researchers and activists from the EU, Mexico, and Brazil worked together to deliver Co-Creation projects in five cities around the world. Co-Creation is both a methodology and a knowledge project that brings together researchers, artists, and stakeholders in order to produce shared knowledge that can challenge, resist, or modify urban stigmatisation (see Chapter 1). Rio de Janeiro was one case among the five. In 2018, more than 20 researchers from the EU and Mexico, NGO members from the EU, and several researchers from Rio de Janeiro, collaborated with local stakeholders in Santa Marta, a favela in Rio de Janeiro's Zona Sul (South Zone). The key community organisation in Santa Marta with whom the project collaborated was Grupo Eco, which is led by Itamar Silva (who co-wrote this chapter). Over the course of five days, researchers, artists, and stakeholders aimed to produce shared knowledge that could challenge, resist, refute, or modify urban stigmatisation. Note that this chapter refers to Co-Creation as a methodology and knowledge project as outlined in Chapter 1; it refers to 'cultural activism' as a broader set of artist-activist-stakeholder practices or projects.

In this chapter, the authors reflect on the Co-Creation process in Santa Marta in 2016–19 by examining the relationships among artists-researchers-stakeholders, and – more intensively – the role of community organisations and activists and likewise the role of the researcher. Like other participatory methodologies, Co-Creation centralises the relationship between academic and non-academic partners (Banks and Hart, 2018). Examining these relationships is a way of 'working the hyphens' (Fine, 1994): that is, the process of examining the relationships between people in research. Fine suggested that, in doing so, writers interrogate how written representations may speak *of* or *for* Others through methodological, ethical, and epistemological considerations, a point reiterated by Ribeiro (2019) in a Brazilian context. A key aspect of this process is placing research and researchers in a broader historical political, economic, and social context. As this Co-Creation project brought together researchers from the Global North with researchers, stakeholders, and artists from the Global South, the reflection here focuses on Global North-South relations.

To guide their reflection, the authors drew on observations from Co-Creation projects in Santa Marta from 2016 to 2019 and conducted interviews with two academic professors in Brazil, two Brazilian NGO leaders, and eight Santa Marta residents and Grupo Eco members aged 18 to 70 in order to gain insight into various moments over Grupo Eco's more than 40-year history.

First, this chapter contextualises Santa Marta and Grupo Eco in terms of the area's historical inequalities and the role that creative expression and activism have played in a post-dictatorship Brazil. Second, it paints a picture of Silva's central role in the history and creative activism of Eco; he is also the leader, gatekeeper, and partner of the Rio Co-Creation case study. The chapter concludes by unpacking some of the elements that should be considered when engaging with local leadership in Co-Creative endeavours.

Co-Creation represents an opportunity for urban marginalised people to contribute to knowledge production across the Global North and South in a way that incorporates different perspectives, traditions, and origins of knowledge. If successful, Co-Creation can contribute meaningfully to the debate around the place of marginalised people in knowledge production. The authors argue that, in order to achieve its aims as a creative, participatory methodology and knowledge project, any Co-Creation project must examine the relationships it builds between its three key actors. To do so requires contextualisation in the country, city, and spaces in which it is undertaken, and indeed the people with whom it works.

Santa Marta and Grupo Eco: popular cultural activism in Rio

Santa Marta is located on the steep hillside of Dona Marta in the historic Botafogo neighbourhood in Rio de Janeiro. Migrants from the north began to populate the hillside during the 19th century, making homes out of wood and stucco, a prelude to the significant Brazilian rural-to-urban shift beginning in the 1940s. Continual population increase through further migration, a lack of water and electricity, and the muddy hillside were challenges residents faced. These were exacerbated by the lack of legal recognition for the settlement, which deprived residents of public services until the 1980s.

Today, houses are made of brick, and running water and electricity have been installed in homes. The residents who now live there (approximately 5,000) are bounded on one side by a wall built by the government to prevent further expansion, and, on the other, by a funicular to transport people up and down the hillside. Still, inadequate rubbish collection and open ditches pose serious health risks in the favela. Santa Marta's history of residential activism to improve this quality of life includes resistance, struggle, sorrow, and hope. Increasingly, activism in Santa Marta, like the rest of Brazil's cities, incorporates artistic and cultural expression.

The terrain for activism, democratic participation, and citizenship in Brazil has shifted over the last 50 years. In the waning few years of the Brazilian civil-military dictatorship in the late 1970s and early 1980s, discernible collective action began to emerge. A prominent example is the mobilisation of the metalworkers' unions and strikes that challenged the military with new leadership for working people, and which gave rise to the Partido dos Trabalhadores (PT) – the Workers' Party – and to the Leftist leader, future President, Luiz Inácio Lula da Silva (known as Lula) (Bourne, 2008). It is from here that forms of collective action reverberated out in the 1980s (Dagnino, 2006; Caldeira and Adriano, 2014). A range of groups grew and strengthened, notably slum movements, Black resistance, gender and sexuality movements, and ecological action. These Leftist movements fostered the emergence of a new political imaginary wherein democratic participation became possible (Dagnino, 2006; Ferrero et al, 2019).

In the 2000s, a new protagonism emerged in the public space of Brazilian cities – partially in response to the formal integration of the Left in formal governmental and bureaucratic systems. Groups of mostly young, black people living in segregated and stigmatised areas, the favelas, mobilised cultural expression and intervention in the form of painting, writing, film, and other digital and electronic media to occupy spaces historically dominated by the upper classes (Caldeira and Adriano, 2014). Using often aggressive language, they denounced the discrimination against them, refuted their positioning as victims, and resignified the city's criminalised spaces (Caldeira and Adriano, 2014). Beginning in São Paulo, such groups spread across Brazil's urban environments, transgressing and even inverting the cultural productions of urban space. As cultural productions continue to be a form through which activism, resistance, and social justice are expressed and might occur, it is at this contemporary juncture in Brazilian history and culture that Co-Creation becomes a suitable academic methodology to contribute to such agendas.

In 1976 in Santa Marta, eight people came together to publish a community newspaper, *The Eco*. Headquartered in Itamar Silva's parent's home, the paper recorded activities in the community and reflected upon the role of the Residents' Association (Pandolfi and Grynszpan, 2003). Over time, and as the group expanded its work in the community with ditch digging and cleaning, building housing, or cultural activities, they became known as 'the Eco people' (Pandolfi and Grynszpan, 2003). Grupo Eco – self-defined as 'a school without walls' – was established. It nurtured two major areas of work: needs within the favela, and those in connection with other favelas, institutions, NGOs, government, or universities in Rio. Explicit in its agenda has been a strong cultural focus. Its initial newspaper, a cultural product itself, included publicising cultural events, like samba and festivals; as it expanded, its cultural expressions did, too. Its annual holiday camp was an example of responding to the total absence of vacations for children in the favela who, by and large, stayed in their homes through the summer months. For children, the opportunity to move beyond the walls of the favela safely was rare. This was the first holiday camp offered in favelas in Rio.

Another cultural output of Grupo Eco was its arts productions, such as theatre, music, and visual art. One notable example is its theatre group, which formed in 1977 to communicate with residents. The impact of the theatre activities, in particular, resonated with residents. One favela resident recounted her experience in theatre with Eco:

> 'I fell in love with theatre. Looking for a theatre group in 1992, I found the Eco theatre group in the nursery at Casa Santa Marta. Itamar was an actor. Eventually he invited me to the Eco group for a Sunday meeting. I was very young and I wanted to be an actress. I took theatre courses in other places and tried to become an actress. The Eco group captivated me, and I started working at the holiday camp' (Favela resident, 43, female)

Through her school and work with Eco, this resident aspired to and then did go to college in pursuit of a degree and profession in communications. She still volunteers with Eco. From her contacts in the communications industry, the news organisation TVT recorded the holiday camps and published a piece on them, a testament to the influence of Eco, its participants, and their ability to speak to broader audiences about the challenges and possibilities in Santa Marta. The theatre group performed in schools, the samba school of São Gonçalo, other favelas of the State of Rio de Janeiro, and in Santa Marta, and other venues during a short series of tours. The group's formation and their performances are reminiscent of the Leftist politics and inspirations of Boal (2006) and Freire (2005): theatre brought residents together, introduced avenues of mobility around the city and beyond, called forward discussion of important issues in the urban margin and its stigmatisation, and brought some of those discussions with them to the places in which they performed.

Perhaps less artistic but no less cultural, another example is from the area of tourism. Another resident is the founder and operator of a tourism initiative in Santa Marta. Born in Santa Marta and a participant in Eco since adolescence, she lives there with her son and mother. From her experience with Eco and while studying tourism at university in the early 1990s, she sought to bring political activism into the domain of tourism. In Santa Marta, she created a social enterprise in her tour to achieve this. She shared that the central aim of her company is "to disrupt favela stereotypes", which she framed like this:

> "We go to discussions with other groups that are developing tourism in other favelas to develop a communitarian tourism base. We do understand that if we do not talk about the favela then people will never come here and will never develop a different perspective of the favela. We have to work very hard with stereotypes. Sometimes, people come in here reinforcing stereotypes rather than deconstructing them." (Favela resident, 45, female)

Walking through the streets and homes in Santa Marta, she shared the favela's history, sought to educate about and provoke consideration of the challenges the neighbourhood faces, and to foster discussion rather than offering a romanticised or stigmatised image. Her efforts directly resonate with the contemporary efforts to resignify the city's stigmatised spaces (Caldeira and Adriano, 2014).

Cultural expression has been a central role for progressive moments, actions and activism in Santa Marta for more than 40 years. Arguably, Eco's 40-year-plus existence resides at the heart of this collective mobilisation. That history is evident, too, when walking through its streets. Graffiti frequently splashes across walls with political messages, such as one cascading colourful representation of Santa Marta with the message, 'The rich want peace to continue to be rich, we want peace to stay alive'. A statue of Michael Jackson about three quarters of the way up the hill celebrates the celebrity-musician from when the area was selected as one site in Rio for the filming of Jackson's video for 'They don't care about us'. That knowledge and statue now helps funnel tourists up the slope to Santa Marta. In its shops, a range of material culture produced by local artists depicts life in the favela; this serves the double purpose of contributing to the local economy and claiming some of the ground upon which favelas are depicted.

For the purposes of Co-Creation this history is important. Artistry and activism have long been present in Santa Marta. Among the three central actors of Co-Creation's methodology – artists-researchers-stakeholders – Eco members and residents form a central part of the favela's stakeholders, while the cultural vibrancy of Santa Marta only expands. A strong historical relationship already existed among the three methodological actors. For the researchers from the Global North who arrived in Santa Marta, the capacity to *do* Co-Creation became a moment for a meeting of knowledges of the Global North and South, and of community activists, artists, and researchers. Itamar Silva, played a pivotal role in this meeting and process, partly because he is an organic intellectual as the next section explains.

Community partners, academics, and organic intellectualism in Santa Marta

Essential to the success of Co-Creation are collaborations with community partners. The community groups and individuals striving to do Co-Creation are numerous and varied. How researchers link up with a community and with whom are points of choice and tension. Working with an entire organisation, people with specific roles, a single individual, a team or group, or an amalgamation of individual activists, artists, or residents – all these bring unique benefits and challenges. Both how people are involved in their community and how they become involved in a project carry significance for the shape, direction, and success of a project. Like other participatory methodologies, Co-Creation raises issues about power relations, hierarchies, and ownership in the research/Co-Creation process, which need to be acknowledged by all participants (Mitchell et al, 2017). The process by which the team of researchers and NGO members established links for the Co-Creation project in Rio de Janeiro, and therefore by which relationships between project members and the community of Santa Marta began to form, occurred through Itamar Silva.

From the beginning, some researchers from the Pontifical Catholic University of Rio de Janeiro (PUC) and Grupo Eco worked with the academic drivers of the project from the Global North in the planning and preparation of the workshop. The research team had immediate access to a researcher-community from previous PUC-Eco collaborations. Because Eco opened up their network, the team were able to access a range of people using cultural practices in response to urban stigma, notably: activist-oriented tourism; other tour operators; graffiti artists such as Tick (see Chapter 16); local residents with whom the research team could speak and conduct activities, such as urban mapping, photography, and food practices; Escola Bola's football players and coaches, with whom the research team spoke and played; and slam-poets with whom the research team performed. Partly this was to assist in the development of the project, but partly also it was to communicate to the research team the scope of cultural activism already happening in Santa Marta. To begin setting in motion all of these opportunities, the Eco group brought the idea of working with the research team up for discussion. Eco acted as an advocate for the project, as it represented a transformative methodology using creativity to combat stereotypes, promote social justice, and account for perceptions of various urban actors. The project also sought to bridge Eco's commitments and agendas.

Since the 1970s, the favela had become a prominent area of study for social scientists, notably among urban studies, anthropology, and sociology. Of this work, Valladares (2019: 135) has raised the question: 'Has the favela become the location of research, rather than its object?' (p.135). The distinction here is important. The former risks reifying the very social stigmas that have claimed a strong representational form through a variety of knowledge sources. Valladares points to three dogmas in academic research: the construction of the favela as a 'different' space, which marks it out as separate; the territorialisation of the favela as a space of and for poverty, which actually fortifies this idea; and the reduction of the idea of the 'favela' into a single association, undermining the diversity, differences and distinctions of favelas while treating them all the same (Valladares, 2019). Santa Marta, in particular, has received considerable attention in the last 15 years because of its designation as the model favela for pacification beginning in 2008, its location within Zona Sul, its spotlighting through investment from the Federal Plan for Growth Acceleration (PAC), and international attention from global sporting mega-events (Gaffney, 2010; Clift and Andrews, 2012). Although Eco's leadership knew well the debates about research in favelas and the challenges/possibilities that it brings, the organisation welcomed the research team in the spirit of collaboration and being part of their fight for social justice, both of which speak to the group's community-driven mindfulness.

Recognising the numerous challenges of Santa Marta residents and based on his lifetime commitment to improving the quality of people's lives, Silva's approach to leadership and political action can be characterised as that of an 'organic intellectual'. Gramsci (2006) suggested that organic intellectuals carry a unique ability to see hegemonic conceptions of the world and bring about modes of thought that challenge and engage with the power structures affronting self-empowerment and sovereignty. Importantly, Gramsci made a distinction between 'traditional' professional intellectuals who have established standing through specialised training, roles, and professions (for example teachers, doctors, lawyers, and so on) with accrued socioeconomic statuses that set them apart from other sections of social and political life, and 'organic' intellectuals who arise within and in response to political moments and the challenges facing marginalised or oppressed groups. In Silva's case, he founded and led Eco while also choosing to work with two NGOs and then the Instituto Brasileiro de Analises Sociais e Economicas (IBASE) – a not-for-profit citizenship organisation founded in 1981 that contributes to public debates on social issues in Brazil and that seeks to build a democratic culture of rights, strengthen associative fabric of civil society, and broaden citizen participation in policy making (IBASE, 2019). Maintaining his connection to Santa Marta and favela life is evident not only in his employment choices but his residential ones, too.

Silva chooses to live in Santa Marta despite having the ability to move out, in what would otherwise be considered an upward socioeconomic change. One professor of sociology who was an intellectual mentor to Itamar spoke about his choice:

> "A striking example is the fact that he did not stop living in the favela, and surely he would have the financial, cultural and intellectual conditions to leave. A lot of people go out and stay connected in a favela, but no longer live there. This is a process of upward mobility that goes beyond the favela's space. Itamar? No, he still lives there. Most of the favela's organic intellectuals leave the favela precisely because they are intellectual and organic. Not Itamar. He makes a point of staying in the favela. For me, it's Itamar's brand." (Interviewee, 70, male)

Silva's choice to live in Santa Marta illustrates the connection he shares with its people and the community while he drives forward a progressive, consciousness-raising agenda. A further example of his strong connection to Santa Marta, the professor noted, are the holiday camps that he runs each year, remarking that Silva takes a break from work to run these. Using his own holiday time away from work, Silva leads Eco in its engagement with between 200 and 300 children from

Santa Marta. In doing so, Silva reiterates the enduring relationship that he has developed with the community. That professor further remarked that he has "tremendous admiration for Itamar" and he is not the only one. There are many scholars who research favelas and who admire Silva because, as the professor went on to say, of his "authenticity as an intellectual of the periphery in general and of the favela in particular .... He is one of the favela's organic intellectuals."

The impact of Silva, Grupo Eco, and their cultural activism is profound. Consider the following testimonies from Santa Marta residents and Eco participants. One woman discussed Silva's and Eco's presence in Santa Marta:

> "Itamar is an adviser, someone you can question. Today, I have a relationship with him of respect. Itamar plants the seed for the future. What is the continuity for Eco? Who are the next to continue it? You can't think of Santa Marta without Eco." (Resident, 26, female)

She also communicated the impact her participation had on her:

> "Today, as an adult you may be able to discern issues of inequality, but when you are a teenager, especially in a favela, it is very difficult for you to do so. It is very difficult for you to position yourself in the world. Saying 'No, I am a beautiful, black woman, I am empowered, I can work in the field I choose' is difficult. Even to create a hope that you can and are capable of achieving is hard. We know the issues that limit our journey. Women in leadership positions are difficult to find, but we cannot lose hope that somehow we can achieve and achieve together. I think that Eco has brought me, or strengthened within me, if not created this feeling that I and we can win. But it is of no use if your community is not with you, thriving together ... . Eco helped me a lot to position myself. I survived in terms of gender, race, being able to speak. I work in an engineering company that has many more men than women. There is the issue of race and gender. I am a woman, black and peripheral." (Resident, 26, female)

Another younger resident went as far as to compare the children who participate in Eco with those who do not:

"Eco has been here for a long time. Everyone knows this. Itamar's ideas spread. Eco is something that cannot die ... something we cannot let die. The children who are not in Eco, unfortunately, are in drug trafficking. There are teenagers who went to my classes, they are trafficking now. I don't keep in touch. They really wanted to show off, to make easy money." (Resident, 18, female)

Like the tourism activist previously quoted, these two women and other residents communicated the relevance and importance of Eco and Silva in improving the lives of those who choose to join Eco. The group's work is a continual community effort to challenge, refute, and combat urban marginality. Silva's character, coupled with his leadership, prominence, and commitment in Santa Marta with Eco, evince the character of an organic intellectual. For the research team, he became the hinge through which the academic-artist-stakeholder relations were made possible.

For researchers seeking to do Co-Creation, recognition and attention must be given to the idea of who has control over a project. Researchers must become comfortable with ceding control. This comes with tremendous upsides in some instances, as well as several challenges. In the Santa Marta case study, links were established with a person and a group with such strong ties to the community that researchers were linked into a network of people and places in numerous ways. Yet, entering into a network of such strong communal ties also brings tension.

Conclusion

The research team's experience of Co-Creation in Santa Marta has led them to recognise that what does and does not work is always contingent on the people in the context of the research itself. In the Santa Marta project, the people with whom the research team collaborated played a pivotal role; these were predominantly Eco and Itamar Silva. The context of Santa Marta, Rio de Janeiro, and Brazil's broader position in the Global South offer further insights into the workings of Co-Creative practices. Through these two important considerations, people and context, this section offers several reflective questions for readers considering Co-Creation as a methodology.

Collaborating in the Global South makes us aware of broader power dynamics. The very authorship of this chapter drew together different positionalities. The first author, Clift, is a cultural studies researcher from the Global North who has limited time and experience in Rio de Janeiro but is learning; he does not have a grasp of Portuguese beyond a basic level. In Santa Marta, he represents an extreme outsider who is anxious about conducting research that colonises urban marginalised people. The second author, da Silva Telles, has worked as a professor of sociology and urban marginality for more than 30 years. Despite this track record and her location within the Global South, she, too, faces challenges around producing knowledge when trying to write not from the point of view of a researcher but rather from the point of view of urban marginalised people. Is it up to academics to write about favelas? Or is it for its residents to do this? Are there ways of producing knowledge that better enable this to occur? These are questions that have been placed on the table of sociology for some time in the Global North and South. The third author, Silva, has a vested interest in the community but he cannot speak for everyone. Inside the favela, he faces the challenge of producing knowledge that is valuable for residents while acknowledging the impossibility of representing everyone. Collectively, the team comes from radically different perspectives. This chapter itself is a good opportunity to discuss and grapple with these challenges.

In the case of Santa Marta and Eco, a rich history of cultural activism and artistry brought together in different ways already exists. It is clear that artistic and creative endeavours in Santa Marta open 'cracks in the system' (Mouffe, 2013). Thus, an important aim of this chapter is to recognise the marvellous social and cultural activism that largely goes unnoticed by academia that tends to see things only through its own theories, methods, and views. Co-Creation is an opportunity to produce knowledge through a variety of perspectives; it is one that can reframe how academic knowledge is produced by doing so more on the terms of those about whom it produces that knowledge. This process, however, is neither simplistic nor straightforward.

Where cultural activism already exists, researchers from both the North and South risk becoming colonisers themselves of knowledge already in existence. Doing so can reify divisions within a city's centre and margin. This can also reify the divisions between the Global North and South wherein the South and urban marginalised people are positioned as underdeveloped and known only through a colonialist or neo-imperialist fantasy. In this framing, researchers from the Global North or South descend upon the favela with knowledge to share or pass on to 'uneducated' or 'impoverished' *favelados*. Through collaboration, knowledge exchange, and communication, Co-Creation as a knowledge project seeks to directly disrupt this danger. In the more collaborative spirit of Co-Creation, the process of creating together enables researchers, artists, and activists/stakeholders to work together to further advance the agendas already set in motion through a new or modified series of actions that develop something that otherwise would not be possible.

The artistic and creative elements of Co-Creation are intended to be the instrument that 'levels' differential voices or footings that systemic power structures typically reinforce (see Chapter 1). Doing so can generate a respectful and mutually beneficial way of advancing socially progressive agendas. In the Santa Marta case study, this resulted in a collective reflection on Santa Marta from a diversity of perspectives – its challenges and potentiality. Only in a few moments in its history have its leaders and activities been brought face-to-face, without tension, to discuss local projects and dynamics. The process of Co-Creation broke some internal resistances that enabled these discussions to happen. Moreover, the role switching between actors enabled a renewal of views of the favela. Residents and leaders who live in a favela can reproduce the favela based solely on their specific struggles and points of view, and thus lose the ability to account for a diversity of actors and the complexity of demands. Artists, residents, leaders, and activists who participated in the project experience Santa Marta a little more broadly, opening views and potentials.

The artist-researcher-stakeholder triad poses an earnest, relationship-focused process for Co-Creation. Who sets the agenda? Engaging with community partners, researchers must recognise that this triadic relationship has several impacts on the possibilities of research. Any entry point into a community opens up opportunities but closes others. In Santa Marta, the Co-Creation project was delimited by working with Silva and Eco. As such, the research team gained access to the people and spaces familiar to this group, but the people who do not regularly engage with Eco were excluded. There is a significant portion of the community that the research team did not reach and there are likely other Santa Marta organisations with whom to work on Co-Creation. One strategy for overcoming this can be 'snowballing' from initial contacts to the wider community. Doing so requires time and care to maintain a positive and productive relationship with those people from whom we snowball. This is a seriously challenging endeavour for work that includes numerous researchers who predominantly live and work in the Global North. Nor can we link up with one person just to get to another, which effectively undermines the collaborative and collective spirit of Co-Creation. For researchers, the agenda must be open to change based on the needs, interests, motivations, and passions of those living within a given context.

Relatedly, in practice how do Co-Creation participants envision their relationship to the people of a project? Co-Creation requires researchers to be diverse in their interactions. In some instances, researchers can lead whereas in others they can be participants. The ability to shift our roles and interactions is always contingent upon the location, the time available to people, language differences, and so forth. How close or how far are the researchers and the place chosen for Co-Creation? In Santa Marta, people are already engaged in the artistry and activism aligned in response to iniquitous conditions.

In this position, researchers must ask: What is our role here? What and how do we contribute? Do we bring anything new to the table? Are we just incorporating these forms of knowledge production in the academy (and in doing so are we at risk of becoming colonisers ourselves)? Are we (academic) reporters? Or are we trying to do something *new* with these groups, where our presence has a positive impact on the artistry-activism already happening? In a context where there is little organisation, such a project would look radically different. Our first task in Co-Creation, then, is to begin to know a place, its people, their organisation, and their histories.

If Co-Creation is to be a successful knowledge project to and for the people for whom it claims to represent, speak, and speak with, then it necessarily must openly reflect upon the relationships it develops in the process of its unfolding. Consider that, with Eco, Itamar Silva has been active in the fight against urban marginalisation in Rio de Janeiro for more than 40 years: who, then, is the 'expert' or 'intellectual' here? Listening is one of the most powerful things researchers can do. Too quickly researchers can become complicit in the writing of the Other (Spivak, 1988; Ribeiro, 2019). Fine (1994) suggested, like Spivak (1988) and Scott (1988), that rather than try to 'know' or 'give voice' researchers should listen to the voices of those Othered, as themselves constructors and agents of knowledge. In this reflective chapter, the research team aimed to listen and write together, a Global North researcher, a Global South researcher, and an organic intellectual of the favela.

This reflective illustration, contextualisation, and working of hyphens compel us to constantly locate our work within broader power formations as we consider the roles of those involved. In Brazil, such considerations assist in thinking through Valladares's (2019) rhetorical question: on whose terms is the favela (re)invented? In thinking through both the processes and products of Co-Creation, asking this question is a necessity in all cities and their margins.

References

Banks, S. and Hart, A. (2018) *Co-producing Research: A Community Development Approach,* Bristol: Policy Press.

Boal, A. (2006) *The Aesthetics of the Oppressed* (translated by A. Jackson), London: Routledge.

Bourne, R. (2008) *Lula of Brazil: The Story So Far,* Los Angeles, CA: University of California Press.

Caldeira, T. and Adriano, S. (2014) 'Gênero continua a ser o campo de batalhas: juventude, produção cultural e a reinvenção do espaço público em São Paulo', *Revista USP,* 102: 83–100.

Clift, B.C. and Andrews, D.L. (2012) 'Living Lula's passion: the politics of Rio 2016', in H.J. Lenskyi and S. Wagg (eds) *The Palgrave Handbook of Olympic Studies,* Basingstoke: Palgrave Macmillan, pp 210–32.

Dagnino, E. (2006) 'Dimensions of citizenship in contemporary Brazil', *Fordham L. Rev.,* 75: 2469.

Davis, M. (2006) *Planet of Slums,* London: Verso.

Ferrero, J.P., Natalucci, A. and Tatagiba, L. (eds) (2019) *Socio-Political Dynamics within the Crisis of the Left: Argentina and Brazil,* London: Rowman & Littlefield International.

Fine, M. (1994) 'Working the hyphens: reinventing self and other in qualitative research', in N. Denzin and Y.S. Lincoln (eds) *Handbook of Qualitative Research,* Thousand Oaks, CA: Sage, pp 70–82.

Freire, P. (2005) *Pedagogy of the Oppressed* (translated by M.B. Ramos), New York, NY: Continuum.

Frenzel, F. (2016) *Slumming It,* London: Zed Books.

Gaffney, C. (2010) 'Mega-events and socio-spatial dynamics in Rio de Janeiro, 1919–2016', *Journal of Latin American Geography,* 9(1): 7–29.

Gramsci, A. (2006) 'Hegemony, intellectuals and the state', in J. Story (ed) *Cultural Theory and Popular Culture: A Reader,* Athens, GA: University of Georgia Press, pp 85–91.

Instituto Brasileiro de Analises Sociais e Economicas (IBASE) (2019) *iBase,* available from https://ibase.br/pt/.

Mitchell, C., De Lange, N. and Moletsane, R. (2017) *Participatory Visual Methodologies: Social Change, Community and Policy,* London: Sage.

Mouffe, C. (2013) *Agonistics: Thinking the World Politically,* London: Verso.

Pandolfi, D.C. and Grynszpan, M. (orgs) (2003) *A Favela Fala: Depoimentos ao CPDOC,* Rio de Janeiro: Editora FGV.

Perlman, J. (2009) *Favela: Four Decades of Living on the Edge in Rio de Janeiro*, Oxford: Oxford University Press.

Ribeiro, D. (2019) *Lugar de Fala*, Chapel Hill, NC: Pólen Produção Editorial LTDA.

Scott, J.W. (1988) 'Deconstructing equality versus difference', *Feminist Studies*, 14(1): 32–50.

Spivak, G.C. (1988) 'Can the subaltern speak?', in C. Nelson and L. Grossberg (eds), *Marxism and the Interpretation of Culture*, Urbana, IL: University of Illinois Press, pp 280–316.

Valladares, L.d.P. (2019) *The invention of the favela* (translated by R.N. Anderson), Chapel Hill, NC: University of North Carolina Press.

16

Artist-researcher collaborations in Co-Creation: redesigning favela tourism around graffiti

Leandro 'Tick' Rodrigues and Christina Horvath

Introduction

As the previous chapters have demonstrated, each Co-Creation experience is unique. Project outcomes and dynamics vary greatly from one project to the other depending on their origins, length, the actors who initiated them and the interactions between the originators and other participants. Workshops can be instigated by academics with expertise in research design, by artists familiar with creative techniques or local actors knowledgeable about issues relevant to the community. Roles are, however, rarely clear-cut and several combinations are possible, including those of artist-researchers, community researchers or community artists.

This chapter explores an artist-driven Co-Creation experience initiated by a graffiti artist from the Global South who is also an activist embedded in a local community. This bottom-up, organic Co-Creation experience was supported by a group of researchers from a Global North university and the analysis presented in this chapter has been produced collaboratively by the artist and one of the researchers. This close collaboration between artist and researchers and Global South and Global North participants presented the two authors with multiple opportunities to observe how trust-based relationships are developed between participants of different backgrounds and to reflect on the role of the artist as the project initiator, as well as on the researchers' contribution to both the creative process and the knowledge production.

The initiative took place in the Rio de Janeiro favela of Tabajaras & Cabritos in July–August 2019. It was designed by graffiti artist Leandro Rodrigues – aka Tick – in collaboration with four social science researchers from the University of Bath and a group of local residents and stakeholders. Its aim was to establish a new walking tour focusing on street art in and around Tabajaras & Cabritos by extending a previous favela tour, which had been discontinued in 2017 due to the increase of violence in the neighbourhood. Including larger sections of the surrounding areas of Copacabana, Bairro Peixoto and Botafogo was seen by Tick as a potential way to make the tour sustainable, as it would allow guides to avoid areas of risk on days of armed conflict in the favela. The redesign also gave the opportunity to shift from the tour's previous focus on favela lifestyle, local history and political resistance to a new narrative about creativity, socially engaged street art and collaboration between artists and communities living on the margin. While this shift required painting additional murals in the area and renovating some of the existing ones, it was seen by the participants as an opportunity to attract new audiences who normally avoid favela tours, change visitors' perceptions about disadvantaged communities, improve residents' skills and self-esteem and create new synergies between them and the visitors.

Situated in the city's South Zone between Copacabana and Botafogo, Tabajaras & Cabritos stretches between the streets of Siqueira Campos and Real Grandeza. It is crossed by a wooded hiking path that offers spectacular views of the city's landmarks. The community's 4,243 inhabitants (Census, 2010) have access to electricity, running water, sanitation and healthcare. The arrival of the UPP (Pacifying Police Unit) in 2010 brought about a period of relative peace and prosperity, which contributed to urban growth, gentrification and rising property prices (Almeida, 2014).

A study undertaken in 2012 by Rio de Janeiro-based business management consultant SEBRAE (Brazilian Support Service to Micro and Small Entrepreneurs in Rio de Janeiro) exposed the favela's potential for alternative forms of tourism including ecotourism, cyclotourism, and community-based, cultural and adventure tourism (Sampaio Correia et al, 2013). It also highlighted that 99 per cent of the residents were favourable to receiving visitors and tourists in the community (Sampaio Correia et al, 2013: 58). The start-up Tabritours, launched in 2012 by certified guide Gilmar Lopes, exploited the opportunities created by the 2014 football World Cup and the 2016 Olympic Games to employ up to 220 residents during these large events. It was, however, discontinued in 2017 after the Olympics were over and the security issues returned (Interview Gilmar Lopes, 2019).

Tick, who initiated the workshop, had been working with Tabritours previously. He was also familiar with Co-Creation methods since he was involved in a previous Co-Creation initiative in the favela of

Santa Marta, Rio de Janeiro, in the summer of 2018 (see Chapters 4, 5 and 15). The communication between Tick and the group of four researchers from Bath was facilitated by the fact that one member of the team was a graffiti writer. After about one year of preparatory planning, Tick invited the researchers, along with local stakeholders and members from the community, to contribute to the collaborative design of an open-air street art gallery and a walking tour in his neighbourhood. The participants agreed on using Co-Creation to develop a shared understanding of local challenges and opportunities which would underpin the tour's narrative. Co-Creation was selected for its potential to make unheard voices emerge and to combine practice-based knowledge that exists within the community with scholarly understandings of sustainable and ethical tourism developed by the researchers. It was anticipated that further reciprocal benefits of using this methodology would include opportunities to test Co-Creation in a context of urban disadvantage and examine its potential to promote an exchange between epistemologies of the Global South and North.

Co-Creation aims to create a safe environment in which all participants commit to respect each other and recognise and mitigate power inequalities existing within the group. In this case, such inequalities included diverging levels of artistic skills, unequal access to financial resources (the initiative used EU funding for the Co-Creation project), and the uneven distribution of academic and community-based knowledge. At the start of the six-week experiment, focusing on the redesign, participants defined Co-Creation as a methodology seeking to counter stereotypes, promoting equality, creativity and new synergies between participants, and encouraging alternative visions that take into account stakeholders' perceptions. The group agreed that, to be successful, the workshop should help them develop a shared vision for the tour, provide participants with new skills and opportunities for self-expression, and increase community members' networks.

Favela tourism in Rio de Janeiro

Tourism in Rio de Janeiro's favelas started in the 1990s and has grown into an industry attracting approximately 40,000 visitors annually (Freire-Medeiros, 2013). In recent years, a wealth of literature has addressed tours that exploit outsiders' curiosity about disadvantaged urban areas in Brazil and elsewhere. Such tours have been referred to as 'slum tourism', 'social tours', 'reality tours', 'cultural tourism', 'poverty tourism' and 'poorism' (Burgold and Rolfes, 2013).

Some suggest that tourists' main motivation for participating in such walks is either a morbid curiosity for poverty or philanthropy. However, Carter (2017) and Dovey and King (2012) have demonstrated that many visitors are less attracted by poverty than by picturesque vernacular architecture, utopic communities and village-like social links. They often see favelas as inventive, creative and resilient communities engaged in a struggle for self-liberation (Carter, 2017: 424). Such qualities particularly appeal to tourists alienated by neoliberalism, solitude, rationalism or lack of agency in the Global North (Carter, 2017: 424). According to Burgold and Rolfes (2013: 166), most favela tours are marketed as 'real' and 'authentic' and, similar to ecotourism or volunteer tourism, they seek to anticipate and counter tourists' moral doubts by projecting themselves 'as a more desirable alternative to usual programmes of mass tourism ... characterised by sameness, crudeness' (170).

Ethical preoccupations are core to most research focusing on favela tours. Scholars often flag up either their morally dubious aspects (such as voyeurism, intrusion into the residents' privacy and dignity, exploitation, and markedly asymmetrical relationships between the tourists and the residents) or their positive, philanthropic goals. Most research suggests that, to be ethical and mutually beneficial for visitors and host communities, tours have to avoid excessive and disrespectful photography and zoo-like sightseeing, and should promote agency, contribute to develop residents' self-esteem and networks, generate material benefits for residents, local entrepreneurs and social projects, and challenge predominantly negative perceptions (dangerous, stagnant, dirty, criminal, lacking hygiene and education) by replacing these with positive attributes (entrepreneurship, initiative, activity, hope, education, culture, creativity and community). Research has also shown that most tours actually do improve tourists' opinions (Burgold and Rolfes, 2013: 167) even if language barriers and asymmetries in income, social status and mobility often impede genuine exchange between hosts and visitors.

While most authors assume that community-based tourism provides 'a meaningful and transformative experience that is rewarding for both tourists and local communities', Dürr and Jaffe (2012) also show that 'cultural productions, from mural to photo exhibitions to movies and socio-religious innovations' allow residents to 'take action themselves, using tourism as a means to advance their goals by representing and performing a more favourable image to a global audience' (2012: 115–6). Therefore, they consider that residents' involvement in organising and guiding tours, setting up museums, and interacting with tourists as artists or artisans provides an opening for more nuanced alternative representations which use global connections to achieve local change (Dürr and Jaffe, 2012: 116).

In his analysis of street art in relation to tourism, Klein (2018) noted that the patrimonialisation of street art and its increasing incorporation into processes of urban regeneration since the mid-2000s resulted in the emergence of initiatives seeking to attract tourists to urban areas prominent in street art production. Graffiti tours call into question conventional oppositions between ordinary and extraordinary and touristic and non-touristic places. They propose multidimensional cultural experiences to satisfy the needs of an emerging market for more differentiated goods and services. Similar to favela tours, street art tourism claims to offer a 'real' and 'authentic' experience to those who seek to discover 'within a controlled and secure framework' (Klein, 2018: 60) an originally criminalised practice born and located in conflicted or segregated neighbourhoods. However, unlike favela tours, which tend to be community-based and mainly attract tourists from other countries or regions, street art tours are generally offered as private products destined for young urban visitors, both foreign and local (Klein, 2018: 65–66). Thus, street art tourism has a stronger potential to attract local tourists who generally shun favela destinations and also a better capacity to revalorise urban areas, change perceptions, divert attention from the extraordinary to the everyday, and create spaces of participation, conviviality and dialogue.

From the researchers' initial review of favela tourism in Rio, it was found that, while there is substantial research on tourism in Rocinha and Santa Marta, tours in other South-Zone favelas such as Tabajaras & Cabritos constitute an under-researched area. To build an understanding of the South-Zone tours currently on offer and their narratives, the team undertook a series of participant observations on walks run by community-based guides in Santa Marta, Vidigal, Cantagalo and Babilônia. Most of these walking tours had a general focus and promoted a historical approach, with the notable exception of the tour in Babilônia which focused on hiking. Guides addressed the origins of the foundation, naming and construction of each favela and emphasised the residents' resistance to material difficulties and political adversity. Visits by famous people (such as the Pope, Michael Jackson or Barack Obama) and cultural products (films, videos featuring favelas) were also mentioned. The presence of crèches, schools, non-governmental organisations (NGOs), resident associations, sport and dance facilities, and other social projects inside the communities was equally highlighted. Guides indicated the best views, but not all of them encouraged tourists to buy local drinks, food or artefacts. Tours were presented as authentic experiences, although it was not always clearly explained how they contributed to the community. The presence of the UPP, police pacification, political and security issues were mentioned sporadically and, in some cases, visitors were warned from taking photographs in certain places.

While street art was visible in most favelas, it was rarely made prominent in the tours. In Cantagalo and Santa Marta, murals representing residents carrying water or construction materials were used as mere illustrations for local history but no attention was dedicated to their aesthetic qualities. In Cantagalo and Vidigal, guides mentioned some local artists and initiatives aiming to establish open-air galleries. However, tours generally failed to discuss how these initiatives related to street art culture in Rio de Janeiro and none of them provided information about the techniques and styles used by the artists. In contrast, a feminist-themed street art tour observed in the city centre around Olympic Avenue provided some biographic data about female artists and a more coherent narrative about their difficulties and messages. Yet contextual information about the city's graffiti scene and artists' distinctive aesthetics were not included in this tour either.

The literature review and the observations allowed the artist and the researchers to develop an in-depth understanding of the niche market on which the tour designed by Tick intended to focus. Developed at the intersection of community-based tourism and street art tourism, the tour in Tabajaras & Cabritos could tap into local guides' knowledge of the community including local history, social projects and lifestyle while also providing information about street art's aesthetic evolution, role and day-to-day functioning in Rio's South Zone and its impact on favela populations. This original and authentic angle appeared to have a strong potential to attract a diverse tourist population including local, Brazilian and foreign visitors, thereby offering multiple opportunities to confront and challenge stereotypes about favelas.

Leandro Tick and socially engaged street art in Rio de Janeiro

This section will introduce socially engaged graffiti artist Leandro Tick (see Figures 16.1 and 16.2). Tick was born in the Northeast of Brazil and arrived in Tabajaras & Cabritos in 1992 at the age of eight. A self-taught artist, he started using spray paint around the age of 13 and completed his first wall in 2001 at the age of 17. He first began to produce murals in the neighbourhood using magazines and relied on

Figure 16.1: Self-portrait by Tick.

Source: Clara Bosso.

online media and contact with other artists to improve his technique. He has progressively developed a figurative style, using bright colours and natural elements including birds, plants, flowers and trees. Today he is known for his photographic portraits, distinctive cityscapes representing symbolic rather than realistic favelas, as well as for his interest in collaborative, participatory projects.

Street art gained prominence in the context of urban marginality in New York in the 1960s and 1970s and spread rapidly across the world as an expression of marginalised urban youth (Klein, 2018: 57). In Brazil, artists have used it as a coping mechanism for the long-lasting

Figure 16.2: Tick painting.

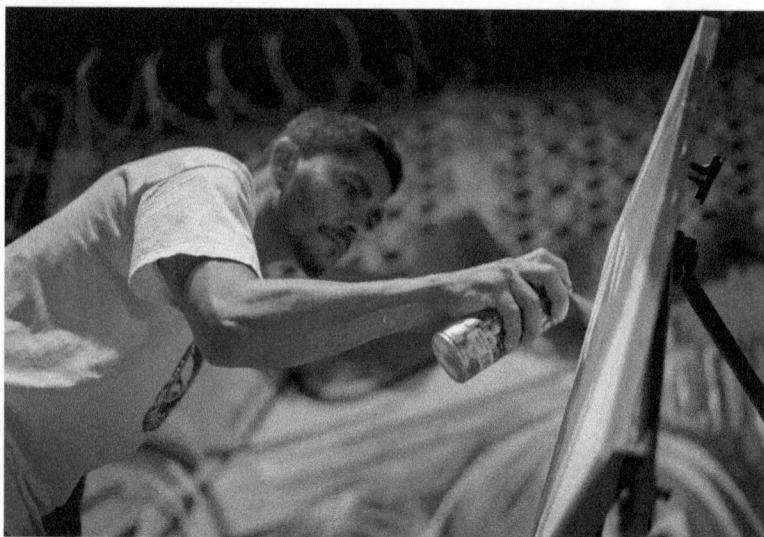

Source: Clara Bosso.

challenges of poverty, inequality, and violence (Bates 2017, Manco et al, 2005). In 2009, the year in which Brazil won the bid for the Olympic Games, the government decriminalised graffiti on buildings produced with the owners' consent. According to Bates, this law reinforced the demarcation between furtive tagging (*pichação*) and street art (*grafite*), the first one engaged in the reproduction of the artists' signatures in a cryptic style, the latter interested in developing a more complex aesthetics with a message. Vital da Cunha (2016: 56) suggests that public (either state or municipal) support for legal graffiti in the run-up to the 2014 and 2016 mega events was part of a broader strategy aiming to improve the city's image after decades of urban violence (on the violence see Soares, 1996; Machado da Silva, 2008) and to resignify Rio de Janeiro as a 'beautiful, lush, harmonious city' drawing on previous stereotypes of the beautiful, sensual, and relaxed '*Carioca* way of being' (Vital da Cunha, 2016: 55). The legalisation, however, has also allowed artists to voice criticism toward social segregation, misgovernment, forced removals, aggressive policing and the assassination of city councillor Marielle Franco in 2018.

According to Vilas Boas, street artists can develop participatory ways of thinking about and occupying public space (2015: 181) thereby activating various concepts of the city as a place of encounter, memory, and artistic and cultural activism. Imas (2014) also notes that favela painting presents a 'discourse of social change and of engagement that invites co-participation and co-creation in order to improve the quality of life of favelas from within' (blogpost). Tick's engagement with the community in Tabajaras & Cabritos is a good example of this. He has developed strong links with his neighbourhood by painting walls both inside Tabajaras & Cabritos and in the surrounding areas. He has collaborated with local businesses, NGOs and institutions, for example by creating scenery for theatre company Abraço da Paz ('Kiss of Peace') in 2014 and by painting a mural in the João Barros Barreto family clinic in 2019.

Tick has been exploring various avenues as an artist, teacher, neighbourhood activist, and event organiser. He has been offering arts workshops to children aged 12–17, initially in Tabajaras & Cabritos and later also in Duque de Caxias with the NGO, Ojubá Axé. In 2006, he brought together over 40 artists for a first encounter entitled 'Graffiti in the favela' in which residents were also invited to participate. He collaborated with the Green Star Movement from the US, participated in the collective exhibit of the group Eixo Rio and hosted several large-scale graffiti encounters, including successive editions of 'Artitude' in 2006, 2008, 2015 and 2018.

In 2007, he co-founded the social project CALLE to attract volunteers to Tabajaras & Cabritos. CALLE, which welcomed volunteers from all over the world, offered art and graffiti courses as well as English, Spanish, yoga, theatre and meditation classes to about 50 young people aged 8–18. Tick was also actively involved in 'Viva Bairro', a cultural project which started in 2015 and sought to identify and involve multiple stakeholders in changing perceptions and improving the environment. In Tabajaras & Cabritos, the project's *main objective was to* integrate existing cultural and environmental initiatives, such as community gardening, environmental education, graffiti classes, the training of young local tourist guides and the signposting and maintenance of tourist trails. Due to worsening insecurity, the end of the project funding and the departure of some core members, many of these activities came to a halt in 2017. Tick, however, remains confident that a street-art-focused walking tour can be made sustainable and would help residents to develop agency, skills and networks. He believes that, as places of creativity where an important part of the origins of Rio de Janeiro's culture resides, favelas will always attract and fascinate visitors. He seeks to promote a form of community-based tourism that would be able to channel this fascination towards equal and mutually beneficial encounters between communities and visitors.

Co-Creating a street art tour in Tabajaras & Cabritos

Dürr and Jaffe (2012) suggest that community-based tours engaging with globally and nationally circulating spatial imaginaries can draw 'on positive images of local cultural achievements … to combat the stigma of poverty, violence and crime' (2012: 120). Street art plays a prominent role in performing cultural resilience, since it simultaneously provides evidence for creativity and local culture, represents collective memory, strengthens resilience and networks of solidarity, and contributes to the residents' self-esteem and well-being. The research in Tabajaras-Cabritos aimed to capture the interplay between the artist, stakeholders and residents by observing three events: a stakeholder consultation meeting, a collective painting and a walking tour designed by Leandro Tick.

The stakeholder meeting took place at the João Barros Barreto family clinic. Tick invited the four researchers and a mixed group of nine residents and stakeholders to get involved in the inception of a walking tour. The stakeholders were social workers, NGO members, and professionals working in tourism, healthcare, sport and education. The vice-president of the Residents' Association and a graffiti artist from Duque de Caxias also joined the meeting. Several participants accumulated different roles and some of them had previously contributed to similar projects in other favelas. The meeting was chaired by the artist, who briefly introduced the two interconnected aims of his initiative: transforming the neighbourhood into an open-air urban art gallery relevant to both local and international audiences, and developing a sustainable walking tour in Tabajaras & Cabritos, Copacabana, Bairro Peixoto and Botafogo with local guides telling the story of the area through street art.

Participants were invited to make suggestions about the project's aims, content and methods. The most important goals emerging from the discussion concerned the involvement of vulnerable young people in collaborative networks and the destigmatisation of the favela. Including teenage residents in creative collaborations was recommended by a health professional as a way to counter tendencies of self-harm among local youths. The founder of an educational NGO saw attracting foreign tourists and changing their preconceptions about favelas as an effective way to act on the perception of Brazilians at the same time.

Participants suggested including art, culture, creativity, gastronomy and social projects into the tour. They recommended strategies successfully tested in other favelas, such as involving local leaders and social projects, constructing networks of solidarity, organising cultural events and a barbecue focusing on collective memory. The latter suggestion was accepted as a means to raise residents' awareness about the project and involve them in selecting themes for the open-air gallery. The invited graffiti artist, Carlos Bobi, talked about the pros and cons of sponsorship and shared his experience of organising the largest charitable graffiti painting in Latin America. This annual event, the 'Meeting of Favela', requires that participating artists engage with local residents and discuss their designs with them in order to obtain their permission to paint. Attracting prominent visitors, foreigners and the press was suggested as a way to avoid the cancellation of collective painting by the police. Finally, participants agreed on meeting on the following Sunday for a barbecue followed by the collective painting of a mural.

The Sunday event brought together the artist, the researchers, and some of the residents and stakeholders. The painting was led by Tick in collaboration with one of the researchers, who is also a graffiti writer. Since the order of the painting and the barbecue was reversed due to logistic reasons, the theme and the design of the painting were improvised rather than discussed and set collectively. The participants painted the word *Co-Criação* ('Co-Creation' in Portugese) on a geometrical background (see Figure 16.3). This simple design allowed even beginners to participate in the colouring. Once the design was completed, the two artists drew the contours and all participants signed their names. At the end, Tick painted a broken guitar and the words '#Pressaõvive'. This was to commemorate Alessandre Duarte, known as Pressaõ, the director of the local samba school, who was killed in a shooting on 17 July 2019. The painting was followed by a barbecue where the participants continued their discussions with other residents.

A week later Tick invited the group of researchers to test the two-hour walking tour he had designed and to comment on it (see Figure 16.4). The tour departed from Copacabana, crossed Tunnel Velho where the group entered Tabajaras & Cabritos on the Botafogo side through the area known as Villa Rica. Participants enjoyed the view on the Lagoa Rodrigo de Freitas and stopped at several murals on the way. Finally, they crossed the centre of the favela where most restaurants and businesses are located and returned to the formal city on Siqueira Campos Street. The tour focused on street art both inside and around the favela and provided explanations about facades and murals created by a variety of artists. It evoked collaborations between various artists as well as occasional sponsorship by local business owners in exchange for advertising. Tick talked about the code of conduct of the artists, the maintenance of open-air artwork and the dynamics of

Figure 16.3: The workshop participants posing in front of the mural they painted together in Tabajaras & Cabritos.

Source: Christina Horvath.

working with the community. The urban development of Tabajaras & Cabritos before, during and after the Olympic Games was equally addressed and some social projects were briefly mentioned. The tour visited several murals painted by Tick himself, including portraits of residents, cityscapes and designs created for institutions and businesses.

After the walk, the researchers provided Tick with their feedback on the tour. They found the combination of the community focus and street art authentic and arguably distinct from all the tours previously observed. Nonetheless, they noted that compared to other walks, Tick's tour was less politically engaged and an overarching narrative was missing. They recommended including more background information about the favela context, as well as the history of street art in Rio de Janeiro with particular focus on prominent artists' styles, aims and political messages. The development of two versions of the same tour, the one diving more in-depth into street art techniques and history and the other providing more details about street art's connection with the favela and its social projects, was also suggested.

Some of the feedback was concerned with organisational and security issues such as keeping the group together, indicating the itinerary and the length of the walk in advance, providing information about the level of walking difficulty, and guidelines on security. Other comments confronted the artist with the expectations of the stakeholders who wanted gastronomy and social projects to be emphasised in the tour. Based on the outcomes of both the stakeholder consultation and the literature review, the researchers recommended that Tick increase the

Figure 16.4: The walk in and around Tabajaras & Cabritos.

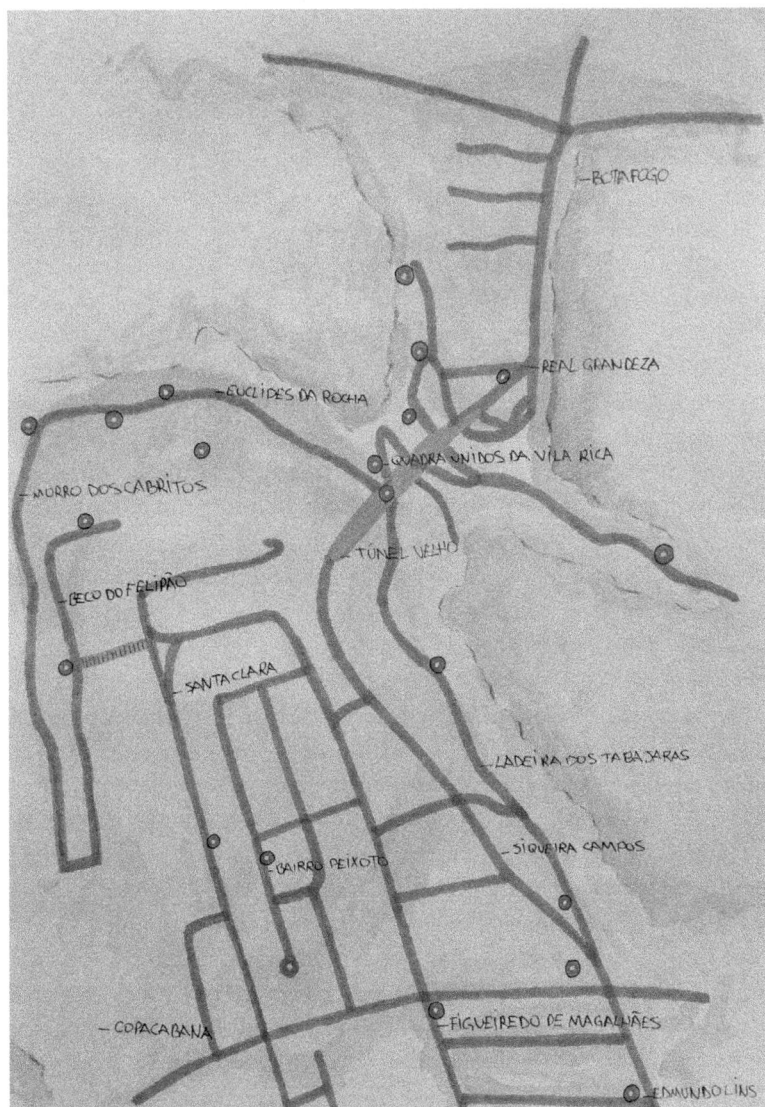

BOTAFOGO

REAL GRANDEZA

EUCLIDES DA ROCHA

QUADRA UNIDOS DA VILA RICA

MORRO DOS CABRITOS

BECO DO FELIPÃO

TÚNEL VELHO

SANTA CLARA

LADEIRA DOS TABAJARAS

SIQUEIRA CAMPOS

BAIRRO PEIXOTO

COPACABANA

FIGUEIREDO DE MAGALHÃES

EDMUNDO LINS

Source: Leandro 'Tick' Rodrigues.

benefits for the community by including a break in a bar or restaurant, encouraging the consumption of food or drinks in the community, and advertising services available in Tabajaras such as the mountain trail or a samba or martial art experience. They also advised facilitating spontaneous encounters between visitors and residents through visits to local institutions and social projects when security permits.

Conclusion

This final section will attempt to assess how Co-Creation worked in this particular case study and to draw some broader conclusions about the role of artist(s), researcher(s) and community participant(s) in Co-Creation projects.

As a socially engaged street artist, Tick was the driving force behind this particular Co-Creation initiative. From the start, he was convinced about graffiti's potential to integrate different viewpoints, record the community's history and memories, and promote fair exchanges of knowledge. As a member of the community, he was familiar with key challenges including insecurity, stigmatisation, isolation and the lack of state and municipal support for community-based art projects. Known in Tabajaras as an independent agent with integrity and authenticity, he was able to successfully mediate between the researchers and the community and use his longstanding networks to involve residents and stakeholders with relevant complementary experience in the dialogue. His participation in previous attempts to develop sustainable community-based tourism also facilitated the exchange between academic and vernacular ways of knowledge production. Due to his familiarity with artistic and pedagogic techniques and his experience of working with his students and other artists, Tick knew how to involve non-artists in the collaborative painting of a mural. Moreover, the involvement of communities in identifying locally relevant themes and the collaborative elaboration of designs were already part of his methodology aiming to promote a positive vision about being a citizen, valuing local history and caring about the place where people live.

Although Tick approved the Co-Creation ethos and had an in-depth understanding of it, this was not always sufficient to keep the process fully in line with the Co-Creation principles. Despite careful planning, the process often took unexpected turns and unfolded in unpredictable ways due to unforeseen circumstances. Thus, the collective painting was preceded by only one consultation meeting with stakeholders, which some key local actors (for example the leader of the environmental education project) were not able to attend. Only the stakeholders residing in Tabajaras took part in the subsequent painting and this was not preceded by collective decision making about the theme and the design. Participants acquired some basic painting skills during the event, experienced feelings of pride and ownership, broadened their networks, engaged in discussion with the researchers and each other, and contributed to shaping the street art tour with their comments. However, they did not become equal partners in the creative process, which remained under the artist's control. This was particularly perceptible when Tick spontaneously added the symbol of the broken guitar to the collectively painted work, turning it into a commemorative wall with a political message relevant to the community.

The experience has also revealed that, while Co-Creation has the potential to enable communities to initiate positive change in their neighbourhoods and develop agency, the process itself is dependent on a number of external factors which cannot be fully controlled by them. It exposed that the time, effort, involvement, dedication, professionalism, and goodwill local actors invest in the process is not always sufficient to fight the problems of insecurity and lack of political support and funding which can affect and undermine the process. Due to the lack of government support for arts-based community projects in Rio de Janeiro's favelas, many residents have lost their faith in state-funded initiatives and feel abandoned. The foreign research funding made available for this case study could only temporarily alleviate the general lack of resources for Co-Creation projects in Tabajaras & Cabritos.

This leads to a reflection about the contribution of the researchers to the Co-Creation process. While the researchers relied on Tick's network to access the community and benefited from his technical aptitude, dedication and leadership throughout the process, they contributed to the project with funding for honoraria, paint and consumables, their experience of academic knowledge production and access to international channels of dissemination. The outcomes of the literature review and participant observation enabled the researchers to critically assess the artist's methods and tour draft and provide him with constructive feedback. Through close collaboration with the artist, they exposed him to different methodologies and ways of knowledge production. Their paper presentations and publications will continue to contribute to the artist's international renown beyond the lifetime of the project. The mural painted with the researchers' support and collaboration has become part of the open-air gallery. We can conclude that the artist-researcher collaboration was ethical and mutually beneficial overall and the underlying power relations were balanced.

Although this six-week experiment did not fully comply with the Co-Creation principles at all times, it contributed to raising the artist's and stakeholders' awareness of ethical issues about community-based tourism, the potential of Co-Creation methodologies and the challenges and possibilities of a street art tour. The tour drafted by Tick was the most Co-Creative outcome of the research insofar as it was shaped by expectations voiced by stakeholders, the artist's street-art-specific knowledge and the researchers' suggestions based on the literature review and participant observation. This collaboration could constitute the first stage of a longer process leading to the consolidation of the street art tour through further Co-Creation events aimed at eliciting feedback from the stakeholders and residents, testing the tour's ability to attract tourists and impact on their views and measuring its impact on the community.

Finally, it is worth reflecting on what makes Co-Creation initiatives successful in general and how they differ from other forms of artist-driven initiatives involving communities. In this particular case study, the Co-Creation was based on a close collaboration between the artist and the researchers which evolved progressively over one year through online correspondence, face-to-face encounters, collaborative work, discussions, and shared social experience. Although the artist had participated in partnerships based on principles similar to those of Co-Creation, these projects did not involve researchers. The contribution of researchers enabled Tick to raise his awareness of the challenges and risks involved in making his street art tour community-based and ethical. The academic research that accompanied and supported the process complemented his practice-based, instinctive understanding of the benefits of tourism for the community. However, this close collaboration between the researchers and the artist may not be necessary in the case of researchers who are also practising artists or of socially engaged artists familiar with academic research methods.

The initiative also revealed that roles such as 'artist', 'researcher', 'community member' and 'stakeholder' are rarely clear cut, Tick being an artist, a community member and a local stakeholder at the same time was a good example of that. Further research would be needed to investigate through a range of different case studies whether the artist's prominence in the elaboration of the collective artistic outcome observed in this case study is a general rule for all artist-initiated Co-Creation workshops. This could also shed light on the importance of the quality of the Co-Created artwork or artefact compared to its contribution to community well-being and collaborative knowledge production.

Acknowledgments

The authors would like to thank all participants of the Co-Creation workshop in Tabajaras & Cabritos for their time, contribution and comments.

References

Almeida, J. (2014) 'Tabajaras and cabritos in Copacabana attract new residents', *Rio on Watch*, 14 May 2014.

Bates, B.R. (2017) 'Participatory graffiti as invitational rhetoric: the case of O Machismo', *Qualitative Research Reports in Communication*, 18(1): 64–72.

Burgold, J. and Rolfes, M. (2013) 'Of voyeuristic safari tours and responsible tourism with educational value: observing moral communication in slum and township tourism in Cape Town and Mumbai', *Die Erde*, 144(2): 161–74.

Carter, C.L. (2017) 'Utopia and the favelas of Rio de Janeiro', *Journal of Literature and Art Studies*, 7(4): 421–28.

Census (2010), Brazilian government, [online] available from https://www.ibge.gov.br/estatisticas/sociais/educacao/9662-censo-demografico-2010.html?t=destaques [accessed 13 August 2019].

Dovey, K. and King, R. (2012) 'Informal urbanism and the aste for slums', *Tourism Geographies*, 14(2): 275–93.

Dürr, E. and Jaffe, R. (2012) 'Theorizing slum tourism: performing, negotiating and transforming inequality', *European Review of Latin American and Caribbean Studies*, 93: 113–23.

Freire-Medeiros, B. (2013) *Touring Poverty*, New York: Routledge.

Imas, J.M. (2014) 'Favela painting: building community, social change and emancipation through an OrgansparkZ/Art installation', [online] available from https://blogs.lse.ac.uk/favelasatlse/2014/10/22/favela-painting/ [accessed 07 June 2019].

Interview Gilmar Lopes, 23 July 2019.

Klein, R. (2018) 'La ciudad y el turismo: experiencias desde la gestión del street art', *Sociologia: Revista da Faculdade de Letras da Universidade do Porto, thematic issue Cidade, cultura e turismo: novos cruzamentos*, 54–71.

Machado da Silva, L.A. (2008) *Vida Sob Cerco: Violência e Rotina nas Favelas do Rio de Janeiro*, Rio de Janeiro: Editora Nova Fronteira – FAPERJ.

Manco, T., Neelon, C. and Lost Art (2005) *Graffiti Brasil – Street Graphics*, New York: Thames and Hudson.

Sampaio Correia, A., Cunha de Oliveira, A.P., Olivieira, A.S., Modesto, J. and das Graças Magnavita, M. (2013) *Estudo de Potencialidades Turísticas Ladeira dos Tabajaras e Morro dos Cabritos*, Rio de Janeiro: SEBRAE.

Soares, L.E. (1996) *Violência e Política no Rio de Janeiro*, Rio de Janeiro: Top Books.

Vilas Boas, V. (2015) 'Artistic engagement as a way of cultural heritage preservation in Rio de Janeiro', *Procedia – Social and Behavioral Sciences*, 184: 180–86.

Vital da Cunha, C. (2016) 'Religion and artification of graffiti in the Olympic city: a look at the walls of Rio', *Streetnotes*, 25: 47–63.

17

Capturing the impact of Co-Creation: poetry and street art in Iztapalapa

Joanne Davies, Eliana Osorio-Saez, Andrés
Sandoval-Hernández and Christina Horvath

Introduction

Various chapters of this book have argued that Co-Creation, as an arts-based knowledge practice, helps improve participants' skills, well-being, social capital, self-esteem and resilience, and that it strengthens community cohesion while also addressing stigmatisation attached to disadvantaged urban areas. This chapter proposes a reflection on whether and how these benefits can be measured.

Evidencing knowledge and transformative change resulting from Co-Creative projects can be challenging for a number of reasons. Arts-based projects tend to produce outcomes which are either intangible (such as shared knowledge, experience or understanding) or creative (such as collective paintings or literary works). While the first type of outcome can be assessed by measuring their transformative impact on behaviour, the second type can only be evaluated using aesthetic criteria which may not be able to take into account the experience produced through the creative process. Moreover, measuring transformative change resulting from Co-Creation projects currently constitutes an under-researched area. Scholarly research has so far mainly focused on impacts emerging from urban regeneration projects (Evans, 2005; Matarasso, 2009) or educational projects (Anderson, 2009; Forrest-Bank et al, 2016; Michels and Steyaert, 2017) Recent research in these areas has drawn attention to the tensions between short-term quantitative approaches and longer-term qualitative approaches (Matarasso, 2009) and has identified indicators likely to demonstrate social transformation, such as a decrease in criminal or antisocial behaviour, a positive shift in reputation attached to a place or group of people or increase in volunteering, public–private–voluntary sector partnerships, educational attainment, individual confidence and aspiration (Evans, 2005: 14–15). Besides, the quasi-experimental design has proven successful in evidencing arts projects' positive effect not only on individuals (Forrest-Bank et al, 2016) but also on families, larger groups (Michels and Steyaert, 2017), neighbourhoods and even entire cities (Anderson, 2009).

In line with these findings, this chapter seeks to test the efficiency of a quasi-experimental mixed-methods approach to evidence Co-Creation's impact and to advance our understanding of knowledge production processes within Co-Creation. Quasi-experimental designs generally require the manipulation of an independent variable using non-equivalent groups, pre-test, post-test, and interrupted time-series designs (Campbell and Stanley, 2015). To achieve this, the authors recruited two non-equivalent groups of participants from two lower-secondary schools in the neighbourhood of Iztapalapa, in Mexico City. The groups were involved in a creative poetry writing workshop which resulted in a collective volume, the painting of a mural illustrating the poems and a public poetry reading event.

Iztapalapa was selected to be the setting of the workshop for being one of the city's most marginalised districts (Mier y Terán et al, 2012) with high levels of violence, unemployment, irregular housing, water scarcity and transportation deficiencies (Vergara, 2009). As a Global South city with striking inequalities in access to culture, education, art (La Silla Rota, 2016) and green spaces (Alvarez, 2012), Mexico City seemed an ideal testing ground for Co-Creation. In addition, the city has a longstanding legacy of arts-based approaches reaching back to the 1920s Muralist movement. For nearly a century, governmental and municipal institutions have been promoting socially engaged art at the neighbourhood level in the city, by sponsoring both bottom-up and top-down projects using public art to spread social and political messages (La Silla Rota, 2016; Folgarait, 2017).

The chapter will first set out the collaborative design of the case study, before discussing how the Co-Creation workshop impacted the participants, their families and the neighbourhood. The authors will then turn to the assessment of the case study, including the evaluation of the quasi-experimental approach to evidence this impact. The chapter will end with a reflection on processes of knowledge production within Co-Creation and some recommendations about how epistemologies from the Global North and South could be combined to improve our understanding of how knowledge is shared in Co-Creative ways.

Co-Creating a poetry workshop in Iztapalapa

This case study was initiated by an interdisciplinary group of researchers from the University of Bath, England, composed of members from the Global North and South. The group organised several stakeholder consultation meetings, involving head teachers, teachers and non-academic staff from the two selected lower-secondary schools in Iztapalapa, members of 'Alas & Raíces' ('Wings & Roots', a governmental organisation having a longstanding expertise of working with disadvantaged groups in Mexico City using arts methods), a collective of four poets called 'Centro Transdisciplinario Poesía & Trayecto', and a street artist, Oscar Román. The aims of these meetings were to carry out an analysis of local needs based on the experience of the school staff and to tap into the partners' respective expertise to develop a series of Co-Creative activities aligned with both the schools' needs and the ten Co-Creation principles advocated in this book. The first five of these principles reflect Co-Creation's inclusive ethos by encouraging participants to build strong, trust-based relationships, commit to mutual respect and address issues related to traditional hierarchies. The other five principles anticipate potential challenges and conflicts which might arise during the collaboration and seek to provide practical guidelines throughout the process (see Figure 1.1, Chapter 1).

The design took as a starting point a model elaborated by the organisation Art from Ashes (AfA, nd), which was modified through a collaborative process to align it with the concept of curricular autonomy. Curricular autonomy is understood as the principle that allows each educational community to decide how to use a certain part of their school day to reinforce key learning, explore other activities with pedagogical value or develop social impact projects (SEP, 2017). Accordingly, workshop objectives were shaped to respond to specific issues identified by school staff, as well as to incorporate methods and techniques that the artists had found effective in similar contexts. A quasi-experimental design (Campbell and Stanley, 2015) was selected for the project's evaluation. The dependent or outcome variables were organised into four conceptual groups, corresponding to the four most pressing issues identified by the school staff: an aggressive/violent school climate, disciplinary problems and low student participation in the classroom, students' lack of interest for community affairs and students' disbelief in their own capacity to make changes in their community.

Two schools participated in the project: one acted as the treatment school and the other as a control school. These roles were assigned randomly. All students at both schools were invited to take part in the project on a voluntary basis. To approach students, the project team visited every classroom to perform a brief poetry reading, explain what the project would involve and invite participants to volunteer. This allowed the grouping of participants by their interest in poetry, so that students from different grades and ages could work in the same curricular space. All participating students were given detailed project information in writing, as well as consent forms for their parents to sign.

First, participants from both schools answered a questionnaire with information about the dependent variables, as well as background information about the schools, themselves and their families ('pre-test'). Subsequently, the students at the treatment school participated in the Co-Creation workshops. These consisted of three sessions of poetry writing over two consecutive days, guiding students through creating first collective and then individual poems. In this framework, writing was used as a tool for the students to develop their voices and perceptions of themselves as actors for positive change in their neighbourhood. The collective production of texts allowed for some painful experiences (such as loss, abuse, abandonment by family members and sexual harassment) to surface. More optimistic feelings (including hope, love and dreams about a better future) were also shared. The mutual support between classmates and the encouragement provided by the poets were expressed through smiles, pats and hugs, making the process emotionally charged.

The following week, the students at the treatment school took part in two street art sessions to create a mural on one of the outside walls of their school, using imagery from their collective and individual poems. This was followed by a public reading of their poems in front of the mural, to which the whole school, parents and the local community were invited. Both the mural and the public event allowed the participants to share their poems with the community of teachers, parents and neighbours and have their voices heard by all. During the reading, each student received a printed copy of a collective volume of their poems entitled *Telesecundaria Iztabalabra: 50 poemas rabiosas de amor y ternura* ['Iztabalabra High School: 50 Enraged Poems of Love and Tenderness'] which contained all four collective and 47 individual poems produced during the workshop. Finally, the students at both the treatment and the control schools answered the questionnaire for a second time ('post-test'). After this, poetry workshops were also delivered in the control school to ensure that the students there also benefited from the experience.

The poetry and street art workshops were specifically designed to strengthen the integral development of students. They privileged an approach to art as therapy rather than skills development or a focus on artistic quality. Using poetry and street art as a means of expression, workshop participants linked artistic production with their emotions both on a personal level and as part of a community. As highlighted earlier, the project was designed to have a positive influence on the selected four target areas (school climate, classroom discipline and student participation in the classroom, student self-efficacy in community affairs, and student participation in the community/ neighbourhood) in order to:

- promote greater respect and tolerance among young people from diverse cultures and backgrounds (improve school climate);
- encourage young people's participation in group settings (increase student participation in the classroom);
- increase young people's self-confidence to promote community participation (encourage greater self-efficacy);
- promote greater respect for poetry and art and their power to change lives and communities (increase community participation).

The impact of the project was expected to extend beyond the level of the school to the entire community. Using creative writing as a process as well as a tool to describe the immediate environment can lead to a deeper knowledge of individual and collective identity. The poetry workshops used the construction of metaphors and other stylistic elements to enable students to express their reality from their own perspective in order to approach the micro-history of their communities from a variety of points of view. In practical terms, outreach to the community was sought through two activities promoting students' civic self-efficacy: the public poetry reading and the painting of the mural on the outside wall of the school.

Quasi-experimental design to measure the workshop's impact

The quasi-experimental design for the Co-Creation project's evaluation is depicted in Figure 17.1. The first school, with 47 participating students (26 boys and 21 girls, aged 14–17), was randomly selected to be the treatment school. The second school, with 33 participating students (12 boys and 21 girls, aged 14–16), was chosen to be the control school.

275

Figure 17.1: Flow of participants through each stage of the evaluation.

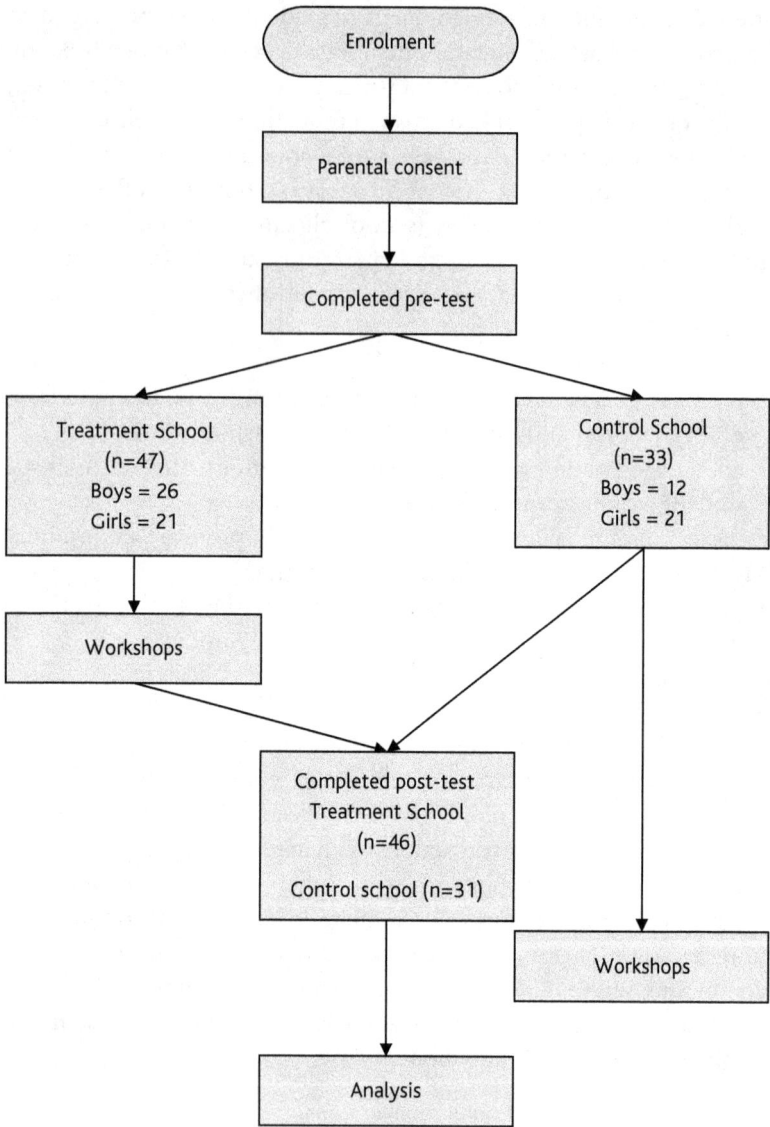

As highlighted in the previous section, a questionnaire that collected information about the dependent variables, as well as background information about the schools, the students and their families, was administered twice in each school (pre- and post-test). In the treatment school, this was administered before and after the Co-Creation activities whereas in the control school this was administered both times *before*

Table 17.1: Themes included in the questionnaire and issues identified in the school and community.

Issues identified in the school and community	Concepts in ICCS
Discipline problems and lack of student participation in the classroom	Open classroom for discussion (7 items)
Aggressive/violent school climate	School climate (7 items)
Students' disbelief in their own capacity to make changes in their community	Student self-efficacy (7 items)
Students' lack of interest or concern for community/neighbourhood affairs	Civic participation (5 items)

the activities took place. The purpose of doing this was to test for differences in the outcome variables between the pre- and post-tests (that is, before and after the project activities). If differences were found in both the treatment and control schools, then such differences could not be related to the project, but if differences were found only in the treatment school, then it could be suggested that these were related to the project.

The questionnaire used items adapted from the International Civic and Citizenship Questionnaire (ICCS) (Köhler et al, 2018), created by the International Association for the Evaluation of Educational Achievement (IEA) and applied in Mexico by the National Institute for the Evaluation of Education (INEE) in 2016. The four main areas identified by school staff during the initial meetings as the most pressing issues in their schools and communities were mapped to the contents of the ICCS background questionnaire, as shown in Table 17.1. The full version of the ICCS background questionnaire can be found in the ICCS User Guide (Köhler et al, 2018).

In addition to the questionnaire, the research design also included a series of 13 qualitative interviews with the head teacher, a classroom teacher and a non-academic staff member at each school, the two staff members of Alas y Raíces, the four poets who led the poetry workshops and the street artist who coordinated the school's mural. The questionnaire data were analysed using SPSS (IBM, 2013), with t-student tests used for comparisons. Interviews were analysed using thematic analysis (Braun and Clarke, 2006).

The following presentation of the results is centred around the four conceptual groupings used in the questionnaire and contains information from the analysis of both the quantitative and qualitative data.

Table 17.2: Results for treatment and control groups concerning how often students raise current political topics for discussion in class.

	N	pre-test	SD	post-test	SD	Diff	t	pp	d
Treatment	44	2.9	1.3	3.5	1.1	0.6	-2.74	0.01	0.41
Control	29	2.4	1.4	2.6	1.4	0.2	-1.72	0.20	0.17

Figure 17.2: Results for treatment and control groups concerning how often students raise current political topics for discussion in class.

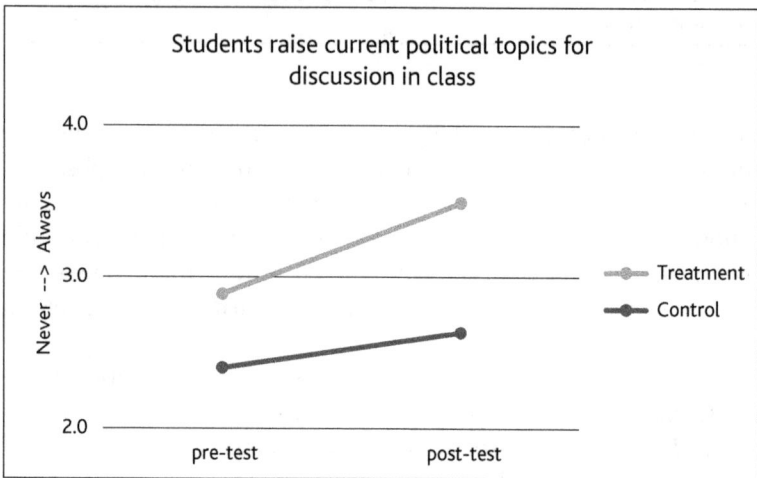

Open climate for classroom discussion

A statistically significant change between the pre- and post-test responses of the treatment group was found in one item within this grouping – that relating to how often students raise current political topics for discussion in class. As can be seen from Table 17.2 and Figure 17.2, there is no statistically significant difference between the pre- and post-test of the control group, t (29) = − 1.72, p > 0.05. The effect size (d = 0.17) is also small. There is however a statistically significant difference between the pre- and post-test responses of the treatment group, t (44) = -2.74, p < 0.01. There is also a medium effect size (d = 0.41). In other words, after participating in the workshop, the average student in the treatment school reported raising political topics to be discussed in class with a higher frequency than 66 per cent of the students before the intervention (see Coe, 2002 for a more detailed explanation of the interpretation of effect sizes).

Interviewees' comments help to understand the improvements evidenced here:

> "During the first questionnaire, the students had many questions about the meaning of spaces for discussion in the classroom …. At the end of the project, there was recognition of these terms and how they are practised because they lived these during the poetry workshops." (Teacher 1)

> "The spaces of creation generated an atmosphere to talk about many things that are not normally talked about in the classroom." (Head teacher 2)

School climate

Statistically significant decreases between the pre- and post-test responses of the treatment group, as well as between the treatment and control groups, were found for two of the questions within this grouping. The results of the first, regarding students' feelings of not fitting in at school, are presented in Table 17.3 and in Figure 17.3, and the results of the second, related to students' fear of being a victim of bullying, in Table 17.4 and Figure 17.4.

As can be seen from Table 17.3, there is no statistically significant difference between the two responses of the control group,

Table 17.3: Results for treatment and control groups concerning students feeling like they do not fit in at school.

	N	pre-test	SD	post-test	SD	Diff	t	p	d
Treatment	43	3.1	1.6	2.5	1.4	-0.6	-2.84	0.01	-0.43
Control	29	2.7	1.3	2.5	1.3	-0.2	-0.67	0.51	-0.12

Table 17.4: Results for treatment and control groups concerning students' fear of bullying at school.

	N	pre-test	SD	post-test	SD	Diff	t	p	d
Treatment	45	2.8	1.5	2.4	1.5	-0.4	-1.91	0.06	-0.28
Control	31	3.1	1.7	2.9	1.4	-0.1	-0.37	0.72	-0.07

Figure 17.3: Results for treatment and control groups concerning students feeling like they do not fit in at school.

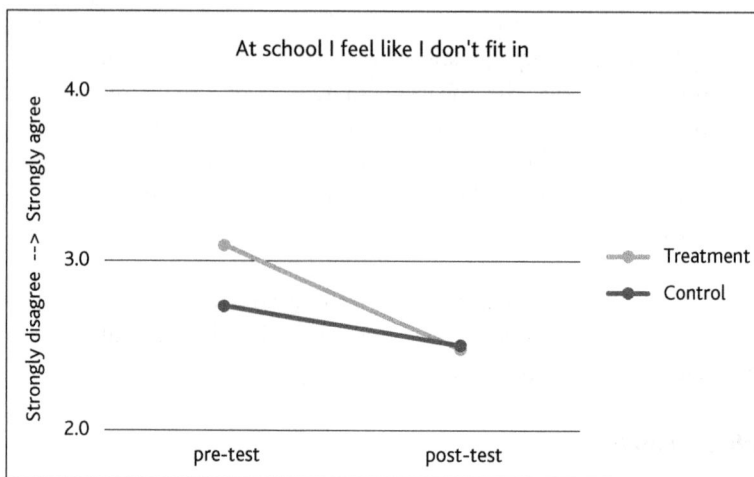

Figure 17.4: Results for treatment and control groups concerning students' fear of bullying at school.

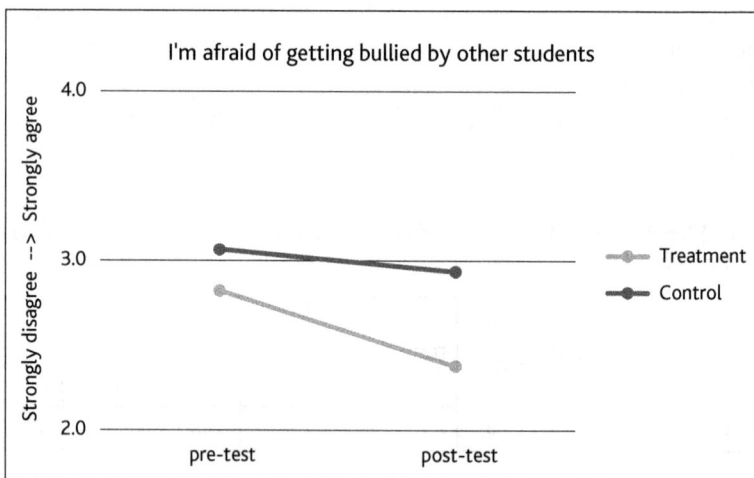

t (29) = -0.67, p > 0.05. The effect size (d = 0.12) is also small. In contrast, there is a statistically significant difference in the pre- and post-test responses of the treatment group, t (43) = -2.84, p < 0.01. There is in addition a medium effect size (d = -0.43). That is, after participating in the workshop, the average student in the treatment school reported that they do not fit in at school to a lesser extent than 66 per cent of the students before the intervention.

As can be seen from Table 17.4, there is no statistically significant difference between the two responses of the control group, t (31) = -0.37, p > 0.05. The effect size (d = 0.07) is also very small. Conversely, there is a statistically significant difference in the pre- and post-test responses of the treatment group, t (45) = -1.91, p < 0.10. There is in addition a medium effect size (d = -0.28). In other words, after participating in the workshop, the average student in the treatment school reported to be less afraid of bullying than about 62 per cent of the students before the intervention.

Comments from the interviewees reinforce the notion of a positive change in school climate:

> 'In the first activities, irreverent language and behaviour were used, because the space lent itself to that, but when we questioned them (me as a facilitator and their fellow students), about their choices – "Why do you say this or that"? – this ensured they thought not only of what they wanted to say but also of those around them listening.' (Poet 1)

> 'The project and especially the final event was a space where young people felt confident in being and saying.' (Head teacher 1)

> 'They were celebrating together, saying "Wow, that's so great".' (Non-academic staff 1)

Student self-efficacy

A statistically significant increase between the pre- and post-test responses of the treatment group, as well as between the treatment and control groups, was found for one question – that relating to students' perceived self-efficacy concerning organising fellow students to make changes within their school.

As can be seen from Table 17.5 and Figure 17.5, there is no statistically significant difference between the two responses of the control group, t (30) = – 0.52, p > 0.05. The effect size (d = -0.09) is also very small. In contrast, there is a statistically significant difference in the pre- and post-test responses of the treatment group, t (43) = 2.26, p < 0.05.

Table 17.5: Results for treatment and control groups concerning perceived self-efficacy in organising fellow students to make changes at school.

	N	pre-test	SD	post-test	SD	Diff	t	p	d
Treatment	43	3.5	1.2	4.0	1.1	0.5	2.26	0.03	0.34
Control	30	3.7	1.2	3.5	1.2	-0.1	-0.52	0.61	-0.09

Figure 17.5: Results for treatment and control groups concerning perceived self-efficacy in organising fellow students to make changes at school.

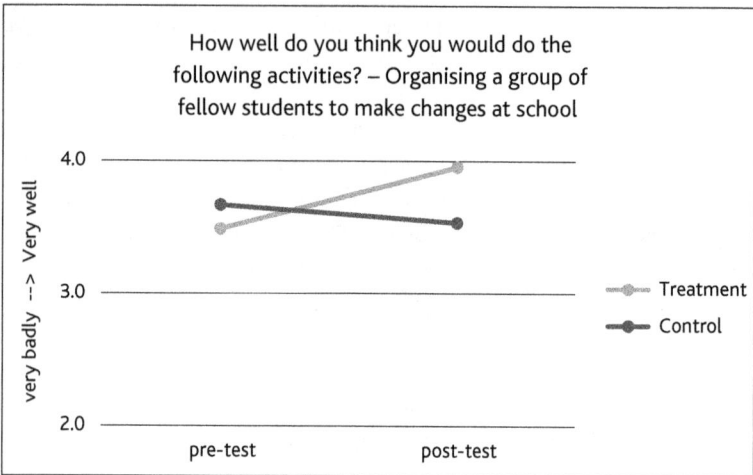

There is in addition a medium effect size (d = 0.34). That is, after participating in the workshop, the average student in the treatment school reported to perceive him- or herself more able to organise other students to makes changes at school than about 62 per cent of the students before the intervention.

Interviewees' comments provide evidence of students' increased capability to speak of and address shared problems and overcome stigma together:

'In the poems, they spoke of their community, their school and feelings, mainly of the affection they were obviously asking for and of the social problems of their community and their need to talk about it.' (Poet 2)

'What hurts was named; the difficulty of life in this community ... Tears that had been held back flowed. It is here that poetry helps to name pain, denounce it and heal it.' (Teacher 2)

'With some students, it was possible to redefine some forms of stigmatisation such as "*pinche marihuano*" ["drughead loser"] and "useless". With poetry these were renamed, it was a way to leave that stigma behind.' (Poet 3)

Civic participation

A statistically significant increase between the pre- and post-test responses of the treatment group, as well as between the treatment and control groups, was found for one question – that relating to students' desire to contribute to an online forum discussing political and social issues.

As can be seen from Table 17.6 and Figure 17.6, there is no statistically significant difference between the two responses of the control group, t (29) = −1.36, p > 0.05. There is a medium effect size (d = 0.25). Conversely, there is a statistically significant difference in the pre- and post-test responses of the treatment group, t (42) = -2.63, p < 0.01. There is in addition a medium effect size (d = 0.41). That is, after participating in the workshop, the average student in the treatment school reported to be more likely to contribute to an online political forum than about 66 per cent of the students before the intervention.

Students' strengthened desire to contribute to discussions on the topics that affect them and those around them, is also evident from interviewee comments:

'Once they participate in the workshops, students develop a series of skills that gradually will become part of the school dynamics and hopefully of the family and the community to which they belong ... They see art as an alternative form

Table 17.6: Results for treatment and control groups concerning students' desire to contribute to an online forum discussing political and social issues.

	N	pre-test	SD	post-test	SD	Diff	t	p	d
Treatment	42	3.5	1.2	4.0	1.0	0.5	-2.63	0.01	0.41
Control	29	3.0	1.4	3.3	1.3	0.3	-1.36	0.19	0.25

Figure 17.6: Results for treatment and control groups concerning students' desire to contribute to an online forum discussing political and social issues.

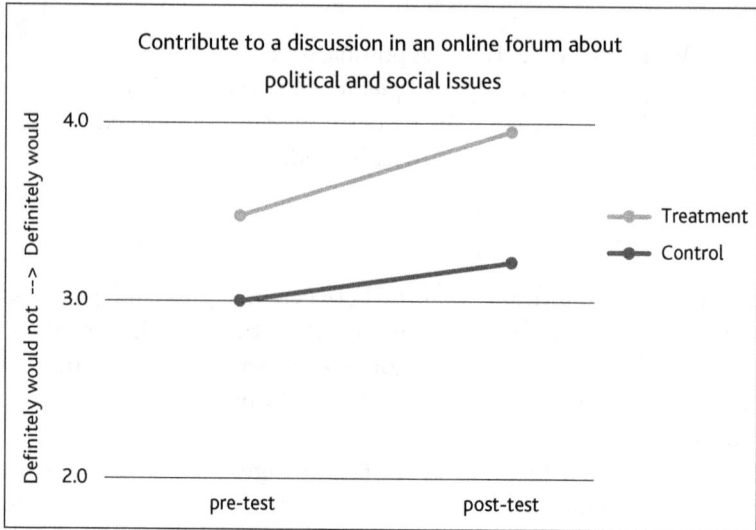

of expression and a tool to look for more opportunities, to express themselves and progress, to change the reality in which they live.' (Head teacher 1)

Overall, we can conclude that although this Co-Creation initiative was modest in its timeframe, it had a positive and relatively significant impact on all four areas evaluated. With regards to the questionnaire, while statistically significant improvements in the responses between the pre- and post-test applications of the questionnaire were not consistent, they were found in at least one item from each evaluated area. Moreover, these gains were only present in the treatment group, which strengthens the evidence in attributing them to the Co-Creation project.

Assessing the Co-Creation process and the measurement tool

The following section will discuss the application of the Co-Creation principles throughout the project and explore the efficiency of the assessment methods used to measure the poetry workshops' impact.

The initiative in Iztapalapa was designed and carried out bearing in mind the ten Co-Creation principles established in Chapter 1 (see

Figure 1.1). Principle 10 ('Creative' outcomes) was particularly prominent insofar as the activities involved creative writing and painting. In line with principle 3 ('Ethical'), academic ethics guidelines were followed at all times and all artists involved in the project received honoraria. Principle 4 ('Shared' outcomes) was guiding the dissemination of the Co-Created poems through the mural painting, public poetry reading and collectively published book. Principles 6 ('Embedded') and 7 ('Aware') were also respected, since the project brought together a range of local actors (school staff, students and artists) and relied on the outcomes of the initial stakeholder consultation meetings to pitch the workshop at social issues relevant to the community. The three stages of the project (planning, execution and evaluation) were also aligned with principle 2 ('Respectful') that advocates mutual respect among participants.

The design of the project, which involved the school staff, researchers, artists, and practitioners, was accomplished in accordance with principles 8 ('Plurivocal') and 9 ('Active'), suggesting that all participants should have their say in the planning of the activities. The Co-Creation ethos also required the acknowledgement and mitigation of the inequalities existing between partners. These included institutional hierarchies within both Alas & Raíces and the team of researchers, the prominence of the epistemologies of the North in the workshop and evaluation design, as well as unequal access to funding and resources (for example, the poets' honoraria were paid by Alas & Raíces while the other activities were co-sponsored by the Mexican Ministry of Culture and the Co-Creation project). These power inequalities were mitigated to some extent by recognising that each partner's specific expertise was equally vital for the project.

The creative stage of the project was affected by the partners' initial decision that only the students and the artists would participate in the creative activities. This division between active participants and facilitators seemed to be necessary to enable peer-groups of teenagers from Iztapalapa to find their own voices and express age- and place-related experience of suffering and rejoicing related to the specific challenges of their local environment (Santos, 2014: 90–3). Nevertheless, this set-up triggered a series of binary divisions between facilitators versus participants, adults versus teenagers and researchers versus researched, which could be considered contrary to principles 1 ('Equal' footing) and 9 ('Active' participation). While practitioners from Alas & Raíces were not present during the workshop sessions, school staff and researchers acted as facilitators and data collectors and these roles excluded them from active participation in the poetry writing and painting. Nonetheless, despite their non-creative roles they participated in the sharing of strong emotions, affect and empathy, which were instrumental to knowledge production and resulted in trust-based relationships (principle 5) not only among the student participants but also between these and the adults present during the workshops, despite the short timeframe of the project and the divisions described here.

The assessment stage of the project was also underpinned by principle 8 ('Plurivocal'). Although the design of the assessment methods was led by the researchers from the Global North, due to their relevant expertise and prominence as the initiators of the project, all adult participants contributed to the process via the initial stakeholder consultation and continuous commenting during and after the creative activities. The choice of combining student questionnaires with unstructured interviews with all partners was motivated by the desire to equalise the balance of power between all adult participants. This format allowed for sharing ideas about the process, its benefits for those involved, and its possible shortcomings.

The quasi-experimental design proved an efficient method overall to evidence transformation in the four targeted areas. It generated a set of data that could be used to fill the gap in the literature about evidencing impact from Co-Creation projects but was also suited to underpin future reports and policy briefs arguing for financial and policy support for Co-Creation activities. The mixed-method approach successfully combined the measurement of behavioural change through quantitative research with insight into the dynamics of the creative process provided by the qualitative research.

However, two important areas remained neglected throughout the evaluation process. The first was the voices of the teenagers mediated by their poems, the second was the embodied knowledge generated through sharing the participants' messages with the larger community. These shortcomings of the evaluation shed light on a particularity of Co-Creation as a knowledge practice, namely that an important part of the knowledge sharing is mediated through the creative process and is therefore inseparable from the participants' bodily sensations, emotions and affects. In the final, concluding section, we will discuss this in more detail with the aim of making some recommendations about how these shortcomings could be overcome in future Co-Creation projects and how the two most challenging areas could be given more prominence in the evaluation design.

Conclusion

There were some important limitations to this study. The first concerned the short timeframe of the case study, which was developed over three months. Such a brief intervention could only generate very modest transformation within the complex environment of the treatment school and the community. The second limitation was related to the role of the researchers, who did not actively engage in the creative activities. Involving them more actively in poetry writing and graffiti painting while simultaneously opening some aspects of the design and research processes to student participants could have resulted in more fluid boundaries and less hierarchical relationships between researchers and non-researchers and artists and non-artists. Finally, evaluating Co-Creation from the perspective of the academic partners and the epistemologies of the North constituted a third limitation. Even if the adopted evaluation design sought to engage with a wide range of actors and stakeholders, the assessment privileged methods developed by scholarly epistemologies of the Global North and was more concerned with the changes in student behaviour and perception than with processes of knowledge production about neighbourhood disadvantage and creative outputs. These, however, proved instrumental in building a shared understanding. Furthermore, while the interviews took into account the voices of school staff, artists and academics involved at all stages of the project, they neglected those of the community (in particular parents' and neighbours' voices) and their reactions to Co-Created outcomes shared with them through the poetry reading and mural. They also did not sufficiently reflect the perspective of student participants whose voices the Co-Creation process was meant to help emerge.

Some of these limitations could be considered as interesting opportunities for future research. Another area to investigate further is the involvement of the epistemologies of the South in the evaluation design. As the case study has revealed, participants' experience of sexual abuse, insecurity, abandonment and demands for love and respect were primarily expressed in a poetic form through linguistic choices including metaphors, exaggerations and occasionally irreverent language. The poems and their graphic illustration via the collectively painted mural did not need to be high-quality artworks to provide insight into what it meant to be a teenager in Iztapalapa and to mediate those affects, passions, beliefs, faiths and values that Santos (2014) calls the 'unsayable'. Epistemologies of the North tend to either ignore creative outcomes or to concentrate exclusively on the message they carry. Thus, even if they attempt to take the participants' poetic claims into account, they are likely to translate these into the neutral, objective and rational language of Global North science, which would inevitably dispossess the participants' emerging voices of their passion, urgency, authenticity and authority.

The workshop in Iztapalapa also revealed that social transformation generated by Co-Creation was principally prompted by the powerful emotions felt by those who witnessed the students' poems. To develop a better understanding of such processes, future workshops should concentrate on embodied ways of producing common understanding and the role that shared narratives of suffering and rejoicing plays in the Co-Creation process. As Santos (2014) argues:

> The epistemologies of the North have great difficulty in embracing the body in all its emotional and affective density, without turning it into one more object of study. ... The epistemologies of the South cannot accept the forgetting of the body because social struggles are not processes that unfold from rational kits. They are complex bricolages in which reasoning and arguments mix with emotions, sorrows and joys, loves and hatreds, festivity and mourning. (Santos, 2014: 20).

It is beyond the scope of this chapter to evaluate existing strategies that seek to close the gaps between Northern and Southern epistemologies and to suggest new ones. However, the authors believe that a dialogue between the two epistemologies is necessary to fully explore Co-Creation's potential to enact positive transformation based on shared understanding. They therefore recommend incorporating recent approaches inspired by the epistemologies of the South such as 'inter-knowledge dialogues' proposed by Dietz and Mateos Cortés (2013) or Esteva (2019), which seek to amalgamate knowledge from the North and the South; strategies recommending 'warming up reason' or '*corazonar*' (Santos, 2014: 97), which argue that knowledge can only turn into action on the condition of being 'soaked in emotions, affections, and feelings' (Santos, 2014: 97); the 'demonumentalising of written knowledge' (Santos, 2014: 188), which seeks to place different cosmopolitics on an equal footing; 'deep listening' (Santos, 2014: 178); and 'democratic negotiation and maintenance of equivalent forms of knowledge in permanent tension' (Lins Ribeiro, 2018: 77). Future Co-Creation initiatives should incorporate some of these strategies not only in the design of their activities but also in the ways they are evaluated.

Note: The authors present their gratitude to all those who helped design and facilitate this Co-Creation intervention in Iztapalapa: Dr Irene Macias and Professor Hugh Lauder (University of Bath); Karloz Atl, Cynthia Franco, Canuto Roldán and Alain Y. Whitaker (Centro Transdiciplinario Poesía y Trayecto); Oscar Román; Anelvi Rivera Milflores and David Hernández Villeda (Alas y Raíces, Secretary of Culture in Mexico); the staff and the students of Telesecundaria 52, as well as Director Irma Hernández.

References

AfA (nd) http://www.artfromashes.org/.

Alvarez, R.F. (2012) 'Neoliberalism and parks: the urban political ecology of green public space in Mexico City', *Sociedad Hoy*, 23: 83–115.

Anderson, B. (2009) 'Affective atmospheres', *Emotion, Space and Society*, 2: 77–81, available from https://doi.org/10.1016/j.emospa.2009.08.005.

Braun, V. and Clarke, V. (2006) 'Using thematic analysis in psychology', *Qualitative Research in Psychology*, 3(2): 77–101.

Campbell, D.T. and Stanley, J.C. (2015) *Experimental and Quasi-experimental Designs for Research*, Chicago: Rand McNally.

Coe, R. (2002) 'It's the effect size, stupid: what effect size is and why it is important', paper presented at the *Annual Conference of the British Educational Research Association*, Exeter, available from: http://www.leeds.ac.uk/educol/documents/00002182.htm.

Dietz, G. and Mateos Cortés, L.S. (2013) *Interculturalidad y Educación Intercultural en México: Un Análisis de los Discursos Nacionales e Internacionales en su Impacto en los Modelos Educativos Mexicanos*, Mexico: SEP-CGEIB.

Esteva, G. (2019) 'El camino hacie el diálogo de vivires', in Santorello, S. (ed) *Entre lo Propio y lo Ajeno: Diálogo y Conflicto Inter-Epistémico en la Construcción de una Casa Común*, Ciudad de Mexico: UIA.

Evans, G. (2005) 'Measure for measure: evaluating the evidence of culture's contribution to regeneration', *Urban Studies*, 42(5/6): 959–83.

Folgarait, L. (2017) 'The Mexican Muralists and Frida Kahlo' in *Oxford Research Encyclopedia of Latin American History*, Oxford: Oxford University Press.

Forrest-Bank, S.S., Nicotera, N., Bassett, D.M. and Ferrarone, P. (2016) 'Effects of an expressive art intervention with urban youth in low-income neighborhoods', *Child and Adolescent Social Work Journal*, 3: 429–41.

IBM (2013) *IBM SPSS Statistics* (Version 22.0), Somers, NY: IBM Corporation.

INEGI (2015) *Principales Resultados de la Encuesta Intercensal 2015*, Mexico City: Instituto Nacional de Estadistica y Geografia, available from https://www.inegi.org.mx/programas/intercensal/2015/.

Köhler, H., Weber, S., Brese, F., Schulz, W. and Carstens, R. (2018) *ICCS 2016 User Guide for the International Database*, Amsterdam: IEA.

La Silla Rota (2016) 'CDMX, la 2da Ciudad con más museos en el mundo', *La Silla Rota*, [online] 13 September, available from https://lasillarota.com/metropoli/-cdmx-la-2da-ciudad-con-mas-museos-del-mundo/124578.

Lins Ribeiro, G. (2018) 'Diversidade cultural como discurso global', in A.C. de Souza Lima, L.F. dos Santos Carvalho and G. Lins Ribeiro (eds) *Interculturalidade(s): Entre Ideias, Retóricas e Práticas em Cinco Países da América Latina*, Rio de Janeiro: Associação Brasileira de Antropologia & Contra Capa: 43–83.

Matarasso, F. (2009) *The Human Factor: Experiences of Arts Evaluation* [online], available from http://web.me.com/matarasso.

Michels, C. and Steyaert, C. (2017) 'By accident and by design: composing affective atmospheres in an urban art intervention', *Organization*, 24(1): 79–104.

Mier y Terán, A., Vázquez, I. and Ziccardi, A. (2012) 'Pobreza urbana, segregación residencial y mejoramiento del espacio público en la Ciudad de México', *Sociologias*, 14(30): 118–55.

Santos, B. de S. (2014) *Epistemologies of the South: Justice against Epistemicide*, New York: Routledge.

SEP (2017) *Autonomía curricular en el Nuevo Modelo Educativo*, Mexico: SEP, available from https://www.gob.mx/sep/documentos/la-autonomia-curricular-en-el-nuevo-modelo-educativo.

Vergara, R. (2009) 'Iztapalapa o el inframundo', *Revista Proceso*, 1704: 26–7.

18

Conclusion: lessons, implications and recommendations

Christina Horvath and Juliet Carpenter

This volume has approached Co-Creation from a variety of different disciplinary angles (planning, political theory, philosophy and literature to name but a few), reflecting the different positionalities of researchers, activists, practitioners and artists from the Global North and South who have contributed to the chapters. It has revealed the hybrid character of the roles that actors can hold and raised further questions about Co-Creation strategies. From their multiple viewpoints, authors have explored the possible aims, outcomes and impacts of Co-Creation, the spaces in which it unfolds and the complex power relations involved in the process.

This concluding chapter will reflect on their contributions, seeking to identify key themes and draw out comparisons between the chapters in order to understand the evolving concept of Co-Creation. It will also highlight emerging directions for further research and formulate some recommendations for activists, researchers, artists, and practitioners interested in pursuing Co-Creation initiatives.

The aims of Co-Creation

The broad scope of areas covered in this volume – ranging from community engagement, civil participation and knowledge production to political activism and advocacy – have raised very different and sometimes contradictory expectations in relation to Co-Creation. Some authors limited Co-Creation's aims to sparking dialogue between individuals, groups and institutions, building or engaging communities, bringing art closer to the underprivileged, awakening civil imagination, and constructing alternative understandings of neighbourhoods and their challenges. Others went further in their claims for transformative change, suggesting that Co-Creation should seek to advance social justice either indirectly, by disrupting traditional thinking and hierarchies and decolonising knowledge production, or directly, by mediating between communities and power holders, balancing interests, and advocating for alternative visions to be incorporated into future policies supported by the state.

These differences raise questions about whether Co-Creation is an actual method or rather an umbrella concept under which very different aims can be brought together and, indeed, whether it has to fulfil all these aims in every particular case in which it intervenes. While one aim of this volume was to address the distinction between 'co-creation' as citizen participation in public policies and Co-Creation, reconceptualised as an arts-based knowledge process acting on the external image and self-perception of disadvantaged communities to promote equality through creativity, the two sets of meanings proved resistant to such separation.

We can conclude that Co-Creation, although it may pursue social justice and community engagement through different means, will always promote agency, collaboration between participants and alternative visions taking into account different perspectives rather than inertia, separation and status quo.

Roles and positionalities

If Co-Creation as a knowledge practice retains some of the original meaning of 'co-creation' as a political process, we need to understand how the term's underlying connotations affect its reconceptualisation as a collaboration between artists, researchers and communities. Does this imply that, like 'co-creation', Co-Creation is possible without artists, researchers or communities?

Research and practice discussed in these chapters have shown the multiple advantages of involving both artists and researchers in Co-Creation. Many artists are familiar with adopting roles of mediators and facilitators and know how to break down inhibitions and incentivise participation through tactics of play and hands-on creativity. They can also play key roles in disrupting hierarchies and encouraging more subtle, tangential and dialogic engagement with issues at stake, as we have seen through the examples of community film making (Chapter 6), the artist-designed playful stakeholder consultation in Greater Paris (Chapter 9), reorientation of community tourism through street art (Chapter 16) and poetry written by teenagers in Mexico City, directing community attention to issues of violence and abuse (Chapter 17). Other chapters have highlighted the added value provided by academic partners who brought not only information and research methods to Co-Creation projects but also material resources, funding, symbolic legitimation and networks that can be key to making the process sustainable, although the limitations of working with academic partners are also recognised in Chapter 12.

Some case studies have also revealed how fluid the boundaries can be between categories such as 'artist', 'researcher' or 'stakeholder'. For instance, Itamar Silva, leader of Grupo ECO in Rio de Janeiro, acted simultaneously as a resident, stakeholder, activist and community researcher in the Santa Marta case study (Chapter 15). Laura Barron (Chapter 11) was able to lead the Street Beats Band project in Vancouver thanks to her dual positionality as artist-researcher. Leandro Tick (Chapter 16) could initiate the collaborative redesign of a community-based walking tour in Tabajaras & Cabritos thanks to his experience and networks as an artist, activist and community member. Familiarity with each other's practices, languages, and methods of knowledge production allowed partners to communicate and build bridges between different disciplines, viewpoints and modes of expression. According to these examples, the overlaps between multiple roles are not only inevitable but a very condition of knowledge sharing among multiple actors. Further research should explore how Co-Creation processes are affected by the positionality of their initiators, whether they are artists, researchers, or communities.

Power and the state in Co-Creation

One of the key underlying themes running through many of the chapters has been the issue of power, and the inequalities that can undermine Co-Creation, for instance through the involvement of the state or power imbalances between participants. A number of chapters draw on examples of experiments between power holders (the state or municipality) and communities (see, for example, Chapters 8, 9 and 13) where Co-Creation is drawn on as a method for dialogue between the two. However, although participants' voices can be brought forth to be heard in novel ways through Co-Creation, they are not necessarily listened to or acted upon by those in power. As a result, the artists and researchers involved in the process run the risk of cooptation and may be discredited in the process, perceived as agents of the state and betraying the trust of community partners.

This raises the question of whether Co-Creation necessarily needs to be a bottom-up process, and whether state-sponsored Co-Creation can ever lead to truly inclusive practices of knowledge production. When powerful state actors are implicated in the process, examples from this volume (for example, Chapter 9) suggest that their hegemonic position in the power hierarchy is likely to dominate the overall relationship between actors. This 'aestheticisation of public policy' may omit the narratives that those in authority chose to ignore. But this also raises questions about whether, in fact, the process of collecting narratives through artistic expression has a value in itself for those who tell their stories, even if those in power are not listening. This 'civil imagination', drawing on an exercise in 'artistic citizenship' (Chapter 3), makes visible the conditions of marginalisation by engaging actors in collaborative art projects that promote and enhance community well-being. This in itself has the potential to create new knowledge and understanding, both within communities and also beyond, which opens up possibilities to challenge traditional perspectives and narratives coming from those in dominant positions.

Process and outcomes

In this volume, the working definition of Co-Creation involves the process of knowledge production through collective creative endeavour. This raises issues about how knowledge production actually takes place, and how communities can both feed in their situated knowledge through artistic creation and also contribute to knowledge dissemination. The authors of Chapter 6 shed some light on this, through a discussion of how young people actively performed an alternative sense of place as a reaction to their local stigmatised community spaces, in highly affective ways. Their Co-Creative project aimed to reconfigure voice, subject, agency and embodiment, to enable young people to tell their story and (re)create the narrative about their experiences of living in a marginalised neighbourhood. Project participants used a variety of multimedia methods to explore their mobility though the neighbourhood and examine their situated and embodied knowledge through creative practices. Their stories were then (re)told through an exhibition involving photos, posters, video and panel talks, as well as an interactive exhibit where audience members could contribute their own ideas. Such an example illustrates how Co-Creative practice can generate affective imaginaries through creative processes, the outcomes of which can then be shared with others through embodied practice.

Outcomes from Co-Creation can take various forms, responding to the call for Co-Creative dissemination. They may materialise in the form of scholarly research papers, presentations or other similar paradigmatic forms of knowledge. But they can also take shape in embedded and embodied forms of knowledge, including artworks that remain in the urban setting under study (such as in Chapter 16), poetry performance (Chapter 17), or more intangible forms of outcomes, such as the interpersonal connections and networks created, and the empowerment of participants as in the case of the Street Beats Band (Chapter 11). One fundamental thread running through these outcomes is the question of accountability, and the justifications provided for the knowledge claims related to these outcomes, in representing the lives and perspectives of others. For this reason, dissemination that is Co-Created is key since it allows participants to tell their own story through appropriate media that expose their knowledge in authentic, powerful ways.

Space and place

The issue of space and place intervenes at various levels in the book. Several chapters investigate whether the neighbourhood is the most appropriate scale for Co-Creation interventions, or whether Co-Creating on wider, municipal, metropolitan, national or even international scales is possible and desirable. While many authors explore Co-Creation at the neighbourhood level (Chapters 4, 6, 13, 17), some look beyond the neighbourhood to a wider grouping of municipalities (Chapter 9), or to the metropolitan level (Chapter 14). The chapters illustrate that the appropriate scale is that which is responsive to the context in which it is designed. In some cases, as shown in Chapter 10 through the example of literary festivals, itinerant events creating their own, nomadic communities can become alternatives to Co-Creation which still successfully address at least some, if not all, aims of Co-Creation.

Also relevant is the definition of a Co-Creation community, and whether it should be place-based or not. The very process of Co-Creation, bringing participants together to share experiences and knowledge, can create communities that did not exist previously, but who interact through embodied actions to reveal forms of knowledge that coalesce around a shared experience and exchange (Chapter 11). Another issue is the role of space and the built environment in processes of Co-Creation (Chapter 7). Urban spaces intervene in the production and reproduction of social practices, and as such, can be an important element in Co-Creation initiatives. Chapter 13 also illustrates this, with the Knowle West Media Centre (KWMC) being a focus, a facility and a space for Co-Creation projects.

At the global level in relation to space and place, the labels North and South have also generated discussion. Authors have not only concurred in saying that a binary North–South divide was artificial (Chapters 2, 4, 5, 15), but they have also demonstrated that such labels were not always relevant and masked more complex differences that were at times more marked than the North–South division. This is not to diminish the important historical differences between global regions, due to colonisation and the enduring postcolonial hegemonic structures that persist today. But it is to recognise that each country, city and neighbourhood is subject to different socioeconomic, political, and historical structures, which impact on the conditions of urban development experienced by local communities.

Impact

The volume has also explored the possibility of measuring impact resulting from Co-Creation (Chapter 17). Beyond the difficulties involved in evidencing and quantifying change in participants' behaviour, this attempt was also confronted with questions about how to interpret creative outputs such as artworks or artefacts and how to take into account emotions and subjective experiences which are intrinsically linked with the process of knowledge production. Who is entitled to measure tangible outcomes such as poems, music performances, murals, photovoice exercises, affective mapping and collaborative video films, as well as the learning processes facilitated by their making and sharing? What is the purpose of evaluating the impact of creative projects on community well-being if not the desire to justify resources dedicated to their production and convince funders of their usefulness, which leads almost inevitably to their instrumentalisation and the denial of their value in themselves? These questions have been touched on in this volume, but would warrant further detailed research, to explore the impacts of Co-Creative projects in more depth, and to examine self-reflexively our own positionality as researchers, artists and participants, in relation to the significance of the evaluation of Co-Creation projects.

When and how to use Co-Creation?

Finally, the authors have also reflected on when to use Co-Creation as a strategy and how to overcome difficulties that may arise throughout the process. From the chapters, it appears that Co-Creation is potentially a lengthy process, since it requires trust that can only be built over time. Moreover, since the process is largely spontaneous, its outcomes are unpredictable to a certain extent. Given that top-down approaches tend to be seen as hijacking the creative process and submitting it to a specific agenda, the best-case scenario may be when communities reach out to researchers and artists, when relationships between the participants are horizontal rather than vertical, when enough time and resources are allocated for the processes without any external pressure (for instance, from the funders) to produce specific outcomes. However, given the current expectations from science, and the structures of funding for creative projects through cultural institutions and academic research, the likelihood of such a constellation is relatively low.

Several chapters have found, however, that Co-Creation was a particularly useful strategy in contexts in which formal kinds of political agency were weak or non-existent. These include situations of political reorganisation, uncertainty (Chapter 5), inequality and oppression (Chapters 3, 4 and 6) in which regenerating a civic capacity allows participants to act as agents involved in the processes of change. This is the case for instance in cities with significant inequalities where the dynamics of change are strong and disruptive and multiplicities of different actors are involved in these processes. Co-Creation in such situations and contexts then helps groups of researchers, inhabitants, artists and other actors become consciously aware of their own individual and collective agency and collectively produce forms of knowledge which recall past, present and future possibilities.

Conclusion and recommendations

This volume concludes with a series of recommendations, derived from the previous chapters, that consider Co-Creation as a process of generating shared understandings and dialogue through creative approaches rather than a methodological toolkit that is applied mechanically regardless of the context. These recommendations are therefore necessarily general, and participants of Co-Creation initiatives are left to adapt them to their own needs.

According to the experience of the authors of this volume, to be successful, Co-Creation should consider adopting the following principles:

- Identify issues that people genuinely care about, as a way to generate participation.
- Open up new possibilities in terms of what can be imagined and what can be made, and allow participants to play leading roles in imagining, designing and building their futures.

- Set overarching common goals around which people from different backgrounds can cluster.
- Establish some ground rules to create safe spaces.
- Encourage cooperative processes in which people with common interests can work together non-hierarchically towards change they want to bring about, using their diverse skills and experiences.
- Identify inequalities between participants (linked to socioeconomic status, age, mobility, North–South divide) and devise strategies (such as a process in which different skills are acknowledged and valued) to balance power hierarchies.
- Concentrate on broad and diverse changes that need to take place. Change may need to happen involving various places, spaces and people, including the participants themselves.
- Nurture intimate exchanges at a smaller scale to develop trust-based relationships and to address hierarchical assumptions.
- Broaden small-scale Co-Creation initiatives to engage with larger communities. This can be achieved by working with young people and involving their families or by creating opportunities that bring people together such as through exhibitions, collective paintings or poetry readings, shared meals or parties.
- Use creative approaches and arts methods to facilitate work across disciplines and power structures, confront ideas on new grounds, express ideas and listen to each other differently, disrupt habitual dynamics of power, express and take criticism.
- Avoid colonising knowledges already in place. Use strategies like 'political listening' to identify these knowledges and use 'scientific' research methods critically (for example, by relying on post-qualitative inquiry and decolonial theory) to balance the epistemologies of the North with an increased focus on flows of affects and emotions.
- Allow participants to contribute as little or as much as they wish at a pace that lets them move flexibly from simple ways of contributing to more lengthy, complex and sophisticated ways.
- Be prepared to cede control over some aspects of the Co-Creation project to other participants.
- Use comparative approaches to identify common problems and seek solutions on a wider scale.
- Close Co-Creation processes with an assessment of whether and how goals have been achieved, and what has been learned.
- Involve participants in 'telling the story', by sharing insights, creating solutions to issues, identifying opportunities and making changes to available infrastructure.

Index

Page numbers for figures and tables appear in *italics*.

recycling *see* binner community,
Vancouver
reflexivity 8
Reid, Elizabeth J. 131
relations between participants
equality 41, 207–8
fluidity of functions 7–8, 174,
178–9, 293
'working the hyphens' 238, 249–51
see also power dynamics; prototyping
research institutions
as hegemonic actors 198, 200
questions of independence 190, 197
researchers
ceding control 247
as collaborators within
communities 3, 11
mobility and internationality 56,
65–6, 79–80, 82
power dynamics 56, 247–8
privileged position of 79–80, 200
questions of independence 190, 197
role and contributions of 250,
267, 292–3
see also relations between participants
residents (community members) 11,
52–3, 65–6, 67
respectful (Co-Creation
principle) *9*, 285
Ribeiro, Djamila 238, 250
Rio de Janeiro (RJMR) *224*
colonialism in city planning 26
political environment 35–6,
77–8, 78–9
urban inequalities 223–5, 237
see also Casa Fluminense; Santa Marta;
Tabajaras & Cabritos
Rittel, Horst W.J. 195, 196
Robinson, Jennifer 24–5, 27,
31, 32, 37
Rodrigues, Leandro (Tick) 243,
253–68 *passim*, *259*, *260*, 293
Rolfes, Manfred 255, 256
Román, Oscar 273
Roy, Ananya 24–5, 25, 27

S

safeguarding 92–3
Said, Edward 57, 60
Sailor, Janna *179*, 181

Saint-Denis, Paris 137, 139–42, *140*
'Football Pitch, Player and Consultant'
project 137, 142–51, *144*
Salles, Écio 155, 157
Salvador, Brazil 36
Santa Marta, Rio de Janeiro 61–2, 80–
3, 238, 239–47, 248, 249
tourism initiatives 242, 257–8
Santaki, Rachid 155, 156, 157, 158,
159, 164–5, 167, 168
Sassen, Saskia 79, 83
Schinke, Robert J. (Blodgett et al) 10
SEBRAE, Rio de Janeiro 254
self-reflection 82
Sen, Amartya 139
Seth, Sanjay 58, 59
shared (Co-Creation principle) *9*,
146, 285
Shaw, Mae 41
Silva, Itamar 62, 238, 240, 243, 244–6,
248, 293
Silverman, Marissa (Elliot et al) 48–9
Simmel, Georg 190, 196–7
smart city programmes *see* Bristol
Approach to Citizen Sensing
social capital 121, 124
social embeddedness 129
social versus artistic outcomes 52,
175–6, 184
song composition 145
South Africa 32
South and North *see* Global North
and South
space *see* urban spaces
street art 255, 257, 258–65
graffiti 64, 242, 257, 260, 261
mural art 37, 105, 107, 258–9, *259*,
263, *264*, 274
Street Beats Band project, Vancouver
(SBB) 177–83, *179*, *180*, *181*,
184, 185–7
Suchmann, Lucy 197, 198
Sustainable Development Goals (United
Nations) 26, *110*, 228, 230
Swindon 91–8
Swyngedouw, Erik 34, 193, 197,
198

T

Tabajaras & Cabritos 254, 261

CPSIA information can be obtained
at www.ICGtesting.com
Printed in the USA
BVHW041128270820
587459BV00005B/149

9 781447 353966